新东方GMAT考试

D0509987

陈向东 / 编著

GMAT
写作高分速成
——ARGUMENT

西安交通大学出版社
XI'AN JIAOTONG UNIVERSITY PRESS

图书在版编目(CIP)数据

GMAT写作高分速成. ARGUMENT / 陈向东编著. —西安：西安交通大学出版社，2013.12

ISBN 978-7-5605-5908-7

Ⅰ.①G…　Ⅱ.①陈…　Ⅲ.①英语—写作—研究生—入学考试—自学参考资料　Ⅳ.①H315

中国版本图书馆CIP数据核字（2013）第319796号

书　　名	GMAT写作高分速成——ARGUMENT	
编　　著	陈向东	
责任编辑	黄科丰	
封面设计	大愚设计	
出版发行	西安交通大学出版社	
地　　址	西安市兴庆南路10号（邮编：710049）	
电　　话	（010）62605588　62605019（发行部）　　（029）82668315（总编室）	
读者信箱	bj62605588@163.com	
印　　刷	北京精乐翔印刷有限公司	
字　　数	170千	
开　　本	880mm×1230mm　1/16	
印　　张	13.75	
版　　次	2014年1月第1版　2014年1月第1次印刷	
书　　号	ISBN 978-7-5605-5908-7/H·1619	
定　　价	35.00元	

前　言

　　全球经济的跌宕起伏，职场上的风云变幻以及MBA就业市场的持续"牛市"使得越来越多的人踏上到国外读商学院的征途。他们希望以国外名牌商学院毕业生的身份以及国际化的视野使自己在未来的职业生涯中步步高升，如鱼得水。然而，到国外读商学院不可避免地要参加GMAT考试。GMAT考试不仅考查考生的语言能力和数学能力，还要测试其头脑反应、逻辑思维和解决实际问题的能力。一般而言，GMAT考试能较真实地反映应试者的英语水平和思维水平，因而受到越来越多的学校和专业的重视与好评。不论在美国还是欧洲，用英语教学的商学院都采用GMAT作为MBA的入学考试。目前，全世界共有近千所大学采用GMAT考试。在中欧和东欧的很多学校，GMAT也是衡量学生分析写作能力的一个重要评判标准。在GMAT考试中，考生的数学成绩基本都很高，而语言与分析写作能取得优异成绩则能够表明"你是一个少有的杰出考生"。因此，想申请到国外商学院读MBA，必须将分析写作能力提高到一定档次。

　　对于那些申请到美国大学读商学院的考生而言，在美国学习，生活，用英语做研究，写论文，查阅资料，做Presentation（演讲性陈述），如果没有一定水准的写作能力是不行的。而且，MBA毕业生六位数的起薪诱惑极大地提高了商学院录取的GMAT分数要求。想从高分林立的竞争对手中脱颖而出，没有优秀的分析写作成绩也是万万不行的。所以，中国考生的英文写作能力受到了空前的挑战。GMAT写作与IELTS、TOEFL iBT写作相比要难得多，其难度与要求与GRE写作相当。但是，GMAT写作的题材更侧重于工商管理和企业经营的内容。2012年6月，GMAT考试做了改革，写作题型只有一种（Argument），而且考题都来源于官方公布的题库，但是这个题库非常庞大。而且，其题目题材范围非常宽泛，涉及工商、管理、社会、人文、教育、环境、建筑、科技等各个方面，既考查考生的知识面，也考查考生的工商管理专业知识。不仅如此，GMAT写作对于考生思维的逻辑性要求也非常高。而中国考生所受的逻辑思维的训练普遍较少，用英文进行逻辑分析更是难上加难。所以，GMAT写作需要考生投入大量的时间和精力。

　　但实际情况是，考生可以用于提高GMAT写作的时间与精力非常有限：他们不但要准备写作，还要花大量的时间记单词、做阅读题和数学题；除此之外，他们还得抽出不少的时间应付专业课和准备申请材料等等。参加工作的考生通常都有处于公司中层以上的职位，不但工作繁忙，而且应酬场合也比较多。现实不允许考生在GMAT写作上花费太多时间，而出国留学又要求考生拥有相对较高的写作成绩。如何在短期内使GMAT写作成绩有明显的提高，已成为困扰广大考生的一大难题。

　　本书针对中国考生在GMAT写作中存在的主要问题，从以下四个方面对如何获得写作高分进行解读：

- **写作入门篇**：根据官方考试指南，全面解答考生在Argument写作方面存在的问题。本篇不但给出了Argument写作的三大策略，还给出了Argument写作的七大步骤，具有很强的实用性和可操作性。此外，本篇还给出了Argument写作的评分标准及官方范文，具有非常强的针对性和指导性。
- **进阶提高篇**：深入分析Argument的命题形式，分类总结Argument的常见逻辑错误，并给出逻辑错误的经典攻击句型和论证方法。为了进一步提高考生的写作基本功，本篇给出了110个Argument写作必备经典句子；为了使考生能快速把握Argument的写作方法，本篇还给出了大量的写作模板和20篇黄金范文供考生参考。范文所涉及的均为近年来考试中出现频率较高的题目，具有很强的针对性。

- **题库突破篇**：面对庞大的题库，全部准备肯定是力不从心，准备一部分又怕有所疏漏。所以，通读提纲不失为一种明智的选择。鉴于此，本篇给出了官方题库所有题目的详细写作提纲，这些提纲不但指出了每一道题目中出现的逻辑错误，而且还对它们进行了有效的攻击，具有较高的参考价值。准确把握每一道题目的思想和内容是正确解题的关键，所以笔者还不遗余力地给出了所有题目的准确翻译。

- **工具素材篇**：俗话说，"熟读唐诗三百首，不会作诗也会吟"。所以，如果时间允许，建议考生背诵本书中的范文。背诵范文不仅可以在短期内有效提高语言质量，而且由于这些文章都是根据GMAT写作题库所涉及的话题内容精心挑选的，因此背诵这些文章还可以在短期内达到丰富思想、为论证提供宝贵素材的目的。但是，有多少考生有背诵几十甚至上百篇范文的精力呢？为此，笔者提出了背句子的概念。在附录部分给出了300个句子供考生背诵，这些句子均选自经典范文或出自大师之手，熟读或背诵对考生的英语表达能力是大有裨益的。

GMAT写作的本质是考查考生对复杂问题的分析能力、论证能力及推理论证过程中对逻辑错误和漏洞的识别能力。所以，要让GMAT写作水平有实质性提高，一方面要通过诵读英文经典提高语言的质量；另一方面，还要通过不断地练习写作来提高语言的驾驭能力和思维的严密性。最后，还应通过广泛的阅读来开阔视野丰富思想，通过与他人的不断交流来磨砺机智、启发灵感。

本书的创作最早可以追溯到2002年。2002年，ETS在GRE测试中取消了中国考生的强项——逻辑部分，加入了中国考生的"软肋"——分析写作。当时笔者正率领团队创建武汉新东方学校，同时担任GRE写作主讲教师，答应为学员们编写一本复习教材帮助他们在短时间内攻克GRE写作考试。同时，我也发现，GMAT考生在写作中也存在同样的问题，考虑到GMAT写作与GRE写作的相似性，在筹划GRE写作的同时，我也时刻关注着GMAT写作，希望能同时写一本GMAT写作方面的书。然而，事与愿违，新东方的快速发展使我卷入了各种各样更具挑战性的管理工作中，使得编著本书的想法一度搁浅。在本书创作期间，我一直像蚂蚁搬家一样地积累，积累，再积累，最终完成了GMAT写作书稿。虽然其中仍有不完善的地方，但是内容已经比较全面。所以，我决定拿出来与考生分享，希望这么多年的努力和积累能对考生提高写作能力和成绩有所帮助。

本书参阅了大量中外相关文献，并得到了很多考生提供的第一手资料。在成书过程中，又得到了易明博士的鼎力帮助，在此表示衷心感谢。

本书虽然经过审慎编校，但由于时间紧张，加上笔者才学所限，恐仍有纰漏之处，尚祈同行和读者不吝指正。

陈向东

使用说明

　　本书旨在用简单、系统、有效和直接的方法，帮助考生在最短的时间内攻破GMAT Argument写作，取得高分。因此，作者在构思本书时，既重视方法，又重视应试技巧；既重视基本功的训练，又重视写作能力的提高。要想从本书中获得最大收益，请参考以下方法使用本书：

　　1. 内容规划：通读第一篇，重视第二篇，熟悉第三篇，诵读附录。

　　2. 时间规划：距考试还有三个月以上的考生，请仔细通读本书，全面准备，争取取得高分，甚至满分；对于时间比较紧迫的考生，请着重阅读本书的第二篇和第三篇，争取在最短时间内实现写作水平质的提高。

　　3. 活用模板：模板的重要性是不言而喻的。要想在考试规定的时间内写出一篇400词以上、有理有据的文章，没有一套成竹在胸的模板几乎是不可能的。所以，本书给出了大量的模板供考生参考和背诵。但是，切记一定不能一字不变地照搬任何模板，否则容易引起作弊嫌疑。最好结合自己的写作习惯和自己总结的范文，制作一份属于自己的模板。

　　4. 强化练习：写作是一项实践性很强的技能。多读多背的最终目标是写出优秀的文章，所以在读和背的同时，必须加强写的训练。只有通过不停地写，才能把读过和背过的东西转化为自己的语言。

　　5. 重视修改：写过的文章一定要反复修改，没有修改的文章就像消化不良的饭。自己修改和他人修改相结合，先自己改，更换词语，变换句式。同时可以参照权威机构的评分标准，对自己的习作进行评估。找出自己的弱点并进行强化练习。修改文章是一个反复的过程，过一段时间后可以把自己以前的习作拿出来重新修改，看看能不能发现以前没有发现的错误，或有没有新的见解要添加进去。不断修改的过程也是不断提高的过程。

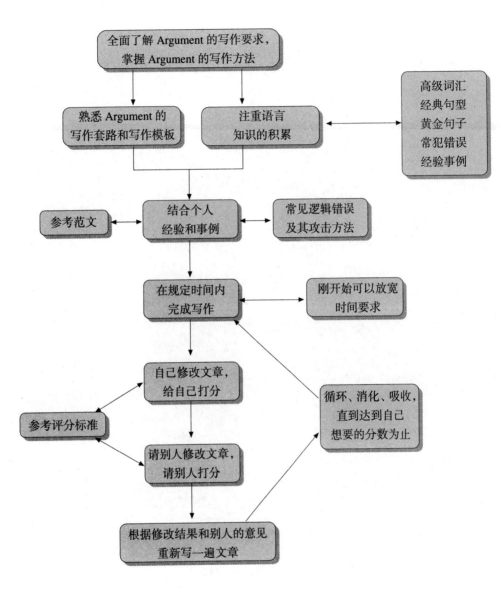

目　录

Part 1　Argument写作总论

Part 2　Argument写作进阶提高

PART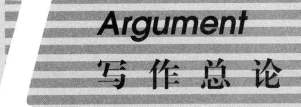
1 Argument 写 作 总 论

- **Argument 写作入门**
- **Argument 写作三大策略**
- **Argument 写作七大步骤**
- **Argument 写作评分标准**

第一章　Argument 写作入门

　　管理学研究生录取测试(The Graduate Management Admission Test, 简写为GMAT)是管理学研究生院用来评估申请者的入学资格, 并预测入学后第一年表现的一种测试。该测试是用英语出题的标准化考试, 整个考试由三部分组成, 其主要形式如下表所示：

Format of the GMAT		
	Questions	Timing
Analytical Writing		
Analysis of an Issue	1 topic	30 minutes
Analysis of an Argument	1 topic	30 minutes
Optional break		5 minutes
Quantitative		
Problem Solving	37 questions	75 minutes
Data Sufficiency		
Optional break		5 minutes
Verbal		
Reading Comprehension	41 questions	75 minutes
Critical Reasoning		
Sentence Correction		
	Total Time	210～220 minutes

　　由于GMAT针对的是MBA (Master of Business Administration)的申请者, 而这些申请者又来自不同的专业和领域, 所以参加GMAT测试并不需要特定的管理知识, 也不需要特定领域的成就。分析写作测试(Analytical Writing Assessment, 简写为AWA)主要是用来评估申请者的分析思维能力以及表达个人观点的能力。商学院在录取MBA申请者时很看重他们的GMAT写作成绩, 在决定是否录取某个申请者时通常会调出他的写作底稿来加以分析。所以, 答好 GMAT写作, 对成功申请MBA是非常关键的。本章介绍GMAT考试的一些基本知识, 主要目的是让考生了解 GMAT考试的内容和特点, 同时也提出一些复习建议, 供考生参考。

一、Argument写作简介

1. Argument写作任务

　　GMAT写作由Issue Task和Argument Task两部分组成。Argument Task, 即"论证辨析"题, 要求考生在30分钟时间内, 对一段推理/论证作一番评估, 指出其推理上的漏洞和论证过程中的缺陷。

　　考试中出现的"Issue"和"Argument"题目涉及商业以及其他各领域所普遍关注的问题。为确保公平性, GMAT写作不要求考生掌握与某一论题相关的专业知识, 只注重考生是否具有一定的分析写作能力。"Issue"与"Argument"这两类题目是互为补充的。第一类题目要求考生陈述自己的观点; 第二类题目要求考生对他人的论述进行评析。这样的考题可以测试考生以下的能力：如何清晰地说明一个较复杂的问题; 如何规范、流畅地陈述观点并为其提供支持证据; 如何通过事实和例证来支持自己的观点、紧紧围绕主要问题展开讨论。这类考题可以有效考查考生的逻辑分析与推理能力。

2. Argument写作题库

GMAT的写作考题基本上都出自管理类研究生录取委员会（Graduate Management Admission Council，简写为GMAC）所公布的题库。考生可以从GMAC的官方网站上免费下载最新的写作题库。考生应当注意的是，题库中的题目可能每年都会有一定的变化。根据最新公布的题库，Issue题目有149道，Argument题目有145道。在考试的过程中，系统会为考生随机抽取一道Issue题目和Argument题目供考生解答。要想取得理想的成绩，考生应该在考前对所有题目进行预习，以节约考试时的审题时间。尽管到目前为止，题库内的考题基本上都考过了，但若对网站上的"机经"进行认真仔细的分析，我们不难发现有些题目考到的概率很高，所以考生在备考时，如果时间比较紧迫，可以着重练习高频题目，从而增加获取写作高分的概率。

3. Argument写作的要求

GMAT写作主要从内容、组织、语言以及结构这四方面来考查考生的写作能力。具体要求如下：

- **内容**：考生通过列举合理的推论性和支持性例子来提出恰到好处的、具有说服力的相关见解和论点的能力。
- **组织**：考生以结构清楚紧凑的行文提出观点的能力。
- **语言**：考生的英语语言支配能力，通过考生的词汇量、措辞(词汇的选择)以及俗语的应用得以体现。
- **结构**：考生对标准书面英语的熟练程度，包括语法、句法(句型结构)以及词汇的应用。

从上面的文字中我们可以看出，拼写和标点不是GMAT写作的评分依据，除非考生犯了过多类似的错误，以致无法有效地表达自己的观点。另外，需要考生引起注意的是，GMAT考试内置的文字处理软件没有拼写和语法检查功能。考生在考场上只能靠自己去避免这类低级错误，虽然GMAT考试不像TOEFL考试那样重视拼写和语法问题，但是从官方给出的范文中我们发现，每篇满分的范文所犯的低级错误都不会超过三个。

4. Argument写作评分解读

GMAC要求所有的阅卷人都采用一致的评分标准。下面是6分(满分)写作的一些基本要求(注意：即使在语法、用词、拼写和标点上出现一点小错误，一样可以得到6分)。

- 写作能够确定论证的主要特征，并进行有一定深度的分析。
- 写作的每一个评论点都有深刻的推理和例证的支撑。
- 写作显示出作者能够熟练运用所掌握的句子结构、词汇、措辞和习惯用语。
- 写作显示出作者对书面英语各个元素掌握得很好，包括语法、句法、拼写和标点，但是允许有一些微小的错误。

对稍低分数的要求与上面的要求相似，分数越低，写作质量的要求也越低。参照GMAC评过分的范文，我们不难发现：无论是Issue还是Argument，在评分标准上都要求：第一，观点要有深度，论证要有说服力；第二，组织要有条理，表达要清晰准确；第三，语言流利，句式复杂，词汇丰富。这三条分别说的是行文的"思想性"、"结构性"和"表达性"，众多获得写作高分的考生都在这三个方面做得很好，我们理所当然也要从这些方面入手，采取"各个击破"的方法剖析GMAT写作的本质，从而得到一个理想的分数。

考生平时在练习时，可以参照上述的三条标准给自己打分。但是GMAC也强调，评分是整体性的，而不是从各个角度分别评分。这就说明，虽然中国考生的语言能力偏弱，但是只要能从其他两个角度给评卷人非常出色的感觉，一样可以拿到高分。因此，在短期内尽力提高语言能力的同时(语言能力的培养不是一天两天可以完成的)，考生在复习时应该尽可能地对题目进行深入的分析，学习高分文章的结构，通过这两个方面的突破来迅速提高写作的整体分数。另一方面，与Issue写作相比，Argument写作对我国考生来讲相对较容易，因此考生获得高分的策略应该是尽量提高Issue部分的写作能力，力保Argument部分获得高分甚至满分。因为如果Argument部分能拿满分的话，Issue部分只需争取在4分以上就可以保证写作总分在5分以上。

5. GMAT写作的阅卷进程及评分方法

考试结束后不久，阅卷人就会批阅考生的写作。写作成绩是一个从0～6分的综合成绩(而不是两个独立成绩)。分数不但会寄给考生，同时也会寄往考生所要求报送成绩的商学院。接下来我们着重介绍写作的阅卷、评分以及分数的报送程序。

(1)人工阅卷

在考试结束后的10到15天之内，考生的两篇GMAT写作就会被送到阅卷人的手中——通常是GMAC聘请的经过专门培训的大学教师。在评阅过程中，考生的写作试卷被随机分发给阅卷人，有关考生的任何信息都被隐藏。一个老师评阅考生的Issue写作，另一个老师评阅Argument写作，通常是独立进行的，他们之间不能相互沟通信息。

所有的GMAT阅卷人都采用"整体"评分法进行评分，他们会根据GMAC给出的评分标准，并结合考生写作的整体质量在0分与6分的范围内打分（以0.5分为一个分数单位），6分是最高分。应当指出，每个阅卷人对考生文章的评阅速度都非常快，不可能很仔细地去看每个细节。考生应该迎合阅卷人的评卷思路，用最规范的结构和最清晰的表达来体现自己的观点：首段要鲜明地提出观点，中间段落层次要拉开，每段的开始应该就是该段的主题句（Topic Sentence）。

(2)计算机阅卷（E-rater）

除了两位阅卷人会对考生的写作进行评分（一人负责一篇）外，还有一个叫做E-rater的电脑评分器也会对考生所写文章的质量进行评估。E-rater的工作原理类似Google这样的互联网搜索引擎。对官方公布的每一篇写作题目，在E-rater使用的数据库内都有上百篇评过分的文章。在评分时，计算机程序先扫描考生的文章，然后再把考生的文章与数据库中相同题目的评过分的文章进行比较。如果你的文章与题库中评过分的6分文章相接近，则考生的文章就被评为6分。如果考生的文章与题库中评过分的5分文章相接近，则考生的文章就被评为5分，以此类推。换句话说，如果考生写的某篇文章与E-rater数据库中对应的高分文章相似，考生就会得到一个高分。

如果了解了E-rater的偏好，那么从E-rater那里"骗取"高分（高于自己写作的应得分）将是一件非常容易的事。在这里，我们并不建议考生本着欺骗E-rater的目的来进行GMAT写作，但是了解E-rater怎样模拟人工进行阅卷对考生来说是非常有帮助的。让我们再来回顾一下评分的四个方面，看E-rater是怎样来分析这四个方面的：

① **遵循题目要求**：对E-rater来说，这一步相当于评价考生的文章是否就给定的题目进行写作。E-rater主要通过分析考生的文章使用题中某些关键词的情况来判断考生是否按照要求答题。所以，在文章中，不仅要出现写作题目中的词语，而且要尽量使用一些高分文章中出现的这些词语的同义词或相关用语。例如，有一篇Issue写作要求考生就下面的论题发表自己的观点："Business leaders have a responsibility to give back to the communities in which they operator." 考生应该在文章中尽量使用上面这句话中的关键字的同义词或相关短语。举例说明如下：

- business leader: entrepreneur, chief executive officer or CEO, corporation, captain of industry, capitalist
- responsibility: obligation, duty, accountability
- related phrases: citizen, shareholder, philanthropy, etc.

② **推理合乎逻辑**：当然，E-rater绝对不具备评价考生的推理过程的能力。E-rater能做的是搜索考生的文章，看考生的文章中是否使用了某些在推理无懈可击的文章中经常出现的过渡词。需要特别指出的是，E-rater会为在文章中使用下列词语的考生加分：

- 证据和结论词语：because, since, for example, therefore, thus, so, etc.
- 对比词语：however, but, although, conversely, nonetheless, still, yet, whereas, etc.
- 承接词语：likewise, similarly, in addition, also, moreover, furthermore, etc.

③ **结构紧凑**：E-rater会为结构通顺的文章加分，这类文章最主要的特征是段落分明——有一个开头段，几个主体段和一个结尾段。并且文章的过渡词使用得恰到好处。

④ **语言规范**：E-rater会为正确使用语法、拼写无误、句法多样（遣词造句）、句子结构丰富的文章加分。为了变换考生的句子结构，考生应该把长句和短句结合起来使用。最后，留出足够的时间来检查语法和拼写错误是非常重要的。

从上面的论述中我们可以看出，电脑评分器主要是对语法、句法（句子结构）、重复性（对同一个短语的过度使用）、句子的长度和拼写进行考查。在很多方面，电脑评分器类似于通用的文字处理软件，如Word和WordPerfect等内置的语法、拼写检查程序。但是ETS特意增加了电脑评分器在某些标准上的评分权重。比如一些操作性失误(标点符号或者拼写问题)就只有很小的权重。而且,电脑评分器会忽视语法的一些灰色区域(比如被动语态的使用),并把阅卷人容易忽视的问题标示出来(比如重复使用的问题)。当然,电脑评分器只是在某些方面能起到一些作用。它无法对考生的思想做出判断,它无法评价考生是如何有说服力地提出并支持自己的看法的,这些问题是阅卷人所要负责的内容。

纵观E-rater的要求,我们看到,结构和句式是很重要的。所以,我们在备考阶段就要从这些方面逐步入手,首先要达到E-rater的要求,进而获得高分。根据考试中心的说法,阅卷人和电脑评分器一起做出的评分结果可以解释超过50个结构性和语言方面的评分标准。每篇文章的最后得分是电脑阅卷和人工阅卷所给分数的算术平均值(除了下面会说到的一种情况)。

(3)GMAT写作成绩的计算方法

考生最后收到的AWA成绩是根据人工阅卷和电脑阅卷的成绩平均后得出的。下面简单介绍一下写作成绩的计算流程。

- **人工成绩:** 一个阅卷人负责给考生的Issue打分,而另一个阅卷人负责评阅考生的Argument,每个阅卷者都会给考生的文章一个整数成绩,从0~6分不等(6分最高)。
- **电脑成绩:** 电脑评分器也会对考生的文章打分,从0~6分不等。
- **例外情况:** 对于任何一篇文章,如果人工阅卷和电脑阅卷的分数相差超过一分,那么就会让另一位经验更丰富的阅卷人重新审阅考生的文章并打分(电脑评出的分数作废)。
- **计算方法:** 每一篇文章的最后得分都是阅卷人和电脑评分器得出分数的平均值(或者是和第二个阅卷人给出的分数的平均值)。
- **近似处理:** 写作的最终得分是两篇文章最终得分的平均值;分数近似到最近的一个0.5分。

为了帮助考生更好地理解AWA分数的计算流程,下面笔者给出了一个具体的例子:

阅卷者	分数	备注
A阅卷人对Issue写作的评分	5	A阅卷人与电脑评分器的分数相差2分,所以取消电脑评分器给出的成绩,而采用另一个阅卷人给出的成绩
电脑评分器对Issue写作的评分	3	
B阅卷人对Issue写作的评分	4	
Issue的最后得分	4.5	A与B给出的成绩取平均
C阅卷人对Argument写作的评分	4	C阅卷人与电脑评分器的分数一致
电脑评分器对Argument写作的评分	4	
Argument写作的最后得分	4	C与电脑给出的成绩取平均
分析写作测试(AWA)的最后得分	4.5	Issue与Argument的最后成绩取平均

更直白地说,考生AWA的最后成绩是4个整数的和除以4,其结果要么是整数,要么是以0.25, 0.5, 0.75结尾的小数。根据分数的近似处理原则,以0.5结尾的成绩不变,而以0.25结尾的成绩向上近似为0.5。同理,以0.75结尾的成绩向上近似为1。比如说,如果考生的Issue和Argument的四个成绩取平均后,分别是4.0, 4.25, 4.5, 4.75分,那么他们最后收到的AWA成绩分别是4.0, 4.5, 4.5, 5分。

(4)GMAT写作成绩的百分位

同多项选择题一样,考生的写作也会有一个从0%~99%的百分位成绩。例如,如果考生的百分位是80%,那就意味着考生的分数高于参加考试的80%的考生(而低于参加考试的20%的考生)。因此,百分位成绩体现的是考生与所有GMAT考生相比而得出的结果,并非考生与写同样题目的其他考生相比较的结果。

(5)向考生和相关学校寄送成绩的服务

在考试以后的10~15天内,考试中心将会把成绩通知单寄给考生。这份成绩单包括AWA成绩,也包括考生的百分位情况。同时，考试中心还将给考生所指定的学校寄出成绩通知单。另外，从2003年开始，学校不但可以收到考生的GMAT成绩单，而且还可以看到考生写的原文。

(6) 学校处理AWA分数的方式

写作分数相对于其他入学要求（即GMAT综合考试、GMAT单科考试、GPA、个人陈述、推荐信，工作经历等）所占的比重之多寡，将由各个研究生院自行决定。招生部门也许会用写作成绩来筛选所有的申请者。或者，他们会用写作成绩来决定取舍两个实力相当的考生。通常来讲，4分以下的分数会被认为写作能力不足，而5分以上才真正属于above-average（5分对应的percentile为67%）。所以，争取考到5分以上应该是每一个考生的奋斗目标。

6. GMAT写作的考试规则

GMAT的两项写作任务（第一部分和第二部分）是连续的（在数学和语文部分之前）。对于GMAT的两项写作任务，考生的工作就是利用计算机化测试系统（CAT）内置的文字处理软件针对题目所给的问题各写一篇相应的短文。对于两种类型的题目——Issue和Argument，每一类在CAT系统内都储存着一百多个题目。每个考试者的题目都是由CAT系统从这个题库中随机抽取出来的。下面是整个写作考试部分的一些需要注意的规则：

1. 每项写作任务的规定时间都是30分钟；
2. 如果考生在30分钟内完成了写作，可以点击计算机屏幕上相应的按钮进入下一个部分；
3. 考生一旦进入下一个部分，CAT系统就不允许再回到前一部分；
4. 在完成写作部分后，做多项选择题前，考生有5分钟的休息时间（但要注意的是在两篇30分钟的写作考试之间并没有休息时间）；
5. 考试时考场提供草稿纸和铅笔，同考多项选择题一样，考生可以在纸上草拟提纲。但考试结束后，必须把所有的草稿纸交给监考人员，不得将其带出考场。

另外，考试时允许使用无声计时器（GMAT机考界面上会显示当前部分还剩余多少时间，所以你可以不带计时器）。

二、Argument写作初探

Argument写作从内容到要求都与Issue写作有较大的不同。两者最为明显的区别是：Issue写作不但要求考生针对某一论题提出自己的观点，而且要求考生对自己的观点进行令人信服的论证；而Argument写作的任务则是要求考生分析一段论述，并评价结论中所给出的理由有什么优点与弱点。Argument写作不要求考生提出自己对某一讨论的问题所持的立场，只要求考生对别人的推理和论证是否可信做一番评论。

Argument题目一般都有这样的结构，如"我们应该做这件事因为它能够完成这个或那个"。从纯粹形式化的观点来看，Argument题目由两个部分构成：第一部分是一句介绍性的话，用来提供论述的背景，这一句话没有逻辑错误可言，其常见的形式如下：

- The following appeared as a memo from...
- The following appeared in a press release issued by...
- The following appeared as part of an article published in...

第二部分是论述本身，是一段完整的逻辑分析，其中有一个陈述阐明了结论，其他的是论述的前提。这些前提也可以被引用作为结论的证据。在Argument的题目中，大多数的论述都涉及提高企业绩效的建议、社区发展规划、教育政策、健康与安全等方面的问题。在第二部分的陈述中，其中肯定包含逻辑错误，这是考生阅读和攻击的重点。考试指令首先要求考生讨论这篇论述的推理怎么样，他们从以下四个方面来详细描述考试要求：

1）考生必须分析原论证的推理过程，评价用来支持原论证的结论或建议的证据的相关性及有效性；
2）考生必须指出文中暗含的支持原论证的假设。如果这些假设有问题的话，考生应该解释为什么会有这样的问题；

3）考生必须引用其他的解释、事实、反例或者其他可以削弱原论述结论的证据；

4）考生必须讨论在原论述的推理过程中还需要加入哪些额外信息才能加强原论证，以及加入哪些额外信息将会削弱原论证的结论。

总之，考生不但要指出题目中的逻辑错误所在，并加以分析，同时应使用举例、比较等议论文的写作手法，证明自己对逻辑错误分析的正确性和充分性。实际上，考试指令并未要求考生在文章中必须包含上面所列出的每一点。然而，如果想获得Argument高分，考生应该在文章中详细地讨论上面所列出的每一项。

1. Argument的构思过程简介

考生有30分钟的时间来构思并完成这篇短文。要想获得Argument写作高分，考生必须要做到以下三点：

1）找出题目中的主要逻辑错误（漏洞）；

2）组织、发展和阐述评论。评论不但要符合逻辑，而且要条理清楚并令人信服；

3）用有代表性的例子和有力的证据来支持自己的见解。

考生在动笔之前，可能需要几分钟好好思考一下；写完之后，可能也需要留些时间再浏览一下写过的内容，并做一些必要的修改。

下面是一道Argument题目：

> The following appeared in an editorial in a Prunty County newspaper.
>
> "In an attempt to improve highway safety, Prunty County recently lowered its speed limit from 55 miles per hour to 45 on all major county roads. But the 55 mph limit should be restored, because this safety effort has failed. Most drivers are exceeding the new speed limit and the accident rate throughout Prunty County has decreased only slightly. If we want to improve the safety of our roads, we should instead undertake the same kind of road improvement project that Butler County completed five years ago: increasing lane widths and resurfacing rough roads. Today, major Butler County roads still have a 55 mph speed limit, yet there were 25 percent fewer reported accidents in Butler County this past year than there were five years ago."

从上面这一段论述中，我们可以看出Argument题干包含三个要素：第一个要素是作者的论点（proposition）、主张（claim）或结论（conclusion）。表明作者主张或结论的信号词主要有so, therefore, consequently, hence, thus, instead等。第二个要素是作者的假设（assumption），即阶段性的小结论或推论，也可以理解为结论成立的基本前提。假设有时在题目中明确陈述出来，有时是隐藏的。第三个要素是作者的论据（evidence），包括事实（facts）和基于事实的谨慎的推理（reasoning）。总之，如果要写好一篇Argument，考生需要关注两点：结论和支持结论的论据。通过认真读题，我们发现本题的结论和论据如下：

结论 （1）The 55 mph limit should be restored.

（2）We should instead undertake the same kind of road improvement project that Butler County completed five years ago, increasing lane widths and resurfacing rough roads.

论据 （1）The safety effort——lowering the speed limit from 55 miles per hour to 45 on all major county roads in Prunty County——has failed. Most drivers are exceeding the new speed limit and the accident rate throughout Prunty County has decreased only slightly.

（2）Butler County completed a road improvement project five years ago: increasing lane widths and resurfacing rough roads. Today, major Butler County roads still have a 55 mph speed limit, yet there were 25 percent fewer reported accidents in Butler County this past year than there were five years ago.

因为Argument的命题目的不是要求说明你相信什么，而是要求评价命题者提出的用于支持结论的理由的好坏。所以，找出题目的结论和论据之后，我们可以从以下几个方面入手来进行分析：

1）论据是否可靠？

2）该段论述是否做了没有证据的假设？

3）结论是否能由论据得出？

4）该段论述是否忽略了其他能够加强或减弱Argument的因素或信息？

接下来，我们从上面四个方面入手，对本题的论据进行分析，并揭示论题论证中的漏洞。

论据（1）表明Prunty县所实施的交通安全措施（lowering the speed limit from 55 miles per hour to 45 on all major county roads）是失败的。其依据主要有两点：第一，"Most drivers are exceeding the new speed limit"；第二，"the accident rate throughout Prunty County has decreased only slightly"。作者的推论实际上已经假设了这样的判断标准：这次交通限速措施若要成功，首先，"Most drivers are not exceeding the new speed limit"；其次，"the accident rate throughout Prunty County must decrease greatly"。这种假设是毫无根据的：一方面司机可能需要一定的时间来适应新的限速，另一方面交通标志的数量不足也会使司机在不知不觉中超出了速度限制。"the accident rate throughout Prunty County has decreased only slightly"也不能说明这次交通限速措施失败了，很可能在实施交通限速措施的主要道路上事故发生率大大下降，而发生在次要路段上的交通事故数量则大幅上升，因而全县的交通事故只是小幅下降。

论据（2）的推理论证也存在很多的漏洞。首先，作者做了不当的纵向和横向类比。五年前可行的事情在今天未必可行；在Butler县可行的办法在Prunty县未必可行。其次，作者犯了"后此谬误（在此之后，因此之故）的逻辑错误"。他怎么知道Butler县交通事故下降25%就是因为那个"road improvement project"呢？没有别的原因吗？第三，作者所说的是"there were 25 percent fewer reported accidents in Butler County this past year than there were five years ago"。注意这里的"reported accidents"，它意味着很可能有些交通事故并未报告、统计上来。所以，很可能那个所谓的"road improvement project"并未使交通事故发生率下降多少。第四，即使Butler县交通事故下降25%是由"road improvement project"引起的，作者也没有给出证据表明Butler县主干道上的交通事故也有大幅的下降。很有可能25%的下降是由非主干道上的交通事故大幅减少造成的。最后，作者并未说明Butler县将交通限速从每小时55英里调低到每小时45英里的情况。那么，他怎能断定这样的措施在这个县没有用呢？也许，Butler县将交通限速从每小时55英里调低到每小时45英里时，主干道上的交通事故发生率会大幅下降呢。

2. Argument写作的注意事项

Argument写作的核心问题是找出原命题中的漏洞。要想顺利通过Argument写作的第一关，考生在平时练习或考试时应当注意以下七点：

1）考生的分析要严格集中在论证的逻辑特征上。正式的写作要求告诉考生不要在文中提出自己对主题的观点。也就是说，考生不必对作者的立场本身表示赞同或反对，而应探讨支持作者观点的推理思路；

2）不应对原题所涉及的话题发表看法，而应评价原论述的逻辑性；

3）不关注原题中的陈述是否精确或真实，而应关注结论和推理是否能有效地从这些陈述中推导而出；

4）区分哪些是证据，哪些是假设（明说的或暗示的），哪些是结论或作者的主张；

5）要密切注意原论述中的信号词（如so, therefore, consequently, however, thus, in conclusion, evidently, hence），因为这些信号词通常表明上下文的逻辑联系；

6）注意原论述的结构或推理思路，看看每一步推理是否合乎逻辑；

7）出题者在每道Argument题目中都有意加入了一些逻辑缺陷，考生必须将其指出并加以讨论。与Issue题目的要求相反，Argument题目的要求并不会"没有正确答案"。这是因为在出Argument题目时，出题者都会毫无例外地在论证中加入一些逻辑问题（缺陷或谬误），为考生提供一些可写的东西。如果考生没有发现论证中"内置"的一些基本问题的话，是拿不到高分的。

3. Argument的内容

根据题目要求，考生必须在Argument写作中完成以下任务（最后一个任务的重要性要低于前三个）：

● 分析文中的推理思路以及证据的使用；

- 评价题目论证思路的说服力(逻辑的合理性);
- 用合理的推理或相关的例证来支持自己的批判;
- 谈谈什么能够让题目的论证更有说服力及/或什么能让自己更好地评价该论证。

在阅读题目的时候考虑以下问题可以让考生的思维保持活跃并把握正确的方向:

- 题目的结论是什么?
- 作者支持结论的理由是什么?
- 作者的题目所依赖的假设是什么?(至少想一个)
- 题目的逻辑是否可信? 如果是,为什么是? 如果不是,又为什么不是?
- 增加什么信息/证据可以加强论证?
- 增加什么信息/证据可以削弱论证?

要获得Argument写作高分,除了指出论证中的关键错误之外,并不要求考生在文中一定包括某些观点、理由、解释或反例等。而且,同Issue一样,Argument写作也没有"正确"或"固定"的写作格式。最后要注意的是,Argument文章不可太短,字数最好在350词左右。从统计上看,个别长度在260词以内的Argument文章有得5分的,但6分Argument文章的长度一般都在350词左右或更长。不过,Argument文章也没必要超过500词,400词就足够了。

Chapter 2

第二章 Argument 写作三大策略

　　尽管考试服务中心明确指出，对Argument写作来说没有所谓的正确的或最好的结构模式，但考生在行文的时候还是要遵循某些策略，否则评卷者将无法理解考生的思路，从而给他们留下不好的印象。

　　同样的，Argument写作也没有"正确"的或"最佳"的段落数。但是，考生必须确保文章有完整的开头、正文和结尾，而且各部分分工明确，上下连贯。正文部分最好不要少于三段，因为每一篇官方范文都至少指出了原命题中三个严重的逻辑错误。如果把每一个逻辑错误作为一个自然段展开论述的话，我们就可以把Argument写成经典的五段式：

　　第一段：开头

　　第二段：正文第一段，论证谬误之一

　　第三段：正文第二段，论证谬误之二

　　第四段：正文第三段，论证谬误之三

　　第五段：结尾

　　全文共计五个意群段。当然，不是说所有的Argument写作都必须是这样的结构。正文段也可以有超过三个或者只有两个意群段（即只对题目中的两个推理／论证谬误进行充分地分析）。

一、开头策略

　　Argument的开头段可以程式化设计，这样既节省时间，又保证质量。大体说来，考生在开头段可以用三到四个句子表达三层意思：

　　1）简洁地复述原文中的结论或主张；

　　2）归纳原论述的假设和／或论据（可以既谈假设又谈论据，也可以只谈假设，或只谈论据）；

　　3）指出原文论证中的问题。

　　根据这几点要求，也针对题库中题目的特点，我们可以用下面给出的几种写作套路来写开头段：

1）The argument is well-presented, but not thoroughly well reasoned. By..., the argument... seems logical.

2）The conclusion in this argument is that... This recommendation is based on the observation that... Meanwhile, the arguer assumes that... This argument is problematic for several reasons.

3）In this analysis, the arguer concludes that... To support this conclusion, the arguer cites the result of a resent survey that... Moreover, the arguer points out that... As it stands, the argument suffers from several critical flaws, as follows.

4）The arguer attempts to convince us that... The major assumptions underlying this argument are... While this argument has some merits, several critical flaws seriously undermine the line of reasoning.

5）The author concludes that... To support the conclusion, the author reasons that... The author also points out that... However, several logical fallacies seriously weaken（undermine, cast doubts on）the validity of the reasoning, making / rendering the argument highly suspect.

6）In this argument, the arguer recommends that... To justify the conclusion, the arguer points out that... In addition, the arguer assumes that / reasons that / cites the example of / cites the results of a recent study that... A careful examination of this argument reveals how groundless it is.

7）In this argument, the arguer cites the evidence that..., based on which he assumes that... Another piece of evidence presented to support the argument is that... In addition, the arguer takes it for granted that... Hence the arguer draws the conclusion that... This argument is flawed in several aspects.

8）Merely dependent on a series of unwarranted assumptions and dubious evidence, the author comes to the conclusion that... On the surface, the argument appears to be somewhat logical, however, this alone neither provides compelling evidence to make the argument sound nor organizes a logical argument in favor of the conclusion.

9）In this argument, the arguer asserts that... The major assumption(s) underlying this argument is（are）that... （and that...） The evidence presented throughout the argument, however, is vague / insufficient / unreliable / doubtful / irrelevant and hence does not lend strong support to what the arguer claims.

10）The arguer's claim that... sounds reasonable at first thought. After all, the arguer does offer some relevant evidence, and the assumptions underlying this argument are not without merits. However, several important concerns, which the arguer fails to address in the analysis, may seriously undermine the argument.

11）In this analysis / argument, the arguer concludes / claims / recommends / predicts / advocates that... To support / strengthen / solidify / justify / substantiate the conclusion, the arguer points out that... / provides the evidence of... / cites the result of the survey of... In addition / Furthermore, the arguer reasons that... However, a careful examination of this argument would reveal how groundless the conclusion is / the argument is unconvincing for（多少个）critical flaws / the argument is problematic for（多少个）reasons / faults with vague, oversimplified and unwarranted assumptions.

12）Merely based on unfounded assumptions and dubious evidence, the statement draws a conclusion that... To support the conclusion, the arguer points out evidence that... In addition, he indicates that... Furthermore, the arguer reasons / asserts / infers that... However, this alone neither constitutes a logical argument in favor of the conclusion nor provides compelling support to make the argument sound. The arguer ignores certain important concerns, which must be addressed to prove. In my point of view, this argument suffers from（多少个）critical flaws.

13）The conclusion endorsed in this argument is that... Several reasons are offered in support of this argument. First of all, the author points out that... In addition, the author reasons that... What's more, he also assumes that... At first glance, the author's argument appears to be somewhat convincing, but further reflection reveals that the conclusion is based on some dubious assumptions and the reasoning is biased due to the inadequacy and partiality of the nature of the evidence provided to justify the conclusion. A careful examination would review how groundless this conclusion is.

14）At first glance, the argument appears plausible, however, strict examination（scrutiny）reveals that it（the author's reasoning）is unconvincing...
  > for several reasons
  > for the following logical fallacies / reasoning errors
  > because it suffers from several critical flaws
  > because several questionable assumptions must be made for the stated evidence to support the author's conclusion
  > because it rests on（depends on, relies on, is based on）several unwarranted（doubtful, problematic, ungrounded, groundless, questionable, gratuitous, dubious）assumptions

　　为了使开头的方式更加多变，考生应当熟记下面的这些关键词，并达到能灵活运用的程度。这样，在练习或考试时，只要结合题目对某些词进行替换，就能打造出属于自己的开头模板。
  • rest on, depend on, rely on, be based on
  • however, nevertheless, nonetheless
  • additionally, in addition, moreover, furthermore
  • unacceptable, unconvincing, unpersuasive
  • ungrounded（groundless）, unfounded, unwarranted

- unsound, weak, unsubstantiated, flimsy, flawed, faulty, fallacious, fallible, erroneous
- doubtful, dubious, doubtable, dubitable, suspicious, suspect
- problematic, questionable

考生在写开头段时，一定要注意以下三点：
1. 复述原题信息要简洁、准确和客观；
2. 在归纳原题信息时尽可能用自己的句式和词汇，但为了能准确表达原文的意思，核心词汇可以保留；
3. 复述原题基本信息时保留原题的时态。分析性动词(对于原文作者的批驳和攻击)用一般现在时，这是全文的基本时态。

二、正文策略

对于正文部分的写作，我们首要关心的是正文的结构，其次是正文展开的攻击策略以及信号词、常用句型等。

1. 正文的结构

正文的结构应尽可能地反映整篇文章的论证过程。考生应该对原论述的论据(evidence)和假设(assumption)、原论述的中间结论(intermediate conclusion)(如果有的话)以及最终的结论(final conclusion)依次进行批驳。如果原论述中有三个明显的漏洞，且把每个漏洞作为一段展开攻击的话，正文部分的结构如下：

1) A first major assumption(about an item of evidence) is needed to justify the intermediate conclusion.
2) A second major assumption (about an item of evidence) is also needed to justify the intermediate conclusion.
3) If the intermediate conclusion is true, a third major assumption is still needed to justify the final conclusion.

对于某些Argument来说，评论的关键在于对该Argument的结论成立所依赖的某个初始假设进行批驳。下面我们给出了这类命题的正文部分结构(分四段论证)：

1) The threshold assumption is needed before addressing the Argument's main line of reasoning.
2) If the threshold assumption is true, a first major assumption (about an item of evidence) is still needed to justify the Argument's conclusion.
3) If the threshold assumption is true, a second major assumption (about an item of evidence) is still needed to justify the Argument's conclusion.
4) Even if all of the foregoing assumptions are true, a third (and final) major assumption is still needed to justify the Argument's conclusion.

当然，大多数的Argument文章并不会完全符合上面所讲到的两种结构，但是考生评论Argument的主要思路都是一样的：理清原文的推理过程，从原文的论据入手，然后考虑原文的假设和中间结论(如果有的话)，最后再考虑原文的最终结论。在Argument正文的写作过程中，考生要注意以下几点：

1) 每一段的第一句话为主题句(Topic Sentence)，指出将要展开分析的逻辑错误；
2) 在写正文时要按逻辑错误来分段，段落的数量一般以三至四段为最佳，先攻击主要的逻辑错误，然后涉及一般性问题。如果某题的逻辑错误多于三个，则可以先用前两段分别攻击两个主要的逻辑错误，其它次要的逻辑错误全部放在正文的第三段；
3) 许多Argument的论断都依赖于某些"初始化"假设(例如，一个含糊不清或未定义的词语的意思)。提出这类假设最合乎逻辑的位置是正文部分的第一段，因为这样将会为考生批驳整篇Argument文章的推理扫清障碍；
4) 许多Argument会依赖于这样的假设：作者建议的行为是达到既定目的或结果的必要、充分或充要条

件。讨论这类假设最合乎逻辑的位置是在正文部分的最后一段，在这一段中，考生承认所有其他假设
是正确的，然后再对该假设进行批驳；

5）有些Argument本身就含有逻辑问题（例如，自相矛盾的建议或目标，循环论证等）。通常，解决这类问题最
合乎逻辑的位置是正文部分的最后一段。在这一段中，考生承认所有其他假设都是正确的，然后再对
该逻辑问题进行批驳。

在大多数情况下，考生可以按照上面所讲的原则来确定主体部分的段数以及段落之间的逻辑顺序。除此
之外，考生还可以考虑下面两方面的内容：

1）Suggestions as to how the Argument can be strengthened

2）Additional information needed to evaluate the Argument

如果时间允许，考生可以在自己的评论中加入以上两方面的内容，其方法如下：

1）把建议（或必要的额外信息）融入到每一个主体段的写作过程中。比如：指出某一个特定的假设要想成
立，需要额外的证据支持；

2）在最后一段，罗列出你的建议（或额外信息）。

2. 正文的攻击策略

在Argument正文的写作过程中，对题目所包含逻辑错误的识别固然重要，但更为关键的是对这些错误和
漏洞的分析，即为什么它们是推理或论证过程中的谬误。这实际上就是如何展开正文段写作的问题。正文的每
一段都要展开来剖析典型的逻辑错误。具体如何批驳是十分灵活的，从总体上讲，主要的攻击策略如下：

1）指出推理或论证中出现的谬误：考生要明确指出：为什么某个地方可以被认为是推理或论证谬误？它
错在什么地方？

2）提出改进建议：指出哪些证据可以加强原论述，或对原论述做出怎样的改变可以使它更有逻辑。

3）寻求其他解释：是否可以设想是其他原因导致了某一结果；是否可以换一个角度解释某一现象。例如，
题目中说事件A是事件B的原因，如果考生认为A不是B的原因，就应该指出真正的原因可能是什么，
并论证这个真正原因成立的可能性。

4）举出反例：假设对原论述不利或削弱其逻辑性的论据出现。同样，假如题目说事件A是事件B的原因，
如果考生认为A不是B的原因，他只需举出若干相反的例证就够了。

5）解剖推理过程：追踪原论述的推理思路，看看它是由哪些要素构成的。

3. 正文部分的转折过渡词

正文段落之间的起承转合以及过渡衔接离不开转折过渡词。正文部分的三个（或四个）段落一般是彼此并
列或层层递进的关系，考生会很自然地运用诸如"First"，"Second"，"Third"，"Last but not least"这样的转折过
渡词或短语。这样的做法无可厚非，但恰恰因为大多数人都会这样做，你不妨对这种账本式的罗列略微做
一些变化。在千篇一律的文章之中，只有你的文章看起来有些与众不同，必然要比别人多一些优势。

1）承上启下

a）In the first place, In the second place, In the third place

b）First of all, In addition, Finally

c）To begin with, Furthermore, Last but not least

d）Most obviously, In addition, Finally

e）The major problem with this argument is that... / Another problem that weakens / undermines the
logic of this argument is that... / Before I come to my conclusion, it is necessary to point out another
flaw that undermine(s) the argument.

2）例证：for example / instance

3）假设：if, even if, given that（考虑到），granted that（承认），only when（只有当），unless, in this / that case , even so, unless the arguer provides substantial evidence regarding / concerning / as to..., the assumption that... is unfounded / problematic / unconvincing

4）推测：it is possible that..., it is equally possible that..., another possibility is that..., it is also likely that..., possibly, perhaps

> 注·意
>
> 以上这些词或者短语要用得自然，不可滥用，以致于满篇都是这些转折过渡词。用这些词的关键在于结合文章的逻辑发展，自然而灵活地应用，只要达到使上下文有机地联系在一起的目的即可。

4. 正文部分的常用句型

正文部分每一段的第一句话通常是该段的主题句（topic sentence），这也是阅卷者必看的一句话。所以考生不但要保证这一句话在语言上精彩、地道，而且要准确无误地描述那个将要攻击的逻辑错误。下面给出了主题句一些常见的表达方法，供考生参考。

1）Another assumption short of legitimacy is the causal relationship claimed between... and...

2）Another reasoning error is that...

3）Another weakness worth pointing out is that...

4）Given that..., the author made a premature conclusion / the author's claim / conclusion is premature.

5）If so, even if..., the argument that... would be seriously undermined.

6）Not only does the author fail to..., but also he fails to...

7）The arguer assumes that... However, no evidence is provided to support this assumption. We are only informed that...

8）The arguer assumes that... may be indicative of... However, there is no clear / compelling evidence to prove that...

9）The arguer assumes that... merely based on the fact that...

10）The arguer commits a fallacy of...

11）The arguer fails to consider / acknowledge and rule out / eliminate / exclude other possibilities / factors that...

12）The arguer fails to consider / fails to take into account / ignores / neglects / overlooks the possibility that...

13）The arguer fails to convince us that...

14）The arguer fails to establish a causal relationship between the fact that... and the assumption / assertion / conclusion that...

15）The arguer fails to establish a causal relationship between... and...

16）The arguer fails to present any information concerning...

17）The arguer fails to provide any evidence to prove that...

18）The arguer fails to take into account（consider / explain）other possible reasons.

19）The arguer ignores other relevant factors concerning...

20）The arguer overemphasizes the importance of...

21）The arguer unfairly assumes that...

22）The arguer's conclusion depends on the questionable assumption that...

23）The argument depends on（rests on / relies on）the gratuitous / unreasonable assumption（s）that...

24）The author provides no justification for...

25）The evidence provided in this argument is not sufficient to validate the assumption that...

26）The evidence / facts cannot lend support to the claim / assumption / assertion that...

27）The fact that... does not ensure that... / does not lend strong support to...

28）The fact that... accomplishes nothing toward bolstering...

29) The fact that... does not necessarily mean that (ensure that)...

30) The fact that... is insufficient to prove / establish that...

31) The fact that... lends no support to the conclusion that...

32) The fact that... says / tells little / nothing (says nothing) about the conclusion that...

33) The fact... does not lend significant support to the claim / assumption that...

34) The fact... is scant evidence that...

35) The first problematic assumption is that / involves that...

36) The first / major problem with the argument is that / involves...

37) The reasoning that... is open to doubt (doubtful / problematic / questionable / unconvincing / unfounded / unwarranted).

38) The second / another assumption (that is) short of / lacking legitimacy / without justification is that...

39) The statistical evidence / the result of the survey upon which the argument relies is too vague to be informative.

40) There are several assumptions that deserve attention.

41) Unless the author can prove that..., the author's claim / assumption / conclusion / assertion that... is unfounded.

42) We are merely informed that... We cannot ensure that / whether...

43) We cannot safely infer that... from the mere fact that...

44) While it is true that..., it is also likely / true that...

三、结尾策略

Argument写作结尾部分的主要任务是总结自己的评论。常见的结尾方式有两种:

1) 客套式结尾: 首先,对题目中的推理做一下纯粹礼节性的肯定,然后指出该论证推理中的问题。

2) 提出希望、建议式结尾: 这样的结尾只是简单地指出题目中推理 / 论证的问题,并给出如何改进的希望和建议。

实际上,将题目中的推理或论证谬误——陈述清楚后,结尾段就显得无关紧要了,所以考生不应在结尾段上花费太多的时间,而应速战速决。如果不幸碰到复杂的题目,有很多逻辑问题需要分析,那么宁可舍弃结尾,也要尽量全面地攻击应该攻击的逻辑错误。为了节省考场上宝贵的时间,考生也可以事先设计好写作模块,以不变应万变。下面给出了一些结尾段的写作模板,供考生参考:

1) As it stands, the argument is not well reasoned. To make it logically acceptable, the arguer should demonstrate that... Additionally, the arguer must provide...

   * evidence to rule out all the above-mentioned possibilities that might weaken the argument.

   * more specific evidence to validate the assumptions.

2) In conclusion, the arguer fails to demonstrate that... To strengthen the argument, the author would have to provide evidence that... To better evaluate the argument we would need information about...

3) In summary, the argument is unacceptable (unconvincing, not convincing) as it stands. To strengthen the argument, the author would have to demonstrate that... To better evaluate the argument, the author must...

4) In conclusion, the arguer fails to justify the claims that... (原论者的结论). To solidify the argument, the arguer should supply more concrete information to demonstrate that... In addition, the arguer would have to rule out(exclude) the above mentioned possibilities that may undermine the argument.

5) In summary, the conclusion reached in this argument is invalid and misleading. To make the argument more convincing, the arguer would have to prove that... Moreover, I would suspend my judgment about the credibility of the recommendation until the arguer can provide concrete evidence that...

6）In conclusion, this argument is not persuasive as it stands. To make it more convincing, the arguer would have to provide more evidence concerning... / provide evidence to rule out other possible causes of... To better evaluate the argument, we would need more information regarding...

7）Overall, the reasoning... seems logical as presented above since... However, before any final decisions are made about..., ... should evaluate all possible alternatives and causes for...

8）To conclude, this argument is not persuasive as it stands. Before we accept the conclusion, the arguer must present more facts to prove that... To solidify the argument, the arguer would have to produce more evidence concerning...

9）To sum up, the conclusion lacks credibility because the evidence cited in the analysis does not lend strong support to the arguer's claim. To make the argument more convincing / To make it logically acceptable, the arguer would have to provide more specific evidence concerning that....

10）To sum up, the conclusion lacks credibility because the evidence cited in the analysis does not lend strong support to what the arguer maintains. To strengthen the argument, the arguer would have to provide more evidence concerning... To better evaluate the argument, we would need more information regarding...

11）To sum up, the conclusion reached in the argument lacks credibility since the evidence cited in the analysis does not lend strong support to what the arguer claims. To make the argument more convincing, the arguer should provide more information concerning... To better evaluate the argument, we need more concrete evidence that... Otherwise the argument is logically unacceptable.

12）To conclude, though the argument seems to be plausible, it is actually neither sound nor persuasive. Not only does it leave out key issues, but also cites in the analysis the evidence, which does not lend strong support to what the arguer claims. To make the argument more convincing, the arguer would have to take the following conditions into consideration... If the argument includes the given factors discussed above, it would have been more thorough and adequate.

13）To conclude, this argument is not persuasive as it stands. Accordingly, it is imprudent for the author to claim that... To make this argument logically acceptable, the author would have to show that... In addition, to solidify the conclusion, the author should provide concrete evidence as well to demonstrate that... Only with more convincing evidence could this argument become more than just an emotional appeal.

本章给出了很多开头、正文以及结尾的模板。这些模板虽然都很精彩, 但仅供参考。千万不要死记硬背这些模板, 因为这样做不但不能获得理想的分数, 而且还会因为涉嫌抄袭而被取消成绩。考生可以熟记这些模板, 并根据这些模板的思路和句型, 灵活地加入一些精辟、美妙的词汇来编制具有自己特色的模板。

第三章　Argument 写作七大步骤

　　一般来说，Argument的写作可分为七个步骤：读题，列提纲，写首段，写主体段，写尾段，文章结构检查，语法和拼写检查。整个写作的流程及每一步所用的参考时间如下图所示：

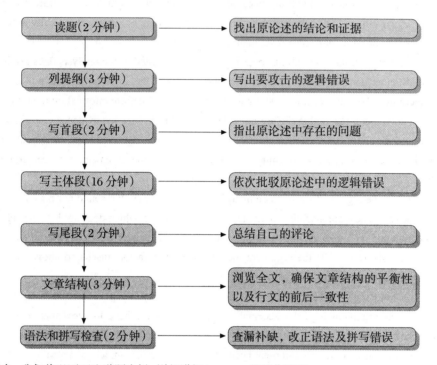

读题(2分钟)	→	找出原论述的结论和证据
列提纲(3分钟)	→	写出要攻击的逻辑错误
写首段(2分钟)	→	指出原论述中存在的问题
写主体段(16分钟)	→	依次批驳原论述中的逻辑错误
写尾段(2分钟)	→	总结自己的评论
文章结构(3分钟)	→	浏览全文，确保文章结构的平衡性以及行文的前后一致性
语法和拼写检查(2分钟)	→	查漏补缺，改正语法及拼写错误

　　接下来，我们将以下面这道题为例，详细讲解Argument的写作流程。

Discuss how well reasoned you find this argument.

The University of Claria is generally considered one of the best universities in the world because of its instructors' reputation, which is based primarily on the extensive research and publishing record of certain faculty members. In addition, several faculty members are internationally renowned as leaders in their fields. For example, many of the faculty from the English department are regularly invited to teach at universities in other countries. Furthermore, two recent graduates of the physics department have gone on to become candidates for the Nobel Prize in Physics. And 75 percent of the students are able to find employment after graduating. Therefore, because of the reputation of its faculty, the University of Claria should be the obvious choice for anyone seeking a quality education.

1. 读题，找出原论述的结论和证据

　　找结论是首要也是最重要的一步。因为只有确定了原论述的结论，才有可能对原文作者的推理或论证展开攻击，这也正是Argument写作的核心任务。有些题目的结论可能不止一个，这时我们根据它们的作用，把它们分为"中间结论（intermediate conclusion）"和"总结论（final conclusion）"。总结论一般是原论述的第一句或最后一句话，以"建议（recommendation）"、"声称（claim）"或"预言（prediction）"等的形式出现，通常由therefore， thus, consequently, so等信号词引导。通过读题，我们发现本题的第一句话和最后一句话分别是原论述的"中间结论"和"总结论"。为了便于分析，罗列如下：

1）**中间结论**：The University of Claria is generally considered one of the best universities in the world because of its instructors' reputation, which is based primarily on the extensive research and publishing record of certain faculty members.

2）**总结论**：Therefore, because of the reputation of its faculty, the University of Claria should be the obvious choice for anyone seeking a quality education.

经过观察，我们发现总结论依赖于中间结论，它们之间的主要逻辑关系如下：

1）The University of Claria is generally considered one of the best universities in the world.（中间结论）

2）Therefore, the University of Claria should be the obvious choice for anyone seeking a quality education.（总结论）

结论通常都是由一些论据（evidence）来支撑的，大多数题目中都有至少两三个论据来支持题目中所提出的结论。本题的论据如下：

1）Several faculty members are internationally renowned as leaders in their fields.

2）Many of the faculty from the English department are regularly invited to teach at universities in other countries.

3）Two recent graduates of the physics department have gone on to become candidates for the Nobel Prize in Physics.

4）And 75 percent of the students are able to find employment after graduating.

列出论据以后，就要认真分析这些论据是如何支持原论述的中间结论和总结论的。特别要留意原论述的结论是否依赖于某些未经证实或不合理的假设。同时，要考虑哪些额外的信息会有助于你对某一个论据是否很好地支持了结论进行评价。除此之外，还要考虑以下两点：

1）原论述本身是否存在逻辑错误（例如，自相矛盾的说法或循环论证等）；

2）原论述是否依赖于某些含糊不清，或未经定义的关键术语。

2. 列提纲，写出要攻击的逻辑错误

毋庸置疑，每一道Argument题目都至少包含三到四个独立的逻辑错误，根据第一步的分析，把这些逻辑错误记录下来。用一分钟的时间考虑，这些逻辑错误是否有重复的地方，或某一个逻辑错误是否可以分成两个独立的问题来讨论。然后，把这些逻辑错误按照它们的严重程度进行排序。在大多情况下，攻击这些逻辑错误的最佳顺序应与它们在原论述中出现的顺序一致。为了方便，我们可以先写出中文的攻击提纲：

1）诚然，该学校在英语和物理方面有非常杰出的人才。但这并不能表明该校的教学质量高，教学效果好；

2）题目中提供的信息太笼统了，学生们无法根据这些信息做出自己的选择；

3）75%的就业率并不能表明该校毕业生的就业前景很好。

相应的英文提纲如下：

1）The fact that the English and Physics departments have excellent scholars does not necessarily mean that their teaching skills and their abilities to pass on knowledge and the love of learning to their students are equally laudable.

2）This evaluation of the University of Claria is too brief and too general.

3）75% employment record is not sufficient to support the assumption that most of the graduates of the University of Claria can find their desired jobs.

3. 写开头段，指出原论述中的推理错误

在开头段不要简单地重复原文的论述，因为阅卷者已经对这些内容非常熟悉了，他们只对考生的评论感

兴趣。一般来说，在开头段考生应该完成以下三项任务：

    1）指出原文作者的结论；

    2）简述原文的推理过程以及支持结论的证据；

    3）指出原文在推理以及论据使用上所存在的问题。

根据以上原则，本题的开头段可以如下：

While the University of Claria appears to have an excellent reputation based on the accomplishments and reputations of its faculty, one would want to consider other issues before deciding upon this particular institution for undergraduate or graduate training. The Physics and English departments are internationally known, but these are only two of the areas in which one might study. Other departments are not listed; is this because no others are worth mentioning, or because no other departments bothered to turn in their accomplishments and kudos to the publicity office?

4. 写主体段，依次批驳原论述中的逻辑错误

考生在主体段要完成的主要任务就是把自己的见解输入到电脑中。在写主体段时，要注意以下几点：

    1）每一个主要的逻辑错误最好用一段展开论述，每段的第一句话是本段的主题句；

    2）对原论述的每一个主要假设，考生至少要举出一个例子（一种情形）来削弱它；

    3）对提纲中任一要点的论述最好不要超过三到四句话。不然就可能来不及讨论原论述中所有的主要错误；

    4）段与段之间的过渡要符合逻辑；

    5）不必为你的论述没有囊括所有可能出现的逻辑错误而担心。阅卷者能够理解考生受时间限制而不能在论述中表达全面。所以，考生只要用心去攻击原论述中最主要以及最严重的逻辑错误就可以了。

根据以上几点以及所列提纲中的要点，正文部分如下：

The assumption is that because English and Physics have excellent scholars on their faculty, their teaching skills and their abilities to pass on knowledge and the love of learning to their students are equally laudable. Unfortunately, this is often not the case. A prospective student would certainly be advised to thoroughly investigate the teaching talents and attitudes of the professors, the library and research facilities, the physical aspects of the departments in which he or she is planning to study, as well as the living arrangements on or off campus, and the facilities available for leisure activities and entertainment.

This evaluation of the University of Claria is too brief, and too general. Nothing is mentioned about the quality of overall education; it only praises the accomplishments of a few recent graduates and professors. More important than invitations to teach elsewhere, which might have been engineered by their own departmental heads in an attempt to remove them from the campus for a semester or two, is the relationship between teacher and student. Are the teaching faculty approachable? Are they helpful? Do they have an interest in passing on their knowledge? Are they working for the future benefit of the student or to get another year closer to retirement? How enthusiastic are the students about the courses being taught and the faculty members who teach those classes? Are there sufficient classes available for the number of students? Are the campus buildings accessible, and how is the University handling all those cars? Is the University a pleasant, encouraging, interesting, challenging place to attend school? What are its attitudes about education, students, student ideas and innovations, faculty suggestions for improvement?

What about that 75% employment record? Were those students employed in the field of their choice, or are they flipping burgers and emptying wastebaskets while they search for something they are trained to do? A more specific statement about the employability of students from this University is needed in order to make the argument forceful.

5. 写结尾段，重述原论述中存在的主要问题

如果论文没有一个独立的结尾段，阅卷者就会认为考生没有按时完成写作。所以，考生要尽量留出一定的时间来完成结尾段的写作，为整篇论述画上一个完美的句号。在结尾段中，不要引入新的论点。下面的两项任务是考生在结尾段应该完成的工作：

1）简明扼要地重述原论述所存在的问题——例如，一系列未经证实的假设（1～2个句子）；
2）指出怎样才能加强原论述的论证，或说明哪些额外的信息将有助于对原论述进行评价（2～3个句子，这一任务也可以融合到主体段的写作过程中）。

本题的结尾段可以如下所示：

The paragraph given merely scratches the surface of what must be said about this University in order to entice students and to convince them that this is the best place to obtain a quality education. Much more work is needed by the public relations department before this can be made into a four-color brochure and handed out to prospective students.

6. 浏览全文，确保文章结构的平衡性以及行文的前后一致

考生一定要留出一定的时间来检查自己的写作，以确保文章结构的合理性和行文的前后一致。检查时，要特别注意每一段第一句话的写法。如果时间允许，考生可以重新组织段落的先后顺序，使得整篇文章在结构上更加符合逻辑。

7. 查漏补缺，改正语法及拼写错误

如同Issue一样，要想获得Argument高分，考生的文章不必没有丝毫的瑕疵。阅卷者不会因为文章中偶尔出现的蹩脚句子，小小的拼写、标点、语法或用词错误而降低分数。利用剩余的宝贵时间去修改文章中自己在无意间犯下的最显眼或最严重的错误。只有当某个词的拼写错误有可能会影响到阅卷者理解考生要表达的意思时，才需要把它改正过来。通常情况下，不必浪费时间去刻意修改标点或小小的拼写错误。

Chapter 4

第四章　Argument 写作评分标准

一、Argument写作评分标准

　　无论E-rater还是阅卷老师，都是按一定的评分标准来给分的。下面给出了GMAC对Argument写作的评分标准，考生在平时练习时，可参照这些标准来给自己的习作打分。当然，也可以按照这些标准的要求来逐步实现取得Argument高分的理想。

SCORE 6（Outstanding）

A 6 paper presents a cogent, well-articulated critique of the argument and demonstrates mastery of the elements of effective writing.

A typical paper in this category exhibits the following characteristics:

- clearly identifies important features of the argument and analyzes them insightfully;
- develops ideas cogently, organizes them logically, and connects them with clear transitions;
- effectively supports the main points of the critique;
- demonstrates control of language, including diction and syntactic variety;
- demonstrates facility with the conventions of standard written English but may have minor flaws.

SCORE 5（Strong）

A 5 paper presents a well-developed critique of the argument and demonstrates good control of the elements of effective writing.

A typical paper in this category exhibits the following characteristics:

- clearly identifies important features of the argument and analyzes them in a generally thoughtful way;
- develops ideas clearly, organizes them logically, and connects them with appropriate transitions;
- sensibly supports the main points of the critique;
- demonstrates control of language, including diction and syntactic variety;
- demonstrates facility with the conventions of standard written English but may have occasional flaws.

SCORE 4（Adequate）

A 4 paper presents a competent critique of the argument and demonstrates adequate control of the elements of writing.

A typical paper in this category exhibits the following characteristics:

- identifies and analyzes important features of the argument;
- develops and organizes ideas satisfactorily but may not connect them with transitions;
- supports the main points of the critique;
- demonstrates sufficient control of language to convey ideas with reasonable clarity generally follows the conventions of standard written English but may have some flaws.

SCORE 3（Limited）

A 3 paper demonstrates some competence in analytical writing skills and in its control of the elements of writing but is plainly flawed.

A typical paper in this category exhibits one or more of the following characteristics:

- does not identify or analyze most of the important features of the argument, although some analysis of the argument is present;
- mainly analyzes tangential or irrelevant matters, or reasons poorly is limited in the logical development and organization of ideas;
- offers support of little relevance and value for points of the critique does not convey meaning clearly;
- contains occasional major errors or frequent minor errors in grammar, usage, and mechanics.

SCORE 2（Seriously Flawed）

A 2 paper demonstrates serious weaknesses in analytical writing skills.

A typical paper in this category exhibits one or more of the following characteristics:

- does not present a critique based on logical analysis, but may instead present the writer's own views on the subject;
- does not develop ideas, or is disorganized and illogical;
- provides little, if any, relevant or reasonable support;
- has serious and frequent problems in the use of language and in sentence structure;
- contains numerous errors in grammar, usage, and mechanics that interfere with meaning.

SCORE 1（Fundamentally Deficient）

A 1 paper demonstrates fundamental deficiencies in analytical writing skills.

A typical paper in this category exhibits more than one of the following characteristics:

- provides little evidence of the ability to understand and analyze the argument;
- provides little evidence of the ability to develop an organized response;
- has severe and persistent errors in language and sentence structure;
- contains a pervasive pattern of errors in grammar, usage, and mechanics that results in incoherence.

SCORE 0（No Score）

A paper in this category is off topic, not written in English, is merely attempting to copy the topic, or consists only of keystroke characters.

二、Argument官方范文

GMAC给出的评过分的范文及其相关的评语对平时写作非常有指导意义。因此，考生要仔细研读这些范文，好好琢磨句法、用词、论据的选择以及论证方法的运用。如果考生细心研究范文，就不难发现高分写作也就是一些共性加上某些个人的创新。

> **注 意**
>
> 为了帮助考生更好地理解评分标准，所有这些范文只是做了格式上的转化，其他的都保持作者完成时的原样(如拼写错误、语法错误、标点符号错误以及多余的空格等问题都没有修改)。

Sample Analysis of an Argument Question 1

The following appeared as part of an article in a daily newspaper:

"The computerized on-board warning system that will be installed in commercial airliners will virtually solve the problem of midair plane collisions. One plane's warning system can receive signals from another's transponder—a radio set that signals a plane's course—in order to determine the

---

likelihood of a collision and recommend evasive action."

Discuss how well reasoned you find this argument. In your discussion, be sure to analyze the line of reasoning and the use of evidence in the argument. For example, you may need to consider what questionable assumptions underlie the thinking and what alternative explanations or counterexamples might weaken the conclusion. You can also discuss what sort of evidence would strengthen or refute the argument, what changes in the argument would make it more logically sound, and what, if anything, would help you better evaluate its conclusion.

❋ 6分范文 ❋

The argument that this warning system will virtually solve the problem of midair plane collisions omits some important concerns that must be addressed to substantiate the argument. The statement that follows the description of what this warning system will do simply describes the system and how it operates. This alone does not constitute a logical argument in favor of the warning system, and it certainly does not provide support or proof of the main argument.

Most conspicuously, the argument does not address the cause of the problem of midair plane collisions, the use of the system by pilots and flight specialists, or who is involved in the midair plane collisions. First, the argument assumes that the cause of the problem is that the planes' courses, the likelihood of collisions, and actions to avoid collisions are unknown or inaccurate. In a weak attempt to support its claim, the argument describes a system that makes all of these things accurately known. But if the cause of the problem of midair plane collisions is that pilots are not paying attention to their computer systems or flight operations, the warning system will not solve the collision problem. Second, the argument never addresses the interface between individuals and the system and how this will affect the warning system's objective of obliterating the problem of collisions. If the pilot or flight specialist does not conform to what the warning system suggests, midair collisions will not be avoided. Finally, if planes other than commercial airliners are involved in the collisions, the problem of these collisions cannot be solved by a warning system that will not be installed on non-commercial airliners. The argument also does not address what would happen in the event that the warning system collapses, fails, or does not work properly.

Because the argument leaves out several key issues, it is not sound or persuasive. If it included the items discussed above instead of solely explaining what the system supposedly does, the argument would have been more thorough and convincing.

文章点评

下面我们将从结构、论证和语言三方面来对该范文进行分析。

结构：该文结构完整，布局合理。开头段一针见血地指出，原题的根本逻辑错误在于用对"预警系统"的描述取代了实质性的论证。正文部分紧紧围绕这一论点展开详尽的分析，并自然过渡到结论，暗示应从上文探讨的几个方面来充实原论证。

论证：逻辑问题分析写作也应遵从议论文的基本写作规律，也就是作者必须在正文部分展开分析，强有力地支持自己在第一段提出的中心观点。该文从三个方面分析了原论证所忽略的重要问题：第一，原论证没有考虑造成空中飞机相撞事故的多种原因；第二，原论证没有考虑飞行员如何使用这种新的预警系统；最后，原论证忽略了商用飞机与其它类飞机相撞的可能性。

语言：该文的语言规范、流畅，句式有变化，体现了作者熟练运用英语写作的能力。有不少句子写得简洁有力，如"the argument never addresses the interface between individuals and the system"。当然，在有限的时间内完成这项写作任务，犯一点语法错误也在所难免。通过阅读我们会发现"the planes' courses, the likelihood of collisions, and actions to avoid collisions are unknown or inaccurate"这句话里措辞拖沓，而且用词也不够准确

（“inaccurate”是不能用来修饰“courses, likelihood, actions”等词的）。

该文的长度为335字，根据评分标准，达到了6分写作的要求。

❋ 4分范文 ❋

The argument is not logically convincing. It does not state whether all planes can receive signals from each other. It does not state whether planes constantly receive signals. If they only receive signals once every certain time interval, collisions will not definitely be prevented. Further if they receive a signal right before they are about to crash, they cannot avoid each other.

The main flaw in the argument is that it assumes that the two planes, upon receiving each other's signals, will know which evasive action to take. For example, the two planes could be going towards each other and then receive the signals. If one turns at an angle to the left and the other turns at an angle to the right, the two planes will still crash. Even if they receive an updated signal, they will not have time to avoid each other.

The following argument would be more sound and persuasive. The new warning system will solve the problem of midair plane collisions. Each plane will receive constant, continual signals from each other. If the two planes are headed in a direction where they will crash, the system will coordinate the signals, and tell one plane to go one way and the other plane to go another way. The new system will ensure that the two planes will turn in different directions so they don't crash by trying to prevent the original crash. In addition, the two planes will be able to see themselves and the other on a computer screen, to aid in the evasive action.

文章点评

下面我们仍从结构、论证和语言三方面来分析这篇文章。

结构：本文从结构上看大体合理，有一个清楚的开头—正文—结尾的布局。但开头太突然，一下子就展开了，没有一个从总体到局部的过渡。一般来说，开头段应是归纳原论证的逻辑关系，并从宏观上指出其基本错误。

论证：本文讨论了原论证所忽略的几种特殊情况。如是否所有飞机都能接收到信号，信号的发出是否及时，预警系统所提供的躲避指令是否明确无误等等。做这样的推测不是完全没有道理，但让人有“欲加之罪”之感，似乎是有意要把对方的观点推到荒谬的极端。此外，作者提出了一个替代性的预警系统，虽然说比原来的考虑要更周全，但作者同样也忽略了一些其他方面的问题，如人与机器的配合。从策略上看，试图在短时间内设计出一个替代性的方案很危险，往往顾此失彼，吃力不讨好。因此，考生应集中精力攻击对方的弱点，而不是试图彻底推翻原论证。

语言：该文在语言上的问题较多，如句子结构单调、重复（比如最后一段的第4和第5句话），变化很少，从头到尾出现了大量的“主—谓—宾”结构。有些用词不够准确得体，如“constant continuous signals”的说法。但文中的语法错误尚不足以影响理解，因此该文还是可以得个及格分。

该文的长度为260字，根据评分标准，达到了4分写作的要求。

❋ 2分范文 ❋

This argument has no information about air collisions. I think most cases happen in new airports because the air traffic is heavy. In this case sound airport control could solve the problem.

I think this argument is logically reasonable. Its assumption is that plane collisions are caused by planes that don't know each others positions. So pilots can do nothing, if they know each others position through the system it will solve the problem.

If it can provide evidence the problem is lack of knowledge of each others positions, it will be more sound and persuasive.

More information about air collisions is helpful, (the reason for air collisions).

文章点评

　　该文结构不完整，论证没有展开，几乎没有什么证据，字数太少（全文108词）。第一段断定飞机失事大多在新机场，这本身就是一个逻辑错误。只有第二段有点相关的议论，而第三段已没有时间完成了。这篇文章在语法、习惯用法以及结构方面犯了很多基本的错误。前后缺乏一致性的问题到处可见，如第二段的"So pilots can do nothing, if they know each others position through the system it will solve the problem"，以及第三段的"If it can provide evidence the problem is lack of knowledge of each others positions, it will be more sound and persuasive"这两句话不但不合语法，而且语意含糊，让人很难理解作者究竟要表达什么观点。参照评分标准，该篇文章只能得2分。

　　为了帮助考生更好地掌握Argument写作，下面给出了另外一篇官方的满分范文：

Sample Analysis of an Argument Question 2

The following appeared in the editorial section of a monthly business news magazine:

"Most companies would agree that as the risk of physical injury occurring on the job increases, the wages paid to employees should also increase. Hence it makes financial sense for employers to make the workplace safer: they could thus reduce their payroll expenses and save money."

Discuss how well reasoned you find this argument. In your discussion be sure to analyze the line of reasoning and the use of evidence in the argument. For example, you may need to consider what questionable assumptions underlie the thinking and what alternative explanations or counterexamples might weaken the conclusion. You can also discuss what sort of evidence would strengthen or refute the argument, what changes in the argument would make it more logically sound, and what, if anything, would help you better evaluate its conclusion.

✻ Answer ✻

The following sample paper would receive the highest rating:

　　This argument states that it makes financial sense for employers to make the workplace safer because by making the workplace safer then lower wages could be paid to employees. This conclusion is based on the premise that as the list of physical injury increases, the wages paid to employees should also increase. However, there are several assumptions that may not necessarily apply to this argument. For example, the costs associated with making the workplace safe must outweigh the increased payroll expenses due to hazardous conditions. Also, one must look at the plausability of improving the work environment. And finally, because most companies agree that as the risk of injury increases so will wages doesn't necessarily mean that the all companies which have hazardous work environments agree.

　　The first issue to be addressed is whether increased labor costs justify large capital expenditures to improve the work environment. Clearly one could argue that if making the workplace safe would cost an exorbitant amount of money in comparison to leaving the workplace as is and paying slightly increased wages than it would not make sense to improve the work environment. For example, if making the workplace safe would cost $100 million versus additional payroll expenses of only $5,000 per year, it would make financial sense to simply pay the increased wages. No business or business owner with any sense would pay all that extra money just to save a couple dollars and improve employee health and relations. To consider this, a cost benefit analysis must be made. I also feel that although a cost benefit analysis should be the determining factor with regard to these decisions making financial sense, it may not be the determining factor with regard to making social, moral and ethical sense.

This argument also relies on the idea that companies solely use financial sense in analysing improving the work environment. This is not the case. Companies look at other considerations such as the negative social ramifications of high on-job injuries. For example, Toyota spends large amounts of money improving its environment because while its goal is to be profitable, it also prides itself on high employee morale and an almost perfectly safe work environment. However, Toyota finds that it can do both, as by improving employee health and employee relations they are guaranteed a more motivated staff, and hence a more efficient staff; this guarantees more money for the business as well as more safety for the employees.

Finally one must understand that not all work environments can be made safer. For example, in the case of coal mining, a company only has limited ways of making the work environment safe. While companies may be able to ensure some safety precautions, they may not be able to provide all the safety measures necessary. In other words, a mining company has limited ability to control the air quality within a coal mine and therefore it cannot control the risk of employees getting blacklung. In other words, regardless of the intent of the company, some jobs are simply dangerous in nature.

In conclusion, while at first it may seem to make financial sense to improve the safety of the work environment sometimes it truly does not make financial sense. Furthermore, financial sense may not be the only issue a company faces. Other types of analyses must be made such as the social ramifications of an unsafe work environment and the overall ability of a company to improve that environment (i.e., coal mine). Before any decision is made, all this things must be considered, not simply the reduction of payroll expenses.

PART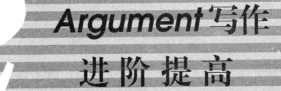

Argument 写作
进阶提高

- **Argument 写作八类逻辑错误**
- **Argument 逻辑错误的经典攻击句型和论证方法**
- **Argument 写作必备经典句子**
- **Argument 写作黄金模板**
- **Argument 黄金范文 20 篇**

第一章 Argument 写作八类逻辑错误

　　Argument主要是要求考生找到原文论断中的逻辑错误（漏洞），然后通过说出其他可能性来攻击这些逻辑漏洞。Argument有漏洞，这个说法既是重复又是一个有力的应考策略。首先，从纯粹形式化的观点来看，陈述仅仅是对归纳性论据本质的描述：除非是演绎性论据（比如，所有的人都会死，哥白尼是人，所以，他会死。）现实生活或归纳性的论点（不像死亡或税收）永远都不是确定的。不论例子多么有力或多么具有综合性，都不能保证百分之百地支持要说明的目标。所以，对给出的任何建议都可以提出反对意见，这样，就解决了Argument的核心问题——找漏洞。再进一步说，Argument题目中的逻辑错误都是出题者预先设计好的。通常，在每一道Argument题目的论述中，考生都可以发现三到四个不同的逻辑错误，出题者就是利用这些推理上的漏洞来考查考生的洞察分析能力。

　　由此可见，找出Argument论述中的主要漏洞是考生得高分的关键。要想快速准确地判断Argument论述中所隐含的逻辑错误，并进行有力的批驳，考生必须具备鉴别典型逻辑错误的能力，并掌握攻击这些错误的方法。

　　通过对Argument题库的深入分析，笔者发现，Argument中的逻辑错误可以分为八类：非因果关系逻辑错误、比较与类比逻辑错误、数据相关逻辑错误、充分条件与必要条件逻辑错误、整体与部分逻辑错误、假定所有的事情都是一成不变类逻辑错误、错误的两难境地类逻辑错误，还有一些不太常见的逻辑错误，我们将其归为一类。接下来我们将按照各类逻辑错误在考试中出现频率的高低来进行讲解，并给出典型逻辑错误最常用的攻击方法供考生参考。

一、非因果关系逻辑错误

　　非因果关系，即"Non-causal relationship"。许多Argument的结论都依赖于某一件事情引起了另一件事情这样的陈述。这些所谓的因果关系可能会基于以下四点得出：（1）两件事情之间存在明显的相关性；（2）两件事情的发生在时间上存在先后关系（一件事情发生在另一件事情之后）；（3）混淆因果关系（把一件事情发生的原因当结果）；（4）因果关系简单化。下面我们将分类进行讲解。

1. 将相关性当作因果关系（Correlation Mistaken for Causation）

　　两件事情之间存在明显的相关性，或这两件事情同时出现。当变量A变化，变量B也相应地变化时，A和B之间可以被认为存在某种相关关系，但二者之间未必就存在因果关系。例如：

　　"In the last several years, whenever sales of personal computers went up, sales of athletic shoes also rose strongly; therefore, buyers of personal computers must have bought athletic shoes as well."

　　凭直觉就判断上述推理是荒谬的。很可能是总体的经济景气造成了各种商品的销售一致看好。把两件事情之间的相关性当作它们之间的因果关系，并以此来得出的结论显然是站不住脚的。请看下面这道例题：

> The following appeared in the editorial section of a local newspaper.
>
> "Commuter use of the new subway train is exceeding the transit company's projections. However, commuter use of the shuttle buses that transport people to the subway stations is below the projected volume. If the transit company expects commuters to ride the shuttle buses to the subway rather than drive there, it must either reduce the shuttle bus fares or increase the price of parking at the subway stations." (Argument 28)

为了使上下班的人能搭乘公交车而不是开车去地铁站，作者提出了两种可行的方案：要么降低公交车的票价，要么提高地铁站附近的停车费。显然，作者认为开车到地铁站的人数与公交车票价或者地铁站停车费之间存在因果关系。而实际情况是前后两者之间虽然存在一定的相关性，但它们之间并没有作者所假定的因果关系。所以这道题犯了把相关性当作是因果关系的逻辑错误（这篇Argument可能还犯有其他逻辑错误，但在这儿我们着重攻击它的因果关系问题）。下面我们将对它就因果关系问题展开攻击：

The argument depends on an unproven cause-and-effect relationship between the unexpectedly low shuttle-bus usage and shuttle-bus fares or station-parking fees. The reason for the unexpectedly low shuttle-bus usage might have nothing to do with either shuttle-bus fares or station-parking fees. For instance, commuter awareness of the shuttle-bus option might be growing more slowly than anticipated. For that matter, many commuters might be wary of riding the buses due to a recent shuttle-bus accident. Without ruling out these and other alternative explanations for the low shuttle-bus usage, the author cannot reasonably conclude that adjusting shuttle fares or station-parking fees will have any effect on that usage.

2. 后此谬误（The "After This, Therefore Because of This" fallacy / Post Hoc Ergo Propter Hoc）

在日常生活中，人们会将一些事情联系在一起，但这些事情之间并没有一定的因果关系，仅有事情发生的先后关系，这时就出现了逻辑推理中的一种错误：后此谬误——对于两个事件，仅由二者的时间先后顺序关系便推出二者之间存在因果关系，即认为先发生事件是后发生事件的原因，而论证中没有充分的证据来论证这个因果关系。例如：

"I found my love after having a special style of haircut, so the haircut must be the reason I found my love." 理了个别致的发型之后，就找到了中意的恋人，于是前者是后者的原因。这可信吗？请考生接着看下面这道题：

> The following appeared in the editorial section of a local newspaper.
> "In the first four years that Montoya has served as mayor of the city of San Perdito, the population has decreased and the unemployment rate has increased. Two businesses have closed for each new business that has opened. Under Varro, who served as mayor for four years before Montoya, the unemployment rate decreased and the population increased. Clearly, the residents of San Perdito would be best served if they voted Montoya out of office and reelected Varro." (Argument 11)

在这篇Argument里，作者建议San Perdito的居民应该让现任市长Montoya下台，而推选前任市长Varro当市长。作者的理由是Montoya当选市长后，San Perdito市的人口下降，失业率上升；而Varro担任市长期间，San Perdito市的失业率下降，人口上升。这样的推理显然是站不住脚的。下面我们将针对该题出现的因果关系问题进行有力的攻击：

The author assumes that the Montoya administration caused the unemployment in San Perdito as well as its population loss. The line of reasoning is that because Montoya was elected before the rise in unemployment and the decline in population, the former event caused the latter. But this is fallacious reasoning unless other possible causal explanations have been considered and ruled out. For example, perhaps a statewide or nationwide recession is the cause of these events. Or perhaps the current economic downturn is part of a larger picture of economic cycles and trends, and has nothing to do with who happens to be mayor. Yet another possibility is that Varro enjoyed a period of economic stability and Varro's own administration set the stage for the unemployment and the decline in population the city is now experiencing under Montoya.

3. 混淆因果关系（Confuse the Cause and Effect）

在Argument中，有时作者会把导致某件事情发生的原因当作结果，而把结果当作原因，从而得出经不起推敲的结论。如下所示：

The following appeared in a memo from the mayor of the town of Hopewell.

"Two years ago, the town of Ocean View built a new municipal golf course and resort hotel. During the past two years, tourism in Ocean View has increased, new businesses have opened there, and Ocean View's tax revenues have risen by 30 percent. Therefore, the best way to improve Hopewell's economy, and generate additional tax revenues, is to build a golf course and resort hotel similar to those in Ocean View."

在这篇Argument中，作者认为Ocean View市经济的腾飞起因于两年前兴建的市高尔夫球场以及度假宾馆。所以作者得出改善Hopewell市经济的最佳方法是建造一个与Ocean View市相似的高尔夫球场以及度假宾馆。作者的推理显然存在两个漏洞：（1）Ocean View市经济的腾飞可能并非起因于两年前兴建的市高尔夫球场以及度假宾馆；（2）即使在Ocean View兴建高尔夫球场以及度假宾馆有助于经济的增长，相同的方法在Hopewell却不一定实用。下面我们针对第一点展开攻击：

It is possible that the mayor has confused cause with effect respecting the recent developments in Ocean View. Perhaps Ocean View's construction of a new golf course and hotel was a response to previous increases in tourism and business development—increases that have simply continued during the most recent two years. Since the mayor has failed to account for this possibility, the claim that Hopewell would boost its economy by also constructing a golf course and hotel is completely unwarranted.

为了使我们的论证显得更有力，我们可以继续列出其他的附加信息来反驳作者的观点：

The mayor fails to account for other possible causes of the trends in Ocean View during the last two years. The increase in tourism might have been due to improving economic conditions nationwide, or to unusually pleasant weather in the region. The new businesses that have opened in Ocean View might have opened there irrespective of the new golf course and hotel. And, the 30% increase in tax revenues might have been the result of an increase in tax rates, or the addition of a new type of municipal tax. Without ruling out these and other alternative explanations for the three recent trends in Ocean View, the mayor cannot reasonably infer based on those trends that Hopewell's economy would benefit by following Ocean View's example.

4. 因果关系简单化（Causal Oversimplification）

在进行推理论证时，在证据不足的情况下，经常会认为一个结果仅由一个原因形成。这种情况就将因果关系简单化了。实际上，这里的因果关系是复杂的。在现实生活中，一个结果可能是多个原因同时发挥作用而引起的，或者一个原因既可能导致A结果，也可能导致B结果。

The following appeared in a memorandum from a vice president of the Megamart department store chain.

"For the third year in a row, the average household income in our country has risen significantly. That prosperity means that families are likely to be spending more time and money on leisure activities. Megamart stores should therefore concentrate on enlarging and promoting its line of products typically used in leisure activities: athletic and outdoor equipment, televisions, gourmet cooking equipment, and luggage and travel accessories."

在上面这篇Argument中，作者认为家庭收入的连续增加必然会导致休闲消费的增加，从而得出了Megamart商场应该把精力集中在休闲消费品上的结论。从表面上看，作者的推理似乎很有道理。然而，仔细分析后，我们发现作者的推理存在严重的漏洞：如果该地居民尚未解决基本的生活需求，那么人们会把增加的收入首先用于购买生活必需品；如果收入的增加是因为人们增加了工作时间（如一人干几份工作），那么，即使收入增加了，人们也没有时间去消遣；如果收入增加了，但同时出现了通货膨胀，那么人们的实际收入并未增加。此外，值得指出的是，收入增加是就全国的平均（注意average这个词）水平而言的，而Megamart商场所在地的居民是否增加了收入，还是一个未知数。作者用于支持他结论的论据显然犯了"因果关系简单化"的逻辑错误。

在GRE的Argument中经常会出现唯一原因与综合原因相混淆的逻辑错误。对于这类错误，我们必须意识到某一个条件可能有助于产生某一个后果（结果），但单单这一个条件又不足以引起这个后果。关于这方面的问题，我们将在"充分条件与必要条件"部分详加讲解。

> **总 结**
>
> 　通过上面的例证及分析，我们发现：两件事情之间的相关性或发生的先后性只是它们之间存在因果关系的一个特征，这些特征并不足以说明这两件事情之间存在一定的因果关系。除非原论证能考虑并排除其他可能引起假定"结果"的因素，否则原论证就不堪一击。

考生为了向阅卷者表明自己已经理解原论证中存在的因果关系问题，需要完成以下三项任务：
☞ 确认原论证所存在的因果关系问题；
☞ 阐明该因果关系存在问题：提供至少一到两个其他可能会造成原论证所论述的某一个结果的原因；
☞ 解释该因果关系问题是如何削弱原论证的。
考生一般至少需要三个句子来完成上面的三项任务（一个句子完成一项）。如果原论证的因果关系中有一个"中间结论"，就可能需要另外的句子，有时甚至是额外的一个段落来讨论中间结论。

完成上面三项任务以后，如果还有时间，考生就可以对该因果关系问题做进一步的讨论：
☞ 说明什么类型的附加信息（比如统计数据）将会有助于证明该因果关系的合理性；
☞ 列举各种附加的必要信息（如：统计数据，成本效益分析以及未来预测等），来确定原论证中假定的因果关系是否存在。

二、比较与类比逻辑错误

比较与类比逻辑错误，即"The Fallacy of Analogy and Comparison"。

1. 错误类比（The Fallacy of Faulty Analogy）

类比推理是通过比较两个相似的事物来进行推理。在GMAT的Argument中可能出现由一个事物（如城市、学校或公司）对另一事物进行类推的情况。进行类比推理时，如果只看到二者在一些方面的相似或是表面上的相似，而忽略其他或深层的不同之处，就得出某种结论，认为它们在其他所有方面也一定都相似，这就犯了错误类比的逻辑推理错误。对于类比问题，除非文章中提供了充分证据支持这种假设，否则其论述就可以受到质疑。

考生为了向阅卷者表明自己已经理解原论证中存在的错误类比问题，需要完成以下三项任务：
☞ 找出有问题的类比（如：发现该类比是原论证成立的一个非常重要的假设）；
☞ 阐明该类比是有问题的：说明类比的两件事情在某一方面或更多方面存在显著的差异；
☞ 解释这些差异如何使类比不能成立，从而削弱原论证的结论。

考生一般至少需要三个句子来完成上面的三项任务（一个句子完成一项）。完成上面三项任务以后，如果还有时间，就可以在论证里加入下面的内容（选择性的）：
☞ 指出作者还需要什么类型的证据来支持他/她的类比。或者，如果原类比确实非常牵强，什么样的证据可以使原论证在没有该类比的情况下更具说服力；
☞ 指出还需要了解哪些内容才能确定支持原论证结论的类比是否合理。

> **注 意**
>
> 　一篇依赖于两件事情（A和B）之间存在可比性的Argument通常会假定如果A与B仅在某一方面相似，那么A就会产生与B相似的结果。关于这一方面的问题，我们将在"充分条件与必要条件"部分详加讲解。

下面这篇Argument中就包含一个有问题的类比：

> The following appeared as part of an annual report sent to stockholders by Olympic Foods, a processor of frozen foods.
>
> "Over time, the costs of processing go down because as organizations learn how to do things better, they become more efficient. In color film processing, for example, the cost of a 3-by-5-inch print fell from 50 cents for five-day service in 1970 to 20 cents for one-day service in 1984. The same principle applies to the processing of food. And since Olympic Foods will soon celebrate its twenty-fifth birthday, we can expect that our long experience will enable us to minimize costs and thus maximize profits."
> (Argument 1)

从题目中我们可以看出，作者试图以来自彩色胶卷冲印行业的经验作为自己结论的证据，这显然是不合适的。当我们将两件事情进行类比的时候，必须注意这两件事情之间是否存在非常明显的可以导致类比无效的差异。下面我们将针对该篇Argument中出现的类比错误进行攻击：

It is highly doubtful that the facts drawn from the color-film processing industry are applicable to the food processing industry. Differences between the two industries clearly outweigh the similarities, thus making the analogy less than valid. For example, problems of spoilage, contamination, and timely transportation all affect the food industry but are virtually absent in the film-processing industry. Problems such as these might present insurmountable obstacles that prevent lowering food-processing costs in the future.

2. 不完整比较或选择性比较(Incomplete or Selective Comparison)

有时作者的结论基于对同类事物的比较，但通常只比较了少数几个方面，或只比较对自己观点有利的方面，同时忽略或压制其他重要方面。根据这样不完整比较或选择性比较得出的结论显然是不可靠的。下面这篇Argument就存在这样的问题：

> The following appeared in an article in a college departmental newsletter.
>
> "Professor Taylor of Jones University is promoting a model of foreign language instruction in which students receive ten weeks of intensive training, then go abroad to live with families for ten weeks. The superiority of the model, Professor Taylor contends, is proved by the results of a study in which foreign language tests given to students at 25 other colleges show that first-year foreign language students at Jones speak more fluently after only ten to twenty weeks in the program than do nine out of ten foreign language majors elsewhere at the time of their graduation." (Argument 36)

在这篇Argument中，作者通过把Jones大学参加该教学方案的学生与其他大学英语专业即将毕业的大学生进行比较，得出了该教学方案非常可取的结论。但是这个比较的过程不一定可靠，因为我们没有关于这个关键比较的具体信息，所以无法判断其可靠性。

The argument is based on the assumption that students from Professor Taylor's program have learned more than foreign language students at other universities. However, we are not given enough information about the study to be sure that this comparison is reliable. For example, the article does not tell us whether the foreign language students at Jones were given the tests; it only reports that the tests in question were "given to students at 25 other colleges." If Jones students were not tested, then no basis exists for comparing them to students at the other universities. In addition, the article does not indicate whether students at all the universities, including Jones, were given the same tests. If not, then again no basis exists for the comparison.

三、数据相关逻辑错误

数据相关逻辑错误，即"Problems concerning data"。题库中有大量的题目都是以调查（study, research, survey, poll）的结果来充当证据的。要对原论证的结论进行驳斥，首先就要对支持这些结论的论据进行有力的攻击。通常来说，我们是从以下两方面来对这些所谓的调查展开攻击的：

（1）调查(study, research, survey, poll)的样本是否具有代表性？

（2）调查(study, research, survey, poll)的程序是否合理，其结果是否可信？

接下来我们将分别对这两类错误进行阐述。

1. 不充分采样错误 (The Insufficient Sample Fallacy)

有些Argument会引用一些来自某项涉及到"样本"的研究、调查或民意测验的统计数据，接着就会得出与该样本代表的更大的集体或人口相关的结论。但是，为了使某一个统计样本能准确地反映一大群人的情况，该样本必须满足以下两条标准：

（1）样本作为整体的一个部分必须具有足够大的数量；

（2）样本在相关的特性方面必须具有整体的代表性。

Argument中引用的来自研究、调查或民意测验的统计数据通常不能满足以上两条标准中的任一条标准。当然，这样的错误都是出题者故意设计的，旨在考查考生是否具有质疑这些证据可靠性的能力。

考生为了向阅卷者表明自己已经理解原论证中存在的统计数据问题，需要完成以下三项任务：

☞ 发现问题：可疑的统计数据是原论证所依赖的一个非常重要的假设；

☞ 阐明问题：说明样本在某些关键方面与选取样本的整体（人口、产品等）是有差异的；

☞ 解释问题：论证这些差异将会如何削弱原论证的结论。

考生一般至少需要三个句子来完成上面的三项任务（一个句子完成一项）。完成上面三项任务以后，如果还有时间，就可以在论证里加入下面的内容（选择性的）：

☞ 指出原论证的作者如何才能证明该样本是具有代表性的，或者在不采用该统计数据的情况下，怎样才能使原论证更有说服力；

☞ 指出还需要了解哪些信息才能确定该样本是否能够代表整体（人口、产品等）的情况。

下面这篇Argument就犯了不充分采样的逻辑错误：

> The following appeared as part of an article in a health club trade publication.
>
> "After experiencing a decline in usage by its members, Healthy Heart Fitness Center built an indoor pool. Since usage did not increase significantly, it appears that health club managers should adopt another approach—lowering membership fees rather than installing expensive new features."

在这篇Argument中，用来作论据的样本太小，作者试图把来自一个健身中心——Healthy Heart健身中心的经验应用到所有健身中心上去，这显然是没有道理的。因为各个健身中心的情况都不一样，适合某一个健身中心的方案不一定适合所有的健身中心。下面是针对该篇论证中出现的样本问题展开的攻击：

The conclusion that installing new features at fitness centers will not increase member usage is based on too small a sample to be reliable. The only evidence offered in support of this conclusion is the fact that Healthy Heart Fitness Center did not experience an increase. Unless it can be shown that Healthy Heart is typical of all fitness centers, the fact that it experienced no increase in member usage is not grounds for concluding that all fitness centers will experience similar results.

接下来我们再看一道有关样本是否具有代表性的例题，与上一题不同的是，在这道题中，样本的选择有问题，从而使得样本不具代表性。

> The following appeared in a newspaper story giving advice about investments.
>
> "As overall life expectancy continues to rise, the population of our country is growing increasingly older. For example, over twenty percent of the residents of one of our more populated regions are now at least 65 years old, and occupancy rates at resort hotels in that region declined significantly during the past six months. Because of these two related trends, a prudent investor would be well advised to sell interest in hotels and invest in hospitals and nursing homes instead."

在这篇Argument中，作者试图选择一个地区的数据来证明他关于投资决策的结论。而他所选择的这个地区如文中所述是一个人口相对密集的地区，从这个地区得出的数据显然不具代表性。下面是针对原论证中出现的样本选择问题而展开的攻击：

The author provides no evidence to support the claim that the population as a whole is aging and that the hotel occupancy rate in general is declining. The example cited, while suggestive of these trends, is insufficient to warrant their truth because there is no reason to believe that data drawn from this unnamed region is representative of the entire country. For example, if the region from which the data was gathered was Florida, it would clearly be unrepresentative. The reason for this is obvious. Florida is populated by a disproportionate number of retired people over 65 years old and is a very popular vacation destination during the winter months. Moreover, resort hotel occupancy in Florida typically declines significantly during the summer months.

2. 有偏采样错误(The Biased-Sample Fallacy)

如前所述，有些Argument基于不充分采样或不具代表性的样本得出了经不起推敲的结论。然而，这不是与统计数据有关的调查存在的唯一问题。如果收集数据的程序(方法)存在问题，那么得到的数据就值得怀疑，从而使得基于这些数据的结论也显得不可信。一项调查的结果要令人信服，必须满足以下两个条件：

(1)对调查的答复必须是可信的(真实且准确)。如果参与调查的人因为某些原因而给出不完整或虚假的回复，那么调查的结果就是有偏差的、不可信的。

(2)收集数据的方法必须公正。如果在调查中，对问题的回答不作硬性要求，或者问题的设计使得参与者易于用某种特定的方式回答，那么这样得到的结果也是有偏差的，或者是不可信的。

考生为了向阅卷者表明自己已经理解原论证中存在的统计数据问题，需要完成以下三项任务：

☞ 发现问题：可疑的统计数据是原论证依赖的一个非常重要的假设；

☞ 阐明问题：根据题目中给出的信息，说出统计数据不可信的一个或多个理由；

☞ 解释问题：说明这些可能有问题的数据会如何削弱原论证的结论。

考生一般至少需要三个句子来完成上面的三项任务(一个句子完成一项)。完成上面三项任务以后，如果还有时间，就可以在论证里加入下面的内容(选择性的)：

☞ 指出原论证的作者如何才能证明这些统计数据是可信的(没有偏见的)；

☞ 指出还需要了解哪些信息才能确定这些统计数据是可信的(没有偏见的)；

☞ 该样本是否能够代表整体(人口、产品等)的情况。

下面这篇Argument就犯了有偏采样的错误：

> The following appeared in a memo from the Director of Human Resources at Newtrue:
>
> "Among Newtrue employees participating in our department's most recent survey, about half indicated that they are happy with our current four-day work week. These survey results show that the most effective way to improve overall productivity at Newtrue is to allow each employee to choose for himself or herself either a four-day or five-day work week."

该篇Argument的结论基于最近的一项调查。根据文中提供的信息，我们无从得知该项调查的问卷中是否有多项工作日方案供应答者选择，也无从得知应答者是否匿名答卷。而这些信息都涉及到调查结果的公正性和可信性。所以，在没有这些信息的情况下，我们完全有理由质疑该项调查的结果是不可信的。请看下面针对这个问题的攻击：

The survey methodology might be problematic in two respects. First, we are not informed whether the survey required that respondents choose their work-week preference between the two alternatives. If it did, then the results might distort the preferences of the respondents, who might very well prefer a work-schedule choice not provided for in the survey. Secondly, we are not informed whether survey responses were anonymous or even confidential. If they were not, then respondents might have provided responses that they believed their superiors would approve of, regardless of whether the responses were truthful. In either event, the survey results would be unreliable for the purpose of drawing any conclusions about Newtrue employee preferences, let alone about how to improve overall productivity at Newtrue.

在考虑涉及到调查的Argument是否犯有"有偏采样错误"时，主要考虑以下几个方面的问题：

（a）Who conducted the survey?（是谁组织了调查？）

（b）Are the statistics misleadingly vague?（数据是否有意模糊？）

（c）When was the survey conducted?（调查在何时进行？）

接下来我们将分别举例说明。

（a）Who conducted the survey?（是谁组织了调查？）

有时调查的结果是否可信，与谁组织了有关调查。如果某人为了自身的利益而组织了某项调查，那么来自这项调查的结果就值得怀疑。请看下面这个例子：

> The following appeared in a memorandum from the human resources department of Diversified Manufacturing:
>
> "Managers at our central office report that their employees tend to be most productive in the days immediately preceding a vacation. To help counteract our declining market share, we could increase the productivity of our professional staff members, who currently receive four weeks paid vacation a year, by limiting them to a maximum of one week's continuous vacation time. They will thus take more vacation breaks during a year and give us more days of maximum productivity."

在这篇Argument中，支持结论的论据来自经理们的报告。因为经理们在假期问题上都有既定的利益，所以来自他们的报告数据公正性就值得怀疑。下面是针对该点的攻击：

The memo provides no evidence that the reports from the managers are reliable. The managers all have vested interests in the vacation policies, and therefore might have fabricated the reports so that the company would adopt policies that they would prefer for themselves. The memo's author must first convince me that the reports are not biased. Then I could begin to consider the department's recommendation.

再看下面这篇：

> The following appeared in a memorandum from the Director of Human Resources to the executive officers of Company X.
>
> "Last year, we surveyed our employees on improvements needed at Company X by having them

> rank, in order of importance, the issues presented in a list of possible improvements. Improved communications between employees and management was consistently ranked as the issue of highest importance by the employees who responded to the survey. As you know, we have since instituted regular communications sessions conducted by high-level management, which the employees can attend on a voluntary basis. Therefore, it is likely that most employees at Company X now feel that the improvement most needed at the company has been made."

在这篇Argument中，即使我们假定该项调查根据员工们的意见把他们关心的问题准确地列了出来，我们仍有理由怀疑"Improved communications between employees and management"是员工们最为关心的问题。因为，如果这份调查表是管理者，而不是根据员工意见制定的，那么员工们最为关心的问题就可能没有被罗列在调查表上。下面是我们针对这一点进行的攻击：

Even if the survey accurately ranks certain issues according to level of employee concern, the highest-ranked issue in the survey might not be the issue about which employees are most concerned. Why? The improvement most needed from the point of view of the employees might not have appeared as one of the choices on the survey. Since the list of improvements presented on the survey was created by management rather than by the employees, the issues of greatest concern to the employees might not be included on the list. Lacking information about how the survey was prepared, it is impossible to assess its reliability. Consequently, any conclusion based on it is highly questionable.

（b）Are the statistics misleadingly vague?（数据是否有意模糊？）

调查过程及结果的叙述应该使用明确的数据，如具体的数字、比例或百分比。有时，为了误导读者，作者可能有意使用一些模糊不清的数据，如"many, a large number of"，表示的数字到底有多少是因人而异的。还有majority和百分比等表达方式，在不知道底数的情况下，我们无法推测到底这个数字是多少。如下例所示：

> The following appeared as a part of an advertisement for Adams, who is seeking reelection as governor.
>
> "Reelect Adams, and you will be voting for proven leadership in improving the state's economy. Over the past year alone, seventy percent of the state's workers have had increases in their wages, five thousand new jobs have been created, and six corporations have located their headquarters here. Most of the respondents in a recent poll said they believed that the economy is likely to continue to improve if Adams is reelected. Adams's opponent, Zebulon, would lead our state in the wrong direction, because Zebulon disagrees with many of Adams's economic policies."

在这篇Argument里，作者为了让选民支持Adams，列出了Adams的一系列"政绩"。作者首先指出该州有70%的工人涨了工资，却没有说明涨了多少。如果工资的上涨幅度跟不上通货膨胀的速度，那么70%的工人涨了工资这件事就不能说明Adams治理有方。作者接着说该州新增了5000个工作岗位，却没说明新增加的就业人数。如果新增加的就业人数远远超过5000，那么Adams在位期间该州的失业率是上升的。虽然有6家公司把他们的总部设在该州，但这6家公司的规模及是否盈利等内容作者却没提及，还有，是否有更多的公司把他们的总部撤离了该州，我们也无从得知。此外，作者也没有说明"most of the respondents"究竟是多少。还有一点就是，与Adam不同的经济政策就一定会使该州走上歧途吗？不一定，因为文中并没有证据表明Adam的经济政策是最好的。请看下面对原论证的驳斥：

First, the statistics are intended to support the main claim that the state is economically better off with Adams as governor. But these statistics are vague and oversimplified, and thus may distort the state's overall economic picture. For example, state workers' pay raises may have been minuscule and may not have kept up with cost of living or with pay for state workers in other states. Moreover, the 5, 000 new jobs may have been too few to bring state unemployment rates down significantly; at the same time, many jobs may have been lost. Finally, the poll indicates that six new corporations located in the state, but fails to indicate if any left.

Next, the poll cited by the author is described in the vaguest possible terms. The ad does not indicate who conducted the poll, who responded, or how the poll was conducted. Until these questions are answered, the survey results are worthless as evidence for public opinion about Adams or his economic policies.

Finally, while we have only vague and possibly distorted evidence that the state is better off with Adams, we have absolutely no evidence that it would be worse off with Zebulon. Given that the state economy is good at the moment, none of the author's reasons establishes that Adams is the cause of this, and neither do they establish that the state wouldn't be even better off with someone else in office.

(c) When was the survey conducted?(调查在何时进行?)

调查的时间也有可能影响调查结果的公正性和可信性。请看下面的例子:

The following appeared in the editorial section of a newspaper in the country of West Cambria.

"The practice of officially changing speed limits on the highways—whether by increasing or decreasing them—is a dangerous one. Consider what happened over the past decade whenever neighboring East Cambria changed its speed limits: an average of 3 percent more automobile accidents occurred during the week following the change than had occurred during the week preceding it—even when the speed limit was lowered. This statistic shows that the change in speed limit adversely affected the alertness of drivers."

在这篇Argument里,作者根据邻近的East Cambria州在过去的十年里一旦改变限速,交通事故率就会上升这个现象,得出了官方改变公路限速的做法危险的结论。然而作者的数据是在一个特殊时间段——改变限速后的一周内得出来的。一方面,事故率上升3%并不能说明大的问题;另一方面,可能改变限速后,部分司机还不适应新的速度标准,所以会导致汽车事故率略有上升。总之,作者得出数据的时间段之特殊性严重地削弱了作者的结论。下面是对原论述在这一点上的驳斥:

It is unlikely that the brief one-week periods under comparison are representative of longer time periods. A difference of only 3 percent during one particular week can easily be attributed to other factors, such as heavy holiday traffic or bad weather, or by problems with reporting or sampling. Had the editorial indicated that several speed-limit changes in East Cambria contributed to the statistic, the argument would be more convincing; but for all we know, the statistic is based on only one such change. In any event, a one-week period is too brief to be representative because it is likely that accidents will occur more frequently immediately following the change, while people adjust to the new limit, than over the longer term when drivers have become accustomed to the change.

四、充分条件与必要条件逻辑错误

充分条件与必要条件,即"Sufficient Evidence and Necessary Condition"。在Argument的题库中,有不少题目的作者会基于以下陈述而建议采取某一项行动:

1) 某项行为是实现某个结果的必要条件;
2) 某项行为是实现某个结果的充分条件。

这两个论断经常在Argument写作中出现，而且都很容易受到攻击。对于第一个论断，作者必须提供证据表明要得到这一结果不存在其他手段（当然，文中通常都没有提供这方面的证据）；对于第二个论断，作者必须提供强有力的证据表明单靠文中提及的行为就能获得预期的结果（通常是不能）。在缺少这些证据的情况下，作者就不能依赖这些论断来支持他的结论。

一篇依赖于这两条论断之一的Argument并不一定要同时依赖于另外一个论断。要认真阅读原论证的论述，因为几个词的不同就可以使句子的意思产生很大的差异。例如，下面是为扭转ABC公司利润下降的状况而给出的几条可选择的建议：

- Unless ABC Company hires the former marketing director of XYZ Company, ABC will not reverse its current profit decline. （雇用XYZ公司的营销主管是ABC公司扭亏为盈的必要条件：只有雇用XYZ公司的营销主管，ABC公司才有可能扭亏为盈。没有XYZ公司的营销主管，其他的方法都无法使ABC公司扭亏为盈。）

- By hiring the former marketing director of XYZ Company, ABC Company will boost its profits. （雇用XYZ公司的营销主管是ABC公司转亏为盈的充分条件：雇用XYZ公司的营销主管，ABC公司就能扭亏为盈。雇用XYZ公司的营销主管这一条件足以让ABC公司转亏为盈；当然不排除还有其他的方法也可以使ABC公司扭亏为盈。）

- In order to boost its profits, ABC Company should hire the former marketing director of XYZ Company. （雇用XYZ公司的营销主管是ABC公司转亏为盈的充要条件。只有雇用XYZ公司的营销主管，ABC公司才有可能扭亏为盈；雇用了XYZ公司的营销主管，ABC公司就能扭亏为盈。）

考生为了向阅卷者表明自己已经理解原论证中存在的必要条件和充分条件问题，需要完成以下三项任务：
☞ 发现问题：原论证依赖的一个非常重要的假设涉及到充分条件或必要条件问题；
☞ 阐明问题：通过举出至少一到两个例子说明：对必要条件问题，指出其他方法也可能达到规定的目标；对充分条件问题，指出其他条件对结果的成立也是必要的；
☞ 解释问题：论证这些充分条件或必要条件问题会如何削弱原论证的结论。

考生一般至少需要三个句子来完成上面的三项任务（一个句子完成一项）。完成上面三项任务以后，如果还有时间，就可以在论证里加入下面的内容（选择性的）：
☞ 指出原论证的作者还需要提供哪些额外信息才能证实某个条件对结论的成立是充分的，还是必要的，或是既充分又必要的；
☞ 指出还需要了解哪些信息才能确定某个条件对结果的成立是充分的，还是必要的，或是既充分又必要的。

1. 充分条件问题（Sufficient-Condition Problems）

The following appeared as part of a letter to the editor of a local newspaper.

"It makes no sense that in most places fifteen year olds are not eligible for their driver's license while people who are far older can retain all of their driving privileges by simply renewing their license. If older drivers can get these renewals, often without having to pass another driving test, then fifteen year olds should be eligible to get a license. Fifteen year olds typically have much better eyesight, especially at night; much better hand-eye coordination; and much quicker reflexes. They are also less likely to feel confused by unexpected developments or disoriented in unfamiliar surroundings, and they recover from injuries more quickly."

在上面的论述中，作者认为良好的体能是安全驾驶所仅需的条件。这样的观点显然是错误的，因为常识告诉我们，对驾驶环境及路面状况的判断，对驾驶行为及行动所造成后果的认知远比良好的体能更重要。请看下面这段文字对上述论述的驳斥：

Even if it is granted that fifteen year olds possess better night vision, reflexes, hand-eye coordination, and are less disoriented in unfamiliar surroundings than older drivers, these abilities do not qualify them to obtain a driver's license. The author assumes that physical capabilities are the only attributes necessary to operate a motor vehicle. But this assumption is clearly mistaken. In addition to these abilities, drivers must be able to exercise good judgment in all types of driving situations and conditions and must be cognizant of the consequences of their decisions and actions when driving. It is because 15-year-olds typically lack these abilities that they are denied driving privileges.

2. 必要条件问题(Necessary-Condition Problems)

The following appeared as part of an article in a popular science magazine.

"Scientists must typically work 60 to 80 hours a week if they hope to further their careers; consequently, good and affordable all-day child care must be made available to both male and female scientists if they are to advance in their fields. Moreover, requirements for career advancement must be made more flexible so that preschool-age children can spend a significant portion of each day with a parent."

在上面的论述中，作者认为服务周到且价格合理的全天儿童看护对希望在自身领域有所发展的男性和女性科学家来说是必不可少的。也就是说，作者认为专业的儿童看护服务中心是男性和女性科学家在研究领域取得成功的必要条件。这样的观点显然是站不住脚的，因为有些科学家可能根本不需要专业的儿童看护服务：他们要么没有孩子，要么孩子已经长大成人，可以自立。即使有孩子的科学家也不一定非得依靠儿童看护中心，因为他们可以委托他们已经退休的父母或比较清闲的亲戚朋友来完成这项任务。请看下面的论述：

In this argument, the author asserts that in order for scientist, male and female alike, to further their career, they must have access to good, affordable, all-day child care. However, the author fails to consider and rule out other options for ensuring proper care for scientists' children during the workday. For instance, a scientist whose spouse (or partner) has time during each day to spend with their child requires no professional day care. Besides, many scientist-parents, including single-parent scientists, might have friends or relatives who can provide child care. Furthermore, childless scientists or scientists whose children are old enough to take care of themselves will have no need for the services advocated in this argument. Thus, to the extent that scientists have other options to ensure day care for their children, the author's assertion that scientists must have access to good, affordable, all-day child care is unwarranted.

3. 充要条件问题(Sufficient and Necessary Condition Problems)

The following appeared in a memorandum from the manager of KMTV, a television station.

"Applications for advertising spots on KMTV, our local cable television channel, decreased last year. Meanwhile a neighboring town's local channel, KOOP, changed its focus to farming issues and reported an increase in advertising applications for the year. To increase applications for advertising spots, KMTV should focus its programming on farming issues as well."

在上面这段论述中，作者认为KMTV将其节目重心转向农业问题是增加广告申请量的充分必要条件，而实际情况并非如此。请看下面的分析：

The argument depends on the assumption that the proposed change is the only way KMTV can stimulate advertising applications. Common sense tells me that there are other such ways—reducing advertising rates, improving programming quality, or extending broadcast range, to list just a few. The author must explain either why none of these options are available or why they would fail to stimulate applications. Otherwise, I cannot accept that the proposed change is necessary. In addition, the author further assumes that the proposed programming change would suffice to bring about the desired increase. However, if it turns out that last year's decline was due to a combination of factors, some of which remain unchanged in the future, a mere programming shift might not have a stimulating impact on applications.

五、整体与部分逻辑错误

整体与部分，即"Composition and Division"。从整体的特征简单地推导出部分的特征，或从部分的特征简单地推导出整体的特征，这是一种典型的逻辑错误。有的Argument会根据某个整体(比如学生、员工或城市)具有的某种特性来断言这个整体中的某一个特殊个体也具备这种特性。反之，有的Argument也会根据某一个特殊个体所具有的某种特性来断言这个整体也具备相同的特性。在任何一种情况下，除非作者给出明确的证据表明该成员可以代表整体(文中通常都不会有这样的证据)，否则原论证就特别易于攻击。

考生为了向阅卷者表明自己已经理解原论证中存在的"整体与部分"问题，需要完成以下三项任务：

☞ 发现问题：原论证依赖于一个非常重要的假设(群体的特性适用于这个群体中的每个个体，或者某一个特定个体所具有的特性也适用于整个群体)；

☞ 阐明问题：指出个体和群体在某些方面是相互区别的(至少举出一个到两个显著不同的地方)；

☞ 解释问题：论证这些用来反驳原论述所依赖的假设的关键差异会如何削弱原论证的结论。

考生一般至少需要三个句子来完成上面的三项任务(一个句子完成一项)。完成上面三项任务以后，如果还有时间，就可以在论证里加入下面的内容(选择性的)：

☞ 指出原论证的作者还需要提供哪些额外信息才能证实某个个体的某些相关的特性与这个个体所在的整体是相似的；

☞ 指出还需要了解哪些信息才能确定某个个体能在多大程度上代表整体。

个体与整体之间的逻辑错误通常可分为三类：(1)适用于整体的原则也适用于整体中的任一个个体；(2)对某个个体适用的东西对整体也适用；(3)从几个个体所具有的某个特性推出整体也具有这个特性(急于概括错误)。

接下来我们分别举例说明。

1. 适用于整体的原则也适用于整体中的任一个个体(What is true for a group is also true for any member)

The following is part of a business plan being discussed at a board meeting of the Perks Company.

"It is no longer cost-effective for the Perks Company to continue offering its employees a generous package of benefits and incentives year after year. In periods when national unemployment rates are low, Perks may need to offer such a package in order to attract and keep good employees, but since national unemployment rates are now high, Perks does not need to offer the same benefits and incentives. The money thus saved could be better used to replace the existing plant machinery with more technologically sophisticated equipment, or even to build an additional plant."

在上面的论述中，作者认为在失业率比较高的时期，Perks没有必要再为员工提供相对较高的薪酬，因为市场会为公司提供很多廉价的优秀劳动力。虽然这样的推理在表面上看来似乎合情合理，但是作者却忽视了一个很重要的问题，那就是Perks公司所从事的业务可能并不具备代表性，可能在众多的失业者中，很少有人能胜任Perks公司的工作。如果存在这样的可能性，那么听从作者的建议显然将对公司的发展带来不良影响。下面是针对该问题的论述：

The author relies on the reasoning that it is unnecessary to pay relatively high wages during periods of high unemployment because the market will supply many good employees at lower rates of pay. While this reasoning may be sound in a general sense, the particular industry that Perks is involved in may not be representative of unemployment levels generally. It is possible that relatively few unemployed people have the type of qualifications that match job openings at Perks. If this is the case, the claim that it is easier now to attract good employees at lower wages is ill-founded.

2. 适用于某一个个体的原则也适用于整体（What is true for a member is also true for the group）

The following appeared in an article in the health section of a newspaper.

"There is a common misconception that university hospitals are better than community or private hospitals. This notion is unfounded. The university hospitals in our region employ 15 percent fewer doctors, have a 20 percent lower success rate in treating patients, make far less overall profit, and pay their medical staff considerably less than do private hospitals. Furthermore, many doctors at university hospitals typically divide their time among teaching, conducting research, and treating patients. From this it seems clear that the quality of care at university hospitals is lower than that at other kinds of hospitals."

在上面的论述中，最严重的错误就是作者用某一个区内的一所大学医院的情况来代表所有的大学医院，然而作者却没有提供证据表明该所大学的医院可以代表所有的大学医院。请看下面的论证：

The most egregious reasoning error in the argument is the author's use of evidence pertaining to university hospitals in this region as the basis for a generalization about all university hospitals. The underlying assumption operative in this inference is that university hospitals in this region are representative of all university hospitals. No evidence is offered to support this gratuitous assumption.

3. 急于概括的错误（The Fallacy of Hasty Generalization）

急于概括是指在证据不足的情况下作出普遍的概括，这实际上是一个归纳推理的错误。在许多题目中，作者往往依据一两个相关的事实，就急于得出结论，而忽略了一些相关的可能得出相反结论的事实或证据，所以也可以称为"Neglect of relevant evidence"。例如：

"Most students in Riverside school must have participated in gang activities, because six students from this school last year were found involved in gang crimes."

这是典型的抓住个别，打倒一片的错误。六个学生怎么能代表全校学生的情况呢？

六、假定所有的事情都一成不变类逻辑错误

假定所有的事情都一成不变，即"Assuming all things remain unchanged over time"。为了给涉及到现在或将来的某个问题提出相关的建议，或得到某个结论，原论证可能会使用一些过去收集的证据。同样，有的Argument也可能会使用今天的数据来预测将来的情况，或为将来提出相关的建议。但是，除非原论证给出明确的证据表

明关键的环境因素会保持不变, 并且在相当长的一段时间内也是不变的(顺便说一下, 关键的环境因素通常是会改变的), 否则原论证就易于受到相应的批驳。

考生为了解决时间变换问题, 需要完成以下三项任务:

☞ 发现问题: 所有的关键因素在研究的时间段内都保持不变的假设站不住脚;

☞ 阐明问题: 举例说明某些条件在不同的时间段是会变化的;

☞ 评价原论证: 根据这些问题来对原论证进行评价。

考生一般需要三个句子来完成上面的三项任务(一个句子完成一项)。完成上面三项任务以后, 如果还有时间, 可以完成下面两项任务中的任一项(选择性的):

☞ 指出要想加强原论证, 作者必须设法使读者相信其他相关的因素在不同的时间段内是保持不变的;

☞ 为了评价文中所提出的建议、预测或其他结论, 列举还需要哪些有关过去和现在(或现在和将来)的环境信息。

1. 过去的情况在今天和将来都保持不变(Past conditions remain unchanged in the present and future)

The following appeared in a memorandum written by the chair of the music department to the president of Omega University.

"Mental health experts have observed that symptoms of mental illness are less pronounced in many patients after group music-therapy sessions, and job openings in the music-therapy field have increased during the past year. Consequently, graduates from our degree program for music therapists should have no trouble finding good positions. To help improve the financial status of Omega University, we should therefore expand our music-therapy degree program by increasing its enrollment targets."

在这段论述里, 作者根据音乐治疗方面的工作机会在过去一年中有所增加这一现象, 得出了增加音乐治疗学位课程的入学人数有助于改善Omega大学的经济状况这一结论。然而, 过去一年的数据显然不足以说明音乐治疗方面的工作机会会一直很多, 所以作者根据去年发生的情况得出有关将来的结论显然是有问题的。请看下面的论证:

The argument depends on the assumption that in the future, there will continue to be sufficient job openings in music therapy for Omega graduates. However, a recent one-year increase is insufficient evidence itself to convince me that this trend will continue, providing a ready job supply for new Omega graduates. Moreover, should this trend actually reverse, then adopting the chair's proposal might result in a decrease in Omega's job-placement rate, which might very well have a negative impact on the school's overall reputation and, in turn, its financial status.

2. 目前的情况在将来保持不变(Present conditions will remain unchanged in the future)

The following appeared as part of the business plan of an investment and financial consulting firm.

"Studies suggest that an average coffee drinker's consumption of coffee increases with age, from age 10 through age 60. Even after age 60, coffee consumption remains high. The average cola drinker's consumption of cola, however, declines with increasing age. Both of these trends have remained stable for the past 40 years. Given that the number of older adults will significantly increase as the population ages over the next 20 years, it follows that the demand for coffee will increase and the demand for cola will decrease during this period. We should, therefore, consider transferring our investments from Cola Loca to Early Bird Coffee."

在这段论述里，作者根据人们在过去40年内对咖啡和可乐的消费情况，结合人口结构在接下来的20年内将发生的变化，推导出咖啡的需求将上升而可乐的需求将下降的结论。作者的结论依赖于咖啡和可乐的供给在接下来的20年里将保持不变这一假设。但这种假设本身是没有保证的，因为事物很少能在不同的地点一直保持相同的状态，也很少能随时间和地点的变化保持不变。请看下面的论证：

The argument assumes that relative supply conditions will remain unchanged over the next twenty years. However, the supply and cost of cola and coffee beans, as well as other costs of doing business as a producer of coffee or cola, may fluctuate greatly over a long time period. These factors may affect comparative prices of coffee and cola, which in turn may affect comparative demand and the value of investments in coffee and cola companies. Without considering other factors that contribute to the value of a coffee or cola company, the firm cannot justify its recommendation.

七、错误的两难境地类逻辑错误

错误的两难境地，即"False Dilemma"。这种逻辑错误是指：把一个复杂问题的解决方法简单地归为非此即彼的两种选择，而忽略第三种方法，这是把复杂问题简单化的一种典型思维方式。因此，这种错误也称为"the either-or thinking"或"the black-white fallacy"。请看下面的例子：

The following appeared in the editorial section of a local newspaper.

"Commuter use of the new subway train is exceeding the transit company's projections. However, commuter use of the shuttle buses that transport people to the subway stations is below the projected volume. If the transit company expects commuters to ride the shuttle buses to the subway rather than drive there, it must either reduce the shuttle bus fares or increase the price of parking at the subway stations." (Argument 28)

为了使上下班的人能搭乘公交车而不是开车去地铁站，作者建议两种可行的方案：要么降低公交车的票价，要么提高地铁站附近的停车费。实际问题比这要复杂得多：如果同时执行这两套方案，也许效果会更得多。另外，为了达到文中所述及的目的，可能还存在其他可行的方案，如果把所有的可行方案综合考虑，也许会得到更好的效果。请看下面的论证：

The author assumes that reducing shuttle fees and increasing parking fees are mutually exclusive alternatives. However, the author provides no reason for imposing an either/or choice. Adjusting both shuttle fares and parking fees might produce better results. Moreover, if the author is wrong in the assumption that parking fees and shuttle fees are the only possible causes of the problem, then the most effective solution might include a combination of policy changes—for example, in shuttle fares, parking fees, rerouting, and rescheduling.

八、其他论证逻辑错误

我们已经对Argument中经常出现的逻辑错误进行了详细的分析。除此之外，Argument中还会出现下面所列出的这些逻辑错误，虽然他们在考试中出现的频率不高，但对它们有所了解还是非常必要的。

1. 考虑问题不全面（Failing to weighing the advantages and disadvantages thoroughly）

为了支持自己的观点，有时作者仅给出对自己观点有利的证据，对该观点不利的因素却从不考虑，这样得出的结论肯定是有问题的，请看下面的例子：

> The following appeared in a memorandum from the business department of the Apogee Company.
>
> "When the Apogee Company had all its operations in one location, it was more profitable than it is today. Therefore, the Apogee Company should close down its field offices and conduct all its operations from a single location. Such centralization would improve profitability by cutting costs and helping the company maintain better supervision of all employees."

在上面的论述中，作者只讨论了集中的有利因素和分散的不利因素，而没有考虑集中的不利因素和分散的有利因素，就匆匆得出了结论。这样的结论显然是经不起推敲的，请看下面的分析：

The author assumes that centralization would improve profitability by cutting costs and streamlining supervision of employees. This assumption is not supported with any data or projections. Moreover, the assumption fails to take into account cost increases and inefficiency that could result from centralization. For instance, company representatives would have to travel to do business in areas formerly served by a field office, creating travel costs and a loss of critical time. In short, this assumption must be supported with a thorough cost-benefit analysis of centralization versus other possible cost-cutting and/or profit-enhancing strategies.

2. 没有限定重要词语（Failing to define important terms）

一篇Argument的论断可能依赖于某一个没有给出详细定义的重要词语，这样很容易使人怀疑这篇Argument结论的正确性。请看下面的例子：

> The following appeared in a speech delivered by a member of the city council.
>
> "Twenty years ago, only half of the students who graduated from Einstein High School went on to attend a college or university. Today, two thirds of the students who graduate from Einstein do so. Clearly, Einstein has improved its educational effectiveness over the past two decades. This improvement has occurred despite the fact that the school's funding, when adjusted for inflation, is about the same as it was twenty years ago. Therefore, we do not need to make any substantial increase in the school's funding at this time."

在上面这段论述中，结论的正确性在很大程度上依赖于人们对"educational effectiveness"这个词的理解。如果我们把"educational effectiveness"等同于升学率，那么作者所引用的数据将会有力地支持该论述的结论。然而，在谈论"educational effectiveness"时，我们关注的不仅是升学率，也许更加关心学生的整体素质是否得到了提高。在这种情况下，作者的结论就会显得苍白无力。请看下面的论证：

We must establish the meaning of the vague concept "educational efficiency." If the term is synonymous with the rate of graduation to college, then the statistics cited would strongly support the argument. But usually we are interested in something more than just the numbers of students who go on to college from a high school; we also want to know how well the school has prepared students for a successful college experience—that is, whether the school has provided a good secondary education. Thus, for the speaker the term "educational efficiency" must essentially carry the same meaning as "educational quality."

3. 循环论证（Circular reasoning）

循环论证是指假定关键性的假设被证明。这种逻辑漏洞通常又叫做"tautology"或"begging the question"。论证的过程为：A→B，B→A。在原题论述中，如果发现有重要假设没有任何论据支持，你就可以就其循环论证的逻辑缺陷展开攻击。

> The following appeared in a letter from the owner of the Sunnyside Towers apartment building to its manager.
>
> "One month ago, all the showerheads on the first five floors of Sunnyside Towers were modified to restrict the water flow to approximately 1/3 of its original force. Although actual readings of water usage before and after the adjustment are not yet available, the change will obviously result in a considerable savings for Sunnyside Corporation, since the corporation must pay for water each month. Except for a few complaints about low water pressure, no problems with showers have been reported since the adjustment. Clearly, restricting water flow throughout all the 20 floors of Sunnyside Towers will increase our profits further."

在上面这段论述里，作者的结论所依赖的关键假设之一就是"The change（restricting the water flow）will obviously result in considerable savings for Sunnyside Corporation." 然而，作者却没有提供限制沐浴喷头流水量之后的实际用水量，他只是想当然地相信现在的用水量一定低于以前的用水量。从逻辑上看，作者并未排除用水量不变甚至有所增加的可能性，因为流水量减小后，人们有可能延长洗澡的时间。

4. 得出的结论在程度或范围上过于广泛（Drawing a conclusion that is too broad in degree or scope）

一篇Argument的结论可能只在某种程度上或只是在某一方面得到了很好的支持。如果其论据不具有针对性，那么结论是非常容易受到攻击的。如下例所示：

> The following appeared in the editorial section of a local newspaper.
>
> "The profitability of Croesus Company, recently restored to private ownership, is a clear indication that businesses fare better under private ownership than under public ownership."

从上面的论述中，我们可以看出作者的结论过于广泛。即使大多数的企业从公有制模式恢复到私有制模式后，利润率提高，我们也得不出企业在私有制模式下比公有制模式下的运营状况要好这样的结论。很有可能那些运营状况良好的公司都是一直保持公有制经济形式的公司。请考生看下面的论述：

Even if most businesses that return from public to private status improve their profitability（"fare better"）as a result, the author's conclusion that private businesses as an entire group fare better than public ones is far too broad. Perhaps the most profitable businesses are the ones that remain public ones forever. If so, then the author would need to narrow his conclusion accordingly.

5. 依赖于模棱两可的证据（Relying on vague or ambiguous evidence）

在一篇Argument中，有些话（词或短语）可能包含不止一个意思，或这些话（词或短语）的意思过于含糊而无法根据它们得到合理的结论。对这类漏洞进行攻击时，要特别留意原论述中用"some, many, 以及several"来代替具体的百分比或数字的地方。

The following appeared as part of an article in the business section of a daily newspaper.

"Company A has a large share of the international market in video-game hardware and software. Company B, the pioneer in these products, was once a $12 billion-a-year giant but collapsed when children became bored with its line of products. Thus Company A can also be expected to fail, especially given the fact that its games are now in so many American homes that the demand for them is nearly exhausted."

在上面这段论述中，作者的结论从某种程度上依赖于一个模棱两可的论据——"Company A's games are now in so many American homes"。因为"so many"是一个不具体的概念，所以上面论述结论的正确性也会受到质疑。请考生看下面对模棱两可的论据所做的分析：

The mere fact that Company A's products appear in "so many" American homes accomplishes little toward showing waning demand for its products, let alone toward showing that the company will fail. To begin with, the term "so many" is too vague to be statistically meaningful. Even if by "so many" the author means "nearly all", perhaps among Americans, the demand for more new Company A games is strong. Moreover, the author ignores foreign markets, which might account for a significant portion of Company A's sales. The greater the demand outside America, the less likely Company A will fail.

6. 同时为两个相对立的目标辩论(Arguing simultaneously for two competing objectives)

在某些Argument中，作者有时会试图同时为两个看起来相互对立的目标辩论。换句话说，如果作者想完成其中的一个目标，就会减小完成另一个目标的可能性。请考生看下面的论述：

The following appeared as part of an article in a popular science magazine.

"Scientists must typically work 60 to 80 hours a week if they hope to further their careers; consequently, good and affordable all-day child care must be made available to both male and female scientists if they are to advance in their fields. Moreover, requirements for career advancement must be made more flexible so that preschool-age children can spend a significant portion of each day with a parent."

在这篇论述中，作者指出科学家要想在他们的研究领域中有所进取的话，他们每周必须工作60到80小时。基于以上事实，作者给出了两条见解：（1）In order for scientists, male and female alike, to further their careers, they must have access to good, affordable, all-day childcare；（2）Requirements for career advancement must be made more flexible so that children of pre-school age can spend significant portions of each day with at least one parent. 如果综合考虑这两条见解，我们会发现第二条见解实际上会削弱第一条。请考生看下面的分析：

In essence, the second assertion serves to undermine the first one. If the children of scientists spend significant time each day with a parent, without compromising to the scientist-parent's career, then all-day child care would seem unnecessary—in direct contradiction to the author's first assertion. Thus, the author must either reconcile the two assertions or choose one assertion over the other.

7. 无理呼吁(Irrational Appeals)

我们在日常生活中，为了使别人相信自己的言论，经常使用 Irrational appeals这种技巧，如"You don't have to think about this, there is no danger of error here"，就是种无理呼吁。Irrational appeals包括诉诸于权威，诉诸于情感等。

8. 人身攻击 (Ad Hominem)

这就是所谓的"Personal Attack"。比如在有些论证中，作者为了反对Jammy的观点会这样说："不要相信Jammy的观点，因为Jammy是个同性恋者。"这显然是在搞人身攻击，我们知道一个人的某个观点是否可信与他或她是否是同性恋者没有太大的关系。

9. 稻草人 (Straw Argument)

树立一个易被攻击的靶子，忽略真正的问题；或者强加一个作者没有提及的易被攻击的问题。

10. 错误权威 (False or Questionable Authority)

在推理中引用没有说服力的权威，或者提供不相关的权威。

第二章　Argument 逻辑错误的经典攻击句型和论证方法

　　找出Argument中的逻辑错误后，还要对其进行攻击。下面给出一些攻击常见逻辑错误的经典句型和模板，供考生参考。

一、常见逻辑错误的经典攻击句型

1. 无效调查

Model 1

☞ The poll cited by the author is too vague to be informative / reliable.

☞ The claim does not indicate who conducted the poll, who responded, or how the poll was conducted.

☞ Until these questions are answered, the results are worthless as evidence for...

Model 2

☞ To begin with, the validity of the survey is doubtful.

☞ Lacking information about the number of employees surveyed and the number of respondents, it is impossible to access the validity of the results.

☞ For example, if 200 employees were surveyed but only 2 responded, the conclusion that... would be highly suspect.

☞ Because the argument offers no evidence that would rule out these interpretations, the results of the survey are insufficient to support the conclusion.

Model 3

☞ We are not informed that how many people were surveyed but did not respond. If, for instance, 500 subjects were studied, but no more than 50 answered the questions, the conclusion would be highly susceptible.

☞ The author fails to point out when the survey was conducted. If the change is very recent, it is possible that insufficient data have been gleaned to draw such a conclusion, an unconvincing one. (If..., before..., ...)

2. 因果关系

Model 1

☞ The author commits the "After This, Therefore Because of This" fallacy.

☞ The author assumes that A caused B.

☞ The line of the reasoning is that because A is before B, the former event caused the latter.

☞ But this is fallacious reasoning unless other possible causal explanations have been considered and ruled out.

☞ For example, perhaps A1 is the cause of these events or perhaps B is caused by A2.

Model 2

☞ The author uses the statistical relationship / positive correlation between A and B to establish causality.

☞ However, the fact that A coincides with B does not necessarily prove that A caused B.

☞ There may be other factors that could have caused B / contributed to B, such as A1, A2, and A3.

Model 3

☞ The author fails to establish a causal relationship between the fact A and the claim B.

☞ This argument is unacceptable if there is no compelling evidence to support the connection between these two events.

☞ Perhaps, for example, ...

3. 无理假设(无前提证据的假设)

Model 1

☞ The author assumes that... will... / A is necessary to B.

☞ However, this is not necessarily the case / no evidence is stated in the argument to support this assumption.

☞ It is possible that... / Perhaps...

Model 2

☞ The author falsely depends on the gratuitous assumption that... (作者的错误前提)

☞ In fact / Actually, this is not necessarily the case.

☞ For example, it is most likely that... (相反例子)

☞ Therefore, this argument is unwarranted without ruling out such possibility.

4. 错误类比

Model 1

☞ Analogies drawn between A and B are highly suspect because there are many serious differences.

☞ While A..., B.... / For example, A..., however, B...

☞ Thus, it is likely much more difficult for B to...

Model 2

☞ The reason / argument rests on the assumption that A is analogous to / similar to B in all respects.

☞ This assumption is weak, since although there are points of comparison between A and B, there are many dissimilarities as well.

☞ For example, A..., however, B...

Model 3

☞ The author also commits the fallacy of "all things are equal".

☞ The fact that this happened two years ago is not sound evidence to draw a conclusion that...

☞ The author assumes without justification that the background conditions have remained the same at different times or at different locations.

☞ However, it is not clear in this argument whether the current conditions at A are the same as they used to be two years ago.

☞ Thus it is impossible to conclude that...

5. 急于概括

☞ Without ruling out these and other possible factors, the author cannot confidently conclude that...

☞ The author assumes too hastily that... necessarily results in... However, it is not the case. If... The author, thus, cannot safely draw any significant conclusion or prediction.

二、常见逻辑错误的经典论证方法

1.因果关系攻击

(1)时序性因果攻击

☞ The author is engaged in "after this, therefore because of this" reasoning. The line of reasoning is that because A happened before B, the former caused the latter. However, this reasoning is fallacious unless other possible causal factors have been considered and ruled out. For example, perhaps C. As a result, any decision aimed at addressing the problem of B must be based on a more thorough investigation to gather data in order to narrow down and locate the actual cause of B.

☞ The author fails to establish the causal relationship between A and B. The sequence of these events, in itself, does not suffice to prove that the former caused the later one. No additional evidence linking the two events is offered in the argument, thus leaving the possibility that the two events are merely coincident rather than causally related.

☞ The author assumes that B caused A. This argument commits the fallacy of assuming that just because A follows B, the second event has been caused by the first. The causal claim based on the correlation is incorrect unless the author can rule out other factors. For example, perhaps... Yet another possibility is that...

(2)先因后果和同时因果都能用

☞ The author's solution rests on the assumption that A is the cause of B. The only reason provided for believing that...can... is that the former proceeded / coincide with the latter, and no additional evidence linking the two events is offered in this argument, thus leaving the possibility that the two events are not causally related but merely correlated. Many other factors can bring about the same result. For instance... In this argument, unfortunately, while temporal precedence / concurrence such as A is one of the conditions required to establish a causal relationship between two events, by itself it is not a sufficient condition. Thus it is groundless to attribute B to A.

(3)同时性因果攻击

☞ The author's solution rests on the assumption that A is the cause of B just because A coincided with B. However, a mere positional correlation does not necessarily prove a causal relationship. In addition, all other prospective causes of B, such as C and D, must be ruled out. Without detailed analysis of the real source of B, it would be groundless to attribute B to A.

(4)因果倒置攻击

☞ It is possible that the author has confused cause with effect. Perhaps A was a response to B. Since the author fails to account for this possibility, the claim that... is completely unwarranted.

(5)因果关系简单化

☞ The author attempts to establish a causal / positive relationship between the fact that... and the claim that... (between two matters... and...). This argument, nonetheless, is based on an oversimplified analysis of the cause of... and the presumptuous correlation accordingly is unacceptable. Actually, it is equally possible that... or it is possible that... Without ruling out such alternative explanation(s) the author can not convince me that... necessarily results in...

2. 错误类比攻击

☞ It is highly doubtful that strategies drawn from A are applicable to B. However, differences between these two clearly outweigh the similarities, therefore making the analogy much less valid. For example, C and D all affect A but are virtually absent in B. Accordingly, we can see that A and B are so dissimilar that B is unlikely to experience the same consequence if it adopts A's strategies.

☞ The author commits a fallacy of false analogy by simply equating A with B. Without better evidence, the stated similarities between A and B are insufficient to warrant the conclusion that A will suffer the same fate（achieve the same result）as B's. It is possible that... and that... If true, these differences may seriously weaken the conclusion based on the similarity（analogy）between A and B.

☞ The author commits the fallacy of "false analogy". The argument rests on the assumption that A is analogous to B in all respects. However, this assumption is weak, since it is highly doubtful that all elements drawn from A are applicable to B. For example, X, Y, Z all affect A, but are virtually absent in B. Differences between the two clearly outweigh the similarities, thus making the analogy invalid.

☞ Although there are points of comparison, many dissimilarities remain. The argument, thus, relying on the assumption that... is analogous to... in all aspects, is weak. It is, for example, possible that... It is also possible that... In either event, only relying on simple mimicry of... there would be little effect.

☞ The author commits the fallacy of "false analogy". It is extremely doubtful that strategies drawn from A are concurrently applicable to B. Because differences between A and B far outweigh the similarities, the application of the same technique in another distinct field or condition with a distinct background is doomed to incompatibility and failure, thereby making the analogy less valid and less legitimate. For instance, ... Accordingly, A and B are so disparate that B is unlikely to accomplish the same result by employing A's strategies.

3. 非此即彼攻击

☞ Last but not least, the author unfairly assumes that a reader must make an either-or choice. However, the argument fails to rule out the possibility that adjusting A and B might produce better results. Moreover, if the author is wrong in the assumption that A and B are the only causes of the problem, then the most effective solution might include a combination of other factors—such as C and D. In any event, the author provides no justification for the mutually exclusive choice imposed on the reader.

☞ The author presents a false dilemma by imposing an either-or choice between A and B, which in fact are not mutually exclusive alternatives. It is entirely possible that the company could employ/utilize A and B at the same time, thus, make the results better. Also, if the author is wrong in assuming that A and B are the only two possible solutions to the problem, then the most effective solution might include other measures such as...

☞ The author unfairly assumes that individuals would have to make an either-or choice. However, the arguer fails to rule out the possibilities that reconciling A with B might yield a middle ground for a better resolution and that the most effective solution, nonetheless, might involve a systematic combination / amalgamation of many relevant techniques and considerations. Specifically, ... In any event, the author provides no justification for the mutually exclusive alternatives.

4. 充分必要性攻击

（1）必要性攻击

☞ The author unfairly assumes that B was determined solely by A. While A is a seemingly important element in determining B, it is hardly the only or even necessarily required element. This assumption overlooks other crucial criteria in determining B—such as C, D. Without accounting for these potential factors, the author concludes too hastily that... is the best way to achieve goals.

☞ Common sense tells me that there are a lot of other ways other than, such as B, C, D, E, to list just a few. （Perhaps one of these would be just as effective as, or even more effective than, the A, the proposed plan.）

（2）充分性攻击

☞ The author's solution rests on the assumption that A is sufficient to achieve the desired goals. However, if it turns out that B is due to a combination of factors, some of which will remain unchanged in the future, such as C and D, only A might have no impact on B.

☞ The author bases his claim partly on the assumption that B is all that required for A（there is no variable alternative means of achieving A except B）. Yet the author presented no evidence that supports this assumption. Although B is an important factor for A, it is hardly the only element required（alternative available）.

☞ The author has focused only on ×××. A more detailed analysis would reveal that other factors far outweigh the factors on which the author focuses. For example, C. Lacking a more comprehensive analysis of the causes, it is presumptuous for the author to claim that ××× solely determined B.

☞ The author unfairly assumes that B is determined and caused exclusively by A. Although A is salient and striking element in determining B, it is not true that other crucial criteria—such as C, D—do not play a more indispensable part in determining B. Without accounting for these underlying pertinent factors contributing to B, accordingly, it is presumptuous for the author to conclude that A is the only determinant.

5. 样本与调查类攻击

（1）选择性样本攻击

☞ The evidence that the author provides is insufficient to support the conclusion draw from it. （One example is rarely sufficient to establish a general conclusion.） Unless it can be shown that A1 is representative of A, the conclusion... is completely unwarranted. In fact, in face of such limited evidence, it is fallacious to draw any conclusion at all.

☞ A threshold problem is that the author provides no evidence to claim that the general group as a whole has the same characteristics. The example cited, while suggestive of this trend, is insufficient to warrant that the sample is representative of the whole group. For example, I question that... Therefore, such evidence would be obviously unrepresentative. In fact, faced with such limited evidence, it is fallacious for the author to draw any conclusion at all.

（2）样本代表性攻击

☞ Another problem is the representativeness of the respondents. Were they representative of all the... ? Were... chosen for the survey chosen randomly or did they volunteer for the survey?

☞ Moreover, a possible methodology problem in the argument is that it is biased. The term "so many" is too vague to be statistically meaningful. It is possible that workers who were more interested in the survey might be likely to respond to the questionnaire. Lacking information about the number of workers surveyed and the number of respondents, it is impossible to assess the validity of the survey. For instance, if 1000 workers were surveyed but only 10 responded, the result is highly suspect. Because the author fails to account for other interpretations, the survey would be useless in regards to the conclusion that...

(3)样本数量攻击

☞ Another problem that seriously weakens the logic of this argument is that the survey cited is based on too small a sample to be reliable. Offered in support of the argument, the only evidence is that.... Unless it can be shown that the sample is typical of a general group, the fact that... is groundless to claim that...

(4)样本不足

☞ The only evidence provided in support of the conclusion is the fact that... The most obvious reasoning error in the argument is the author's use of evidence pertaining to A in X region as the basis for generalization about A. Unless it can be proved that X is typical of A, the fact that... is not a basis for concluding that A as a whole will experience similar results.

(5)样本时效性攻击

☞ Last but not least, another flaw that significantly undermines this argument is that the author neglects to indicate how recently the survey was conducted. When used to generally claim a particular group, the samples should be close enough to support the generalization, in order to prevent historical changes from invalidating the generalization. All we know is that the survey is recently published. The older the survey is, the less reliable the results to demonstrate that...

(6)调查的可靠性

☞ The author fails to point out how the survey was conducted. If they conducted it themselves, and the question is..., it is obvious that if... Or if these questions were leading, people might respond with expected answers, thus the results would be unconvincing.

☞ Samples for the survey should be statistically reliable. Unfortunately, from the survey we find little sign of such procedures for sampling, thus making it doubtful whether the respondents constitute a sufficiently large sample to be representative of the overall population of the nation.

☞ Since the arguer makes a claim about..., in general, samples for the survey should be able to represent all... However, from the survey quoted in this argument, we find no sign of such procedures for random samplings, and have good reason to doubt if the sample is representative enough to reflect the general altitude of... as a whole.

☞ From the survey we find little sign of such procedures for random sampling, thus casting doubt on whether the respondents are representative of the overall population of the nation. If the subjects are only limited to a certain city or geographic region, the results of the survey will be unconvincing.

☞ The claim does not provide evidence to confirm the reliability of the poll / study, because the poll / study fails to indicate who conducted it, who responded, or how the poll / study was conducted to lend credibility to these claims. Moreover, while the phrase "study / poll suggests" may appear...

☞ The author provides no evidence to justify that the procedures of the survey quoted in the argument are from a randomly sampling, thus, lacking such evidence, I have good reason to doubt if the respondents of the survey are representative of the overall group of people who... That is to say, it is entirely possible that those who... were more likely to respond to the survey or even were chosen to respond to it. In short, without more specific information about the survey showing its statistical reliability, the author cannot rely on it to draw any convincing conclusion about...

☞ The statistical evidence in the argument is somewhat problematic since the poll cited by the author is described in the vaguest possible terms: no details such as that how the poll was conducted and who responded have been indicated. Consider if thousands of people are surveyed but only several responded, then the results are worthless as evidence for... Therefore, lacking this relevant information it is not possible to assess whether this is the case as claimed.

☞ The argument depends on the assumption that customers who did not complain were actually satisfied with... However, the evidence offered is insufficient to support that claim. It is entirely possible that people express their displeasure simply by not returning the complaint sheets or by not coming to the shop any more. Therefore, the greater percentage of such people, the weaker the argument's evidence as a sign of customers' satisfaction with... is. Lacking more concrete information about customers' attitudes, the author cannot assume that the great majority of customers are pleased with the change.

☞ What's more, the methodology of the survey is problematic for two reasons. For one thing, we are not informed whether the survey provided only 3 alternatives. If it did, the respondents, who might very well prefer another choice not provided in the survey, might be forced to leave out their preferences. Also, we are not informed whether the survey responses were anonymous or confidential. The respondents might supply responses favored by their superiors who might have conducted the survey. Both events would make this survey unreliable, let alone be the basis for drawing the conclusion that...

6. 整体与部分攻击

☞ The author unfairly presuppose that（小范围中这样）suffices to infer（大范围也这样）, for there are all kinds of crucial differences between（小范围和大范围）. It is just as likely that... Consequently, unless it can be shown that... is typical of a general group, the author cannot justify this recommendation that...and moreover, implementing the author's suggestion might amount to poor advice.

☞ The argument depends on the assumption that..., however, this is not necessarily the case.（While it is true that... it is not true of everyone.）

☞ The most egregious reasoning error in this argument is the author's use of evidence pertaining to particular / general group as the basis for a general / particular group. Without better evidence that... it is equally possible that... or that... If so, these facts will certainly serve to undermine the author's argument to a large extent.

7. 非此即彼（二选一，忽略其他同类）

☞ The author's recommendation rests on the unlikely assumption that the company has only two alternatives... and... In all likelihood... can engage one of many other... instead. Thus, to some extent the author recommends... over not just... but over any other... the recommendation is unwarranted.

8. 急于概括

☞ There is no thorough lost-benefit analysis in the argument. If the increase of cost outweighs that of benefits... will be in danger of losing rather than gaining money. Also, the author neglects the fact of competition.

☞ The author commits a fallacy of hasty generalization. Even if..., it does not follow that... It is highly possible other factors may have contributed to... For instance, ... Besides, the arguer does not provide any solid information concerning... Unless..., which is unknown for this argument, there is guarantee that...

9. 差异概念攻击

☞ To begin with, we must establish the meaning of the vague concept A. If the term were synonymous with B, the evidence cited would strongly support the argument. However, A may be defined in other terms such as C and D. Accordingly, the author has drawn the conclusion too hastily due to the ignorance of other definitions of A.

10. 范围内推攻击

☞ What's more, the most egregious reasoning error in this argument is that the author uses evidence pertaining to a general group on the basis of a particular B. Even if the reasoning may be sound in general sense, the particular situation in which B is involved may not be representative of the entire general group. It is possible that... If this is the case, the claim that... is ill founded.

11. 一成不变攻击

☞ Moreover, the author unfairly assumes that A will remain unchanged in the future. However, a mere recent one-year A is insufficient to claim that. Statistics from such limited anecdotal evidence are not a good indicator for this trend. In addition, it is possible that in the future, this trend will greatly fluctuate or even reverse, then the adoption of the author's proposal might give birth to B. However, it might also have a negative impact on C1 and, in turn, C2. Admittedly, this argument would be even weaker as time goes by.

☞ Committing the fallacy of all things are equal, the author unfairly assumes that past experiences are applicable to present situations, that the same technique drawn from past incidents may now function effectively, and that this tendency will remain stable over the next several years. Statistics from the past, nevertheless, are not a verifiable indication of further permanent trends because of alterations in the background, along with unexpected fluctuations within A. For instance... Accordingly, lacking evidence proving that this trend may continue, this hypothesis is unfounded.

12. 以偏概全攻击

☞ The author relies on the dubious supposition that... can... without sacrificing the... The line of reasoning fails to consider the benefits... might bring harm as well, ... might occur. In fact, (这个决定的坏处) After assessing the situation more comprehensively, it may turn out that the advantages far outweigh the disadvantages. Since the reasoning lacks a complete analysis of the condition, the forecast of... cannot be taken seriously.

13. 言行不一

☞ The author appreciates who's strong commitment to something to some extent. However, we know the fact that to make a commitment is one thing, but to keep it is far more difficult. There is no indication that they might fulfill their promise. As a consequence, the author cannot make any prediction.

第三章 Argument 写作必备经典句子

下面这些句子都是从大量的阅读中收集到的Argument中可能会用到的经典句子。这些句子不要求背诵，但希望考生能够熟读。建议考生最好先把这些句子翻译出来，然后看着译文把这些句子用自己的话译成英文，最后把自己的语言与原文进行对比，反复练习，不断提高自己遣词造句的能力，最终写出属于自己的闪光句子。

1. A six-month period is not a particularly long time frame for the citizens to determine that the speed limit has influenced the number of automobile accidents in the area.

2. A third problem with the argument is that the statistical evidence upon which it relies is too vague to be informative.

3. According to the memo, companies are urged to follow this code, but there is no evidence whatsoever to show any serious commitment on the part of those companies other than their overt agreement to abide by it.

4. Accordingly, this assumption is simply an unproven claim.

5. Admittedly, the vice president's reasoning linking employee benefits with company profits seems reasonable on the surface.

6. An additional reason given in support of this recommendation is that Solario's chief executive was a member of the financial planning team for a company that has shown remarkable growth since its recent incorporation.

7. Any adverse change in those factors will have a negative impact on the company's profitability.

8. Any further link between these two phenomena requires more evidence and is not justified by the data available.

9. Are there more people in Forestville than there were six months ago? If so, there may be an increased number of accidents due to more automobiles being on the road, and not because of the increased speed limits.

10. As it stands, this argument suffers from three critical flaws.

11. But any conclusion at this stage is premature in the absence of a comprehensive examination of the school's educational competence.

12. But no evidence is provided to show that this explanation is correct.

13. But the problem is that the two situations are not similar enough to justify the analogical deduction.

14. But we are told nothing about the way the poll was conducted and how well it represents public opinion.

15. Common sense tells us that a photographer can succeed by working in both media.

16. Comprehensive analysis is necessary to identify the actual cause(s) of the company's lower profits.

17. Consequently, it is unlikely that the machines pictured in the magazine will be of much use in helping maximize the fitness levels of the town's residents.

18. Consequently, the mere fact that Company A holds a large share of the video-game hardware and software market does not support the claim that Company A will also fail.

19. Consequently, unless the author can demonstrate that the city will incur expenses that are not covered by the increased revenues from these projects, the author's concern about these issues is unfounded.

20. Contingencies such as market changes, competition, material and labor costs, changes in legislation, and national or international economic cycles can all lead to decreased profits.

21. The economy, as we know, is influenced by the combination of a host of factors, local, national and international, political, social, and technological.

22. Experience alone is far from being enough to guarantee minimized processing costs.

23. Factors such as funds, the teaching staff 's computer skills, and the relative importance of other teaching objectives all have some bearing on the extent of computer-aided instruction.

24. Finally, in asserting that organic farming is financially unwise because it is motivated by environ-mental instead of economic concerns, the speaker unfairly assumes that a practice cannot be both environmentally and economically beneficial.

25. Finally, the author unfairly trivializes the severity of rural crime by comparing it with urban crime.

26. First of all, while asserting that real incomes are rising, the author provides no evidence to support this assertion.

27. For a couple of reasons, this argument is not very convincing.

28. From the survey quoted in the argument, however, we find no sign of such procedures for random sampling, and have good reason to doubt if the sample is representative enough to reflect the general attitudes of all workers as a whole.

29. Given that Olympic Foods does benefit from lowered processing costs due to its experience, the prediction about maximum profits is still lacking the solid ground.

30. However, before any final decisions are made about a reduction in the speed limit, the citizens and officials of Forestville should evaluate all possible alternatives and causes for the increased number of accidents over the six-month period as compared to Elmsford.

31. However, the author fails to acknowledge and rule out other possible causes of such accidents.

32. However, the citizens of Forestville are failing to consider other possible alternatives to the increase of car accidents after the speed limit was raised.

33. However, this is not necessarily the case.

34. However, unless the original cast and production team are involved in making the sequel, there is a good chance it will not be financially successful.

35. However, while the poll establishes a correlation between reading the ad and purchasing sale items, and also indicates a correlation, though less significantly, between reading the ad and buying non-sale items, it does not establish a general causal relationship between these events.

36. If so, even though 3 percent more accidents occurred after the change, the author's argument that changing the speed limit increases the danger for drivers is seriously flawed.

37. If the subjects for the study were randomly chosen and represent a diverse cross section of the population of

shampoo users, the results will be reliable regardless of the number of participants.

38. If this will be the case, then the increasing number of middle-aged people in the future will not necessarily mean an increase of business volume in department stores.

39. In addition, the arguer reasons that 15-year-olds are physically more capable than older drivers of performing the various skills associated with driving a vehicle and thus should be eligible to get a license.

40. In addition, while it is true that many voters change their minds several times before voting, and that some remain undecided until entering the voting booth, this is not true of everyone.

41. In any event, the advertisement provides no justification for the mutually exclusive choice that it imposes on the writer.

42. In the first place, a great deal of empirical evidence shows that sequels are often not as profitable as the original movie.

43. In this argument the arguer concludes that the Appogee Company should close down field offices and conduct all its operations from a single, centralized location because the company had been more profitable in the past when all its operations were in one location.

44. In this argument, the planning department of an investment firm reached the conclusion that the firm should encourage investment in Solario—a new manufacturer of solar-powered products.

45. It appears reasonable, therefore, for the citizens to focus on these trouble spots rather than to reduce the speed limit in the entire area.

46. It does not naturally warrant the conclusion that movie violence has significantly contributed, and thus causes increased rates of urban crime.

47. It is equally possible that legislators can concurrently address both areas of concern.

48. It is possible that fees paid by movie studios for screenplays will decrease in the future relative to those for book rights.

49. It is possible that the sales trend in a particular location is not representative of sales in other regions.

50. It is possible that there are younger, more inexperienced, or more elderly, unsafe drivers in Forestville than there are in Elmsford.

51. It is unlikely that the brief one-week periods under comparison are representative of longer time periods.

52. Lacking more specific information about how the other employees responded, it is impossible to assess the reliability of the survey's results or to make an informed recommendation.

53. Moreover, I would suspend my judgement about the credibility of the conclusion until the arguer can present more factual evidence to rule out the possibility that is listed in my analysis above.

54. Moreover, the author fails to consider and rule out other factors that might account for proportional decreases in spending on food.

55. Moreover, the author provides no evidence that the realism of color photography is the reason for its predominance.

56. Not only does the arguer fail to see the ecological advantages of preserving the trees, he also fails to see the obvious economic advantages of doing so.

57. One can infer from the survey's results that a full one third of the respondents may have viewed the current

benefits package unfavorably.

58. Opening subsidiaries may coincide with changes in the above-mentioned factors and the consequent impact on the company's profitability.

59. Opinions should be judged by their own merits, and should not be dismissed merely because they are voiced by a few people.

60. Overall, the reasoning behind decreasing Forestville's speed limit back to what it was previously is logical as presented above since the citizens are acting in their own best interests and want to protect their safety.

61. Since no effort was made to gather information about the spending amounts of the shoppers who had not read the ad in Gazette, the possibility cannot be excluded that the average amount spent by a shopper did not vary significantly, whether the shopper had read the ad or not.

62. Since the arguer makes a claim about workers in general, the workers sampled for the survey should be representative of all workers.

63. Since the difficulties inherent in this process make it hard to predict whether the result will be a success or a failure, the conclusion that the sequel will be profitable is presumptuous(武断的).

64. Substantiating this assumption requires examining the proper duty of government.

65. The arguer draws the conclusion that photographers who work in color hold a competitive advantage over those who work in black-and-white.

66. The arguer employs two lines of reasoning to reach this conclusion.

67. The argument fails to rule out the possibility that a writer engages in both types of writing as well as other kinds of writing.

68. The argument ignores the factors—such as initiative, creativity, technical skills, and business judgment—that may be more important than the choice of medium in determining success in photography.

69. The argument provides no direct information as to the degree to which the public's demand for restaurants is satisfied by the supply from the industry.

70. The argument relies on the assumption that the legislators in question(所讨论的) have the opportunity to address urban crime problems.

71. The argument simply equates success with movie ticket sales, which is unwarranted.

72. The author assumes that physical capabilities are the only attributes necessary to operate a motor vehicle.

73. The author ignores other likely benefits of agricultural technology that affect food prices only indirectly or not at all.

74. The author is presenting a false dilemma by imposing an either-or choice between two courses of action that need not be mutually exclusive.

75. The author's conclusion that switching to incineration would be better for public health is seriously undermined.

76. The author's implicit claim that incinerators are economically advantageous to landfills is poorly supported.

77. The author's proposal is inconsistent with the author's conclusion about the consequences of adopting an ethics code.

78. The basis for this recommendation is the expectation that solar energy will soon become more cost efficient and attractive than other forms of energy.

79. The editorial fails to take into account possible differences between East and West Cambria that are relevant to how drivers react to speed-limit changes.

80. The example cited, while suggestive of these trends, is insufficient to warrant their truth because there is no reason to believe that data drawn from this unnamed region is representative of the entire country.

81. The fact that the nearby city has a weaker economy does not prove that the city will not contribute significantly to tax revenues.

82. The fact that the student performance improved after the application of interactive computer instruction does not necessarily imply that the new teaching method is responsible for the achievements.

83. The major problem with the argument is that the stated similarities between Company A and B are insufficient to support the conclusion that Company A will suffer a fate similar to Company B's.

84. The mere fact that ticket sales in recent years for screenplay-based movies have exceeded those for book-based movies is insufficient evidence to conclude that writing screenplays provides greater financial opportunity for writers.

85. The other premise in the argument that centralization would improve profitability lends little support to the argument because its own credibility is suspect.

86. The problem is that the two situations are not similar enough to justify the analogical deduction.

87. The statistics offered in the announcement warrants only the conclusion that the decline of The Mercury's circulation and the alleged competitor, the lower-priced newspaper The Bugle, coexisted in the past five years.

88. The survey on which the argument relies lacks credibility and therefore does not lend strong support to the conclusion.

89. There is also the possibility that The Mercury's declining circulation has little to do with The Bugle.

90. There is no data available, however, to support any causal relation between the number of people watching TV programs about the visual arts and the number of people visiting art museums.

91. There is no evidence whatsoever to indicate that the water is solely responsible for the health condition of the local people.

92. Therefore, any decision aimed at addressing the problem of falling circulation must be based on more thorough investigation to gather sufficient data in order to narrow down and locate the actual cause(s) of the problem.

93. This assumption overlooks other criteria for determining a bridge's importance—such as the number of commuters using the bridge, the role of the bridge in local emergencies and disasters, and the impact that bridge closure would have on the economies of nearby cities.

94. This assumption presents a false dilemma, since the two media are not necessarily mutually exclusive alternatives.

95. This editorial asserts that West Cambria should not change its highway speed limits because such changes adversely affect driver alertness and are therefore dangerous.

96. This expectation is based on recent declines in the cost of equipment used to convert solar energy into electricity and on new technologies that are being developed for this purpose.

97. This observed phenomenon says little more than that these two events are synchronic.

98. Thus, the author unfairly assumes that highly-rated public television programs are widely viewed, or popular.

99. To begin with, the author fails to consider health threats posed by incinerating trash.

100. To begin with, this argument depends on the assumption that providing a greater range of subjects and a larger library will alleviate the students' chief sources of dissatisfaction.

101. To find the exact cause or causes of economic ups or downs, all the factors that have significantly impacted the economy should be examined.

102. To support this claim, the editorial cites statistics indicating that whenever East Cambria changed its speed limits, an average of 3 percent more automobile accidents occurred during the week after the change than during the week preceding it, even when the speed limit was lowered.

103. To support this conclusion, the arguer claims that the greater realism of color photos accounts for their predominant use in magazines and portraits.

104. We do not have any evidence suggesting that the increase or decrease of the number of TV program viewers will cause a similar increase or decrease in the number of museum visitors, or vice versa.

105. When samples are used to make general claims about a particular group, they need to be close enough in time to the generalization they are supporting, so that historical changes will not invalidate the generalization.

106. While this argument has some merits, there are a few assumptions that deserve attention.

107. While this may be true in some cases, it is equally possible that only companies with products that are already best-sellers can afford the higher ad rates that popular shows demand.

108. Without further investigation, any claims made about the effectiveness of the radio ad are doubtful even though the café's business increased.

109. Without knowing the extent and nature of the damage resulting from the bad publicity or the reason for the violation, we cannot accept the author's conclusion.

110. Without any evidence, we cannot accept the author's conclusion that no government funds should be directed toward maintaining the Styx River Bridge.

第四章　Argument 写作黄金模板

　　前面几章里，我们已经提供了大量的开头段、主体段和结尾段的写作句型以及写作模板，同时我们也介绍了Argument常见逻辑错误的攻击方法；除此之外，我们还收集了110个Argument写作必备的经典句型。把所有这些综合在一起，就能构成一篇篇完美的写作模板。本章列出一些全篇文章的写作模板，以便考生能快速入手Argument。考生也可以根据本章的方法，参考前面几章的内容，并结合自身的特点，撰写出适合自己的独特模板，从而为Argument写作高分奠定坚实的基础。

一、简化模板

　　先列出一个简化模板，供考生入门之用。看过简化模板后，考生对一篇Argument写作该怎么构思就会有一个比较清楚的认识了。

The author concludes that _____, because _____. The author's line of reasoning is that _____.
This argument is unconvincing for several reasons; it is _____ and it uses _____.
First of all, _____ is based upon the questionable assumption that _____. However, _____.
Moreover, _____.
Secondly, the author assumes that _____. However, _____. It seems equally reasonable to assume that _____.
Finally, _____. The author fails to consider _____. For example, _____. Because the author's argument _____.
In summary, I agree that _____. However, _____; on balance, _____.

二、自由组合式模板

开头段模板

- In this argument, the arguer concludes / recommends / suggests / claims / predicts that...
- The author cites... as an example in support of this recommendation. (Optional—In addition, the arguer provides the evidence that...)
- At first glance, the author's argument appears to be somewhat convincing / appealing / attractive, but thorough examination reveals that the argument is problematic because of several critical flaws that are discussed below.

第二段

- In the first place, the argument commits a fallacy of causal oversimplification.
- The arguer recklessly assumes that...
- However, the fact that A occurred after B doesn't necessarily prove that the former event is caused by the latter. (However, the fact that A coincides with B does not necessarily prove that A caused B.) Therefore, the argument is groundless unless other possible explanations have been considered and ruled out.
- For example, the cause of A might be E1. Or E2 could also lead to... Yet another possibility is that C.

Chapter 4

第三段

- In the second place, even if it were the case that... another problem that seriously weakens the logic of this argument... It is entirely possible that... For instance, A.

第四段

- Finally / Furthermore / Admittedly, it is imprudent for the arguer to claim / assume that... In any case, the author has failed to demonstrate a logical connection between A and B（A is not a sound evidence to draw a conclusion that B.）

结尾段

- In conclusion, the argument is not well reasoned and therefore misleading because of the logical flaws discussed above.
- To make the argument more persuasive, the arguer would have to... Furthermore, the arguer should...

三、总模板

这篇模板的主体段对很多常见的逻辑错误进行了攻击，所以称之为总模板。考生在写作时，一篇Argument中出现的逻辑错误通常不可能会有这么多，所以可以根据实际情况选择使用。如果感觉内容不够多，可参阅前面几章的内容。

模板1

开头段：

In this argument, the author concludes that... To support his conclusion, the author points out that... In addition, the author reasons that... Furthermore, he also assumes that... At first glance, the author's argument appears to be somewhat appealing, while a close examination will reveal how groundless it is. We do not have to look very far to see the invalidity of this argument. This argument is problematic for the following reasons.

主体段

Firstly, this argument rests on a gratuitous assumption that... However, the assumption is questionable because the author provides no evidence to support this argument. The arguer fails to take into account other facts that might contribute to the result that... It is likely that... It is also likely that... Any of these scenarios, if true, would show that... Therefore, this argument in question should not to be accepted without ruling out such a possibility that...

Secondly, the argument commits the logical fallacy of "after this, therefore because of this". In no case can the mere fact that... be cited as evidence to support the assumption that there is a causal-effect relationship between A and B. Moreover, that just because B can be statistically correlated with A does not necessarily mean that A is the cause of B. In fact, the author has obviously neglected the possibility of other alternative facts such as..., or... may contribute to a certain extent to B. It may be only a coincidence that... Unless the author can rule out other factors relevant to... this assumption in question cannot be accepted.

Thirdly, the evidence that the author provides is insufficient to support the conclusion drawn from it. One example is rarely sufficient to establish a general conclusion. Unless the arguer can show that A1 is representative of all A, the conclusion that B... is completely unwarranted. In fact, in face of such limited evidence, it is fallacious to draw any conclusion at all.

Fourthly, the argument has also committed the fallacy of false analogy. The argument rests on the assumption that A is analogous to B in all respects, and the author assumes without justification that all things are equal, and that the background conditions have remained the same at different times or at different locations. No evidence is provided to support this assumption. However there are all kinds of important differences between... and other... making the analogy less than valid. For example, A... however, B...Thus lacking this assumption, the conclusion that... is entirely unfounded.

Last but no least, the validity of the survey on which the argument relies is doubtful in itself. The survey cited by the author is too vague to be informative. The claim does not indicate who conducted this survey and when and how the survey is conducted, neither does it mention what is the sample size, or how the samples are selected. Until these questions are answered the results of this survey are worthless as evidence to support that...

Besides, the author assumes that A and B are mutually exclusive alternatives and there is no room for a middle ground. However, the author has never offered any reasons or evidence for imposing an either-or choice. Common sense and observation tells us that joining A and B might produce better results.

结尾段

In conclusion, the arguer fails to substantiate his claim that... Because the evidence cited in the analysis is too weak to lend strong support to what the arguer claims. To strengthen the argument, the arguer must convince us that... In addition, the arguer would have to provide more precise information to support his claim.

另外一种结尾

In conclusion, it is imprudent for... to... solely on the basis of the evidence presented. Because the evidence cited in the analysis is too weak to lend strong support to what the arguer claims. To make the argument more convincing, the arguer should provide more substantial evidence concerning that... Moreover, I would suspend my judgment about the credibility of the recommendation（conclusion）until the arguer could provide concrete evidence to rule out all the above possibilities that I analyzed.

模板2

In this argument, the author concludes that _____. At first glance, the author's reasoning seems to be appealing, but while clearly examining the author's reasoning, we may find it unconvincing. The argument contains several facets that are questionable.

First of all, the author's evidence is insufficient to support the conclusion. _____. Common sense tells us that _____. It is possible that _____. Obviously, the author does not provide enough information on the subjects of _____. One specific example cannot generate the general conclusion. Therefore, faced with such limited evidence, the conclusion is unwarranted.

Secondly, the author makes an oversimplified analogy between _____ and _____. In most instances, this is an unwarranted assumption for the simple reason that things rarely remain the same over extended periods of time / from place to place. As we know, many factors should be taken into consideration, such as the demographics of the population, and the geographical and physical terrain of the two different areas _____.

In addition, the author commits a "after this, therefore because of this" fallacy. The causal relationship between the cause of _____ and the effect _____ is unwarranted. It is well-known that _____. This is fallacious reasoning unless the author can provide persuasive evidence to rule out any other possibilities.

To sum up, the conclusion lacks credibility. Regardless of who the author is, he or she has overlooked or chosen to ignore many aspects of his or her conclusion. To strengthen the conclusion, the author should give more evidence about the above-mentioned possibilities.

四、万用模板

如果考生不能确定理由点，比如不确定具体是什么逻辑错误，可以直接套用下面的模板，非常实用。

模板1

In this argument, the author relies on anecdotal evidence about _____, as well as the unreliable statistics (comparison) about the general trends among_____, to convince us of the conclusion that_____. This argument—that appears to be reasonable at first glance—suffers some critical flaws that seriously undermine the conclusion after close scrutiny, and accordingly is not thoroughly well-reasoned. The main flaws of the argument should be discussed respectively.

In the first place, the argument is fraught with vague and unwarranted assumptions that_____—rather than some phenomenon—was responsible for _____. In fact, more discerning inspection reveals (discloses) that other factors far outweigh the factors that the author presents. For example, _____. For that matter, _____ is surely attributed to _____. It is also possible that_____. Hence, without weighing and then eliminating these and other possible causal explanations contributing to the long-term trend endorsed in the argument, the author can not solely attribute B to A while convincing us of the suspect conclusion.

Secondly, even if_____, the argument relies on an additional assumption—which renders it unconvincing as it stands—that_____. Offered in the argument, the only evidence is that_____. Lacking the firm support, it might be the case that, if so, it turns out that_____. It may also be possible that_____. Since the author fails to account for this possibility, he or she can not convince us of the assertion that_____, let alone the groundless conclusion.

Finally, granted that the author justifies all the foregoing assumptions, the conclusion remains doubtful since the arguer fails to consider alternative means available. The example of _____ cited, while meaningful in regards to this trend, is insufficient to guarantee that _____ since the arguer does not offer any evidence to support that _____ is sufficient for_____, nor does he take into account other concerns pertinent to the conclusion. Common sense tells us that _____. By the same token, it is possible that_____. And the claim is completely unwarranted. Thus, in face of such limited anecdotal evidence, it is fallacious for the author to draw any conclusion at all.

In conclusion, this argument, while seemingly well-supported at first, has several flaws as discussed above. Hence it is unacceptable and not persuasive as it stands. It could be substantiated by providing more solid evidence that_____. In addition, to further bolster the conclusion, the arguer should furnish a demonstration concerning_____. Accordingly, only with more logical reasoning could this argument be more than just an emotional appeal.

模板2

In the argument, the arguer concludes that _____. To buttress the argument, the arguer refers to the fact that _____. The arguer further suggests that _____. While the argument appears plausible at first glance, it is not without loopholes and generalities that seriously damage its validity. Clearly, the arguer fails to address a number of factors that are vital to substantiating the conclusion.

In the first place, the arguer rests on a dubious assumption that _____. However, no further information or specific information is provided to bolster this assumption and establish the correlation. As a matter of fact, it is quite likely that _____ . For example, imagine that _____ . Therefore, without further exploring the dissimilarities between A and B, the argument cannot safely jump to the conclusion.

In the second place, even if _____ . is / are practical, there is no guarantee that _____ . And the arguer commits another fallacy that _____ . For instance, in fact, _____ （举例说明）. Without carefully examining these possible changes, the arguer is simply shooting in the dark and jeopardizing all the efforts to reach his / her conclusion.

In conclusion, the arguer, by leaving out the above-mentioned factors, tries in vain to justify the argument. To better bolster his argument, the arguer needs more data and analysis to smooth out all the wrinkles in the line of reasoning. In assessing whether A can succeed by following B, I would recommend, from a business point of view, that research on business feasibility encompassing the factors discussed above will be instrumental in minimizing any potential risks.

五、其他黄金模板

下面的这些模板只是把一篇Argument的构思过程列了出来，而把具体的内容省去了。考生在写作时可以结合具体的题目，根据括号内的中文提示，把省略的内容加上，写出一篇结构合理、内容完整的文章。

模板1（注重类比关系）

The author asserts that _____ （重复作者的见解）. However, I believe that the argument is highly dubious, because it commits several logical mistakes which are addressed below.

First of all, the argument depends upon a misleading comparison between A and B. A _____ （A的情况）. On the other hand, B _____ （B的情况）. As a result, _____ （A与B不具可比性）.

Secondly, one of the speaker's assumptions is that _____ （作者的假设）. However, _____ （假设的缺陷）It is possible that _____ （相反的可能性）. For example, _____ （举例说明）

Finally, the author claims that _____ （找出作者的另一处错误）. It's also wrong because _____ （说明原因）.

Since the author makes many logical errors, his opinion is highly suspect. If he were to consider the above problems and significantly improve his logic, the argument would be much better.

模板2（注重类比关系）

The conclusion of this argument is that _____ （作者的结论）. The author employs several lines of reasoning to reach this conclusion. For one thing, the author reasons that _____ （作者得出结论的第一个依据）. For another, the author reasons that _____ （作者得出结论的第二个依据）. This argument is unconvincing for several reasons.

To begin with, the author assumes that there are no relevant differences between A and B. This assumption is clearly mistaken. The major difference between A and B is that A _____ （A的特性）, while B _____ （B的特性）.

Secondly, the author claims that _____ （作者的另一处错误论述）. But he / she fails to support this argument because that _____ （说明其错误的原因）.

In conclusion, the author's argument fails to take into consideration important differences between A and B, and he / she also makes other mistakes. So, _____ （总结论点）.

模板3(注重类比关系)

In this memorandum, _____ (重复结论及论据). The reasoning of the argument, however, is biased due to the inadequacy and partiality of the evidence provided to justify the conclusion.

In the first place, we may give allowances to the belief that generally speaking A _____ (A的情况). But this does not sufficiently assure that the same tendency applies to B _____ (B的情况). Therefore, _____ (A与B不具可比性).

Secondly, the author provides no evidence to support the claim that _____ (指出作者论述的另一处错误). We need to point out that _____ (错误的原因).

Finally, when the speaker draws his conclusion, he unfairly assumes that _____ (得出结论的一个假设). However, _____ (说明假设的错误).

To strengthen the argument, the author must present more evidence that _____ (得出结论的依据). The speaker must also provide information about _____ (正确得出结论的信息) as well.

模板4(注重因果关系)

The author recommends that _____ (作者的论述). Two reasons are offered in support of this recommendation. First, _____ (作者的第一个证据). Second, _____ (作者的第二个证据). The argument is unconvincing because the speaker oversimplifies the problem and its solutions.

First of all, the author's line of reasoning is that A was the cause of B. However, _____ (A与B之间存在的联系), it does not establish a general causal relationship between A and B. For instance, _____ (举例说明). Thus, _____ (结论错误).

There may be other possible causes for B. Perhaps _____ (导致B的第一个原因); or perhaps _____ (导致B的第二个原因). Any of these scenarios, if true, would show that _____ (A不一定是导致B的原因). Without taking these factors into consideration, we cannot accept the author's conclusion.

In summary, the persuasiveness of the argument made by the author is undermined by the lack of fairness in the reasoning that _____ (总结论点).

模板5

Citing the evidence that _____ (作者得出结论的根据), the author asserts that _____ (作者的结论). This assertion is not convincing because _____ (结论错误的原因).

The major problem with the argument is that _____ (作者论述中的第一个逻辑错误). It is entirely possible that _____ (得出与结论相反的方面). For instance, _____ (举例说明).

Another problem with the argument is that _____ (作者论述的第二个逻辑错误). There are many other facts that might account for _____ (得出结论的其他原因). For example, _____ (举例说明).

Last but not least, the argument ignores other factors—such as _____ (作者忽视的因素).

With essential information still in lacking, there is no ground to support the conclusion. Therefore, it is questionable whether _____ (总结论点).

模板6(注重因果关系)

Based upon B, the author argues that A. I find the author's reasoning is unconvincing in two respects.

The argument concludes that _____ (作者的结论). Very likely, but not necessarily, other factors—such as _____ (其他因素) are ignored as possible causes for B. The argument can be sustained only if these and other possible factors can be completely ruled out as contributing to B.

Furthermore, the entire argument depends on the assumption that _____ （作者的假设）. The author provides no evidence to support this assertion; moreover, it might be false. For example _____ （举例说明）.

Since the author commits the above-mentioned logical mistakes and fails to consider the whole situation comprehensively, his ideas should not be adopted. If he or she wishes the idea to be of any value, he has to take the following conditions into consideration _____ （使论述更加严密的因素）.

模板7

The author argues that _____ （作者的陈述）. This line of reasoning is unconvincing for a number of reasons.

The primary problem with the argument is the author's unwarranted assumption that _____（作者无根据的假设）. Consequently _____ （结论错误）.

Another problem with the argument is that the author's conclusion that _____ （作者结论）. However, the author provides no evidence to substantiate this assumption. It is possible, for instance, _____（得出相反结论）.

Finally, the author ignores some other factors that may effect the situation. For example, _____ （举例说明干扰结论的其他因素）.

In sum, the author provides an incomplete analysis of the problem and, as a result, provides a questionable solution. To better bolster the argument, the author should _____ （增加论述严密性的建议）.

模板8

In this memo, the author concludes that _____（作者的结论）. The author reasons that _____（作者的论据）. The author's reasoning is unconvincing, since it suffers from two critical problems.

In the first place, the argument rests on the assumption that _____ （作者的假设）. However, the author provides no evidence that this is the case. It is possible that _____ （得出相反的结论）.

Secondly, perhaps there are other factors relevant to _____ （影响结论的其他因素）. For example, _____ （举例说明）.

Finally, the author provides no support for the claim that _____ （作者论述中的另一处错误）.

In conclusion, the author's argument is unconvincing as it stands. To strengthen the argument, the author must _____ （增加论证严密性的建议）.

模板9 (注重数据)

The argument is severely weakened by the confused logic in its reasoning process. According to the statistics cited, the author concludes that _____ （作者的结论）. For the most part this argument is well-reasoned; a few concerns must be addressed, however.

To begin with, the statistics cited in the editorial may be misleading because _____ （数据误导的原因）. For example, _____ （举例说明）.

Moreover, the author assumes that _____ （作者的假设）. This assumption is unwarranted. If it turns out, for example, _____ （举例说明）.

If the argument is meant to be convincing, it still needs to be substantiated with specific information about

_____（正确得出结论的其他因素）.

模板10（注重数据）

Based upon some statistics that indicate _____（数字表明的现象）, the author argues that _____（作者的结论）. But the reasoning in this argument is problematic in several respects.

The main problem with the argument is that the statistics cited could be misleading, because the reason why _____（得出结论的原因）is not specified. For instance, _____（文中的数字）does not necessarily mean that _____（得出结论的原因）. Therefore there is no way to _____（得出结论）.

Secondly, the author unfairly assumes that _____（能够得出结论的其他必要条件）. This is not necessarily the case. It is possible that _____（作者不合理的假设）.

Lastly, the author fails to indicate that _____（驳斥假设）.

In summary, the author provides an incomplete analysis of the problem and, as a result, provides a questionable solution. To strengthen the argument, the author must provide evidence that _____（作者的另外一处逻辑错误）.

本章介绍的模板都很精彩，对考生的Argument写作应该说是很有帮助的。但考生该怎样正确使用这些模板呢？下面是使用模板的注意事项：

1. **正确看待模板**：模板的重要性是不言而喻的。要想在考试的半个小时内写出300词以上的优秀文章，没有一套现成的模板，几乎是不可能的。

2. **活用模板**：不要一词不变地照搬本书中或别人撰写的模板，因为这样容易引起作弊的嫌疑。考生最好结合自己的习惯和自己总结的范文，制作一份自己的模板。

3. **模拟练习**：模拟练习时养成良好的习惯。一般来说，花1分钟读题，用2～3分钟在草稿纸上快速地列出要写的3个要点。最后留3分钟左右的时间检查错误。要注意的是，列要点及检查这两个步骤非常重要，最好不要省略。

4. **模拟练习总结**：模拟练习时，每练一次，总结一次。一是总结碰到类似的题目时如何展开，二是继续熟悉模板，背熟模板。最后要做到一列出要点，细节的东西就在脑子里自然再现，先说哪句话，后说哪句话，这些话之间是怎样的逻辑关系都成竹在胸。

5. **根据模板练习**：一般而言，考试前一个星期定下模板套路即可。然后在考前的每一天都要写一篇Argument，并且要在规定的30分钟内写完，培养自己在有限的时间内完成写作的感觉。

6. **仿真模考**：考试前两天仿真模考一次。紧张起来，就当是正式考试一样。这样在正式考试时，写作思路才能流畅。不能指望在考试时超水平发挥，尤其是写作。没有大考前的仿真模拟，考试时难免会手忙脚乱。

Chapter 5

第五章　Argument 黄金范文 20 篇

本章所选的这20个题目是近几年来考试频率相对较高的题目。考生可以先从这20个题目入手，把最常考的题目一一攻破，然后再着手准备其他考试频率相对较低的题目，这也是准备GMAT写作必须遵从的一项原则。

> **① The following appeared as part of an annual report sent to stockholders by Olympic Foods, a processor of frozen foods.**
> 下文摘自一家奥林匹克食品公司———家冷冻食品公司——提交给股东的年度报告：

"Over time, the costs of processing go down because as organizations learn how to do things better, they become more efficient. In color film processing, for example, the cost of a 3-by-5-inch print fell from 50 cents for five-day service in 1970 to 20 cents for one-day service in 1984. The same principle applies to the processing of food. And since Olympic Foods will soon celebrate its twenty-fifth birthday, we can expect that our long experience will enable us to minimize costs and thus maximize profits."

随着时间的推移，企业学会了更好的工作方法，从而提高了效率，因此加工成本逐步下降。以彩色胶卷为例，冲印一张3×5英寸照片的成本从1970年的50美分并需耗时5天降至1984年的20美分，且只要1天就可完成的水平。同样的规律也适用于食品加工业。由于奥林匹克食品公司马上就要举办它的25周年庆典大会了，我们可以凭借长期的从业经历来实现成本最小化，从而达到利润最大化的目标。

In this report, the author concludes that 25 years of experience in the food processing industry will enable Olympic Foods to minimize costs and thus maximize profits. To support this conclusion, the author cites the general principle that "as organizations learn how to do things better, they become more efficient." The author also states that trends in the color-film processing industry indicate a decline in the costs of film processing over a 24-year period. Based on these facts, the author is confident that Olympic Foods will maximize its profits. However, close scrutiny reveals that these facts provide little credible support for the author's conclusion.

To begin with, the argument is based on the assumption that Olympic Foods' 25 years of experience will automatically result in minimal costs and maximum profits. However, there is no guarantee that this is the case. Nor does the author cite any evidence to support this assumption. It seems likely that Olympic Foods has learned little or nothing from its 25 years in the food-processing business. With this in mind, the assertion that efficiency increases as time goes by holds little ground.

Secondly, the author attributes the cost decline in the color film processing industry to its 24-year history. Although experience may contribute to the cost decline, it certainly is not the only factor that contributes to determining the processing cost. There is no causal relationship between a company's history and its ability to maximize profits. Perhaps the increased efficiency results from employing new technologies or machines, which have taken over work previously done by hand. To make the argument more convincing, other factors that may contribute to the reduced cost of color film processing should be considered and ruled out.

Finally, even if the cost decline in the color film processing industry is largely due to long-term experience, it does not follow that Olympic Foods can maximize profits by its long experience. The food processing industry is not analogous to the color film processing industry. Differences between the two industries clearly outweigh the similarities, thus making the analogy less than valid. For example, problems of spoilage, contamination, and timely transportation all affect the food industry but are virtually absent in the film-processing industry. Problems such as these might present insurmountable obstacles that prevent lowering food-processing costs in the future.

In sum, the conclusion that Olympic Foods will enjoy minimal costs and maximum profits in the future is indefensible based on the evidence. To strengthen the argument, the author must provide specific evidence that the company has learned how to do things better as a result of its 25 years of experience. To better assess the argument, I would like to know more supporting examples drawn from film processing industry with closer similarities to the food-processing industry.

② The following appeared in a memorandum from the business department of the Apogee Company.
以下摘自Apogee公司业务部的一份备忘录：

"When the Apogee Company had all its operations in one location, it was more profitable than it is today. Therefore, the Apogee Company should close down its field offices and conduct all its operations from a single location. Such centralization would improve profitability by cutting costs and helping the company maintain better supervision of all employees."

当Apogee公司的所有业务集中于一个地方时，它的赢利水平要比现在高。因此，Apogee公司应该关闭它在其他地方开设的办事处，而把业务集中到一个地方。这样的集中不但可以降低成本，而且有助于公司更有效地监控员工，从而提高公司的盈利能力。

Based on the fact that Apogee Company had been more profitable in the past when all its operations were in one location, the author concludes that Apogee should close down field offices and conduct all its operations from a single, centralized location. I find the author's position unjustified in several critical respects.

First of all, the argument commits the fallacy of "After This, Therefore Because of This". The author assumes the decentralization of operation locations to be the only reason profits decreased only because the Apogee Company had been more profitable before the decentralization. This assumption is questionable because the author provides no evidence to support it. As a matter of fact, there may be other factors that could have caused the decline. It is entirely possible that management has become lax regarding any number of factors that can affect the bottom line; such as inferior products, careless product pricing, inefficient production, poor employee expense account monitoring, ineffective advertising, sloppy buying policies and other wasteful spending. Without ruling out all these factors or presenting stronger evidence, the author cannot reasonably ascribe diminishing profits to the practice of decentralization.

Secondly, the argument relies on the assumption that centralization would improve profitability by cutting costs and streamlining supervision of employees. However, the author fails to provide any evidence to support this assumption. In addition, this assumption is problematic as it takes no account of cost increases and inefficiency that could result from centralization. For example, Apogee's representatives would have to travel to do business in areas formerly served by a field office, incurring travel costs and wasting time. In a word, this assumption must be supported with a complete cost-benefit analysis of centralization versus other possible cost-cutting and / or profit-enhancing strategies.

Finally, even if Apogee succeeded in the past because of centralization, this strategy would not necessarily guarantee a similar success today. Since the market, competitors, customers and Apogee's business are changing all the time, the statistics from the past are not necessarily representative of the status quo or a good indicator of future trends. Therefore, Apogee should constantly look forward and make effective strategies, rather than simply use old ways of doing business.

In sum, the author fails to convince me that Apogee should close field offices and centralize. To strengthen the argument, the author must rule out factors other than decentralization that might be affecting current profits negatively and demonstrate how centralization would cut costs.

> ⑥ **The following appeared as part of an article in a magazine devoted to regional life.**
> 下文摘自一份地方生活类杂志上的一篇文章：

"Corporations should look to the city of Helios when seeking new business opportunities or a new location. Even in the recent recession, Helios's unemployment rate was lower than the regional average. It is the industrial center of the region, and historically it has provided more than its share of the region's manufacturing jobs. In addition, Helios is attempting to expand its economic base by attracting companies that focus on research and development of innovative technologies."

企业在寻找新的商机或者新的办事处时，应该关注Helios市。即使在最近的经济萧条时期，Helios市的失业率也比地区平均水平低。它是该地区的工业中心，以前也曾为本地区创造了非常多的制造业就业机会。另外，Helios正试图通过吸引那些专注于新技术研发的公司来拓展自己的经济基础。

In this argument, the author concludes that the city of Helios is a good choice for corporations seeking a new location or new business opportunities. To support this conclusion, the author points out that Helios's unemployment rate remained lower than the regional average even in the recent recession. The author also points out that Helios is the industrial center of the region and provides most of the region's manufacturing jobs. Moreover, it is argued, Helios is trying to attract companies that focus on research and development of innovative technologies. As the following discussion shows, the author's argument is not well supported by the evidence.

First, the author fails to establish a causal relationship between the low unemployment rate and great opportunities for new corporations. Perhaps the low unemployment rate during a recession suggests that the city has a labor shortage. Consequently, corporations that require large numbers of workers would not find Helios attractive. The fact that few persons are out of work may also suggest that new corporations will have to either attract new workers to Helios or pay the existing workers higher wages in order to entice them away from their current jobs. Neither of these alternatives seems alluring to companies seeking to relocate. In short, the low unemployment rate in Helios may actually mean that the city is a poor place to locate a new business.

Secondly, the argument is based on the assumption that Helios is well equipped to support all types of corporations. However, the author provides no credible evidence to support this assumption. It is entirely possible that there are not enough workers with new skills, since the city has traditionally provided a large amount of manufacturing jobs. Also, the author cannot rule out the possibility that the resources required by research and development of new technologies are too short in Helios to ensure the development of such companies. On the contrary, the status of the Helios as a manufacturing center will likely mean that it is equipped to effectively handle manufacturing businesses. Its labor supply, energy resources, regulatory environment, support businesses and infrastructure are likely well suited to manufacturing companies rather than corporations that focus on research and development of innovative technologies. In short, without credible evidence, the author's prediction that Helios is an ideal place for new business opportunities is dubious at best.

To sum up, the author fails to provide compelling evidence that Helios is an ideal place for the further development of corporations. To strengthen the argument the author must provide clear evidence that there is enough labor force in Helios to meet the needs of new corporations, and that the workers in Helios have the skills required by research and development of innovative technologies. To better evaluate the argument, I would also need to know what specific measures have been taken by Helios to attract companies that focus on research and development of innovative technologies.

"The common notion that workers are generally apathetic about management issues is false, or at least outdated: a recently published survey indicates that 79 percent of the nearly 1,200 workers who responded to survey questionnaires expressed a high level of interest in the topics of corporate restructuring and redesign of benefits programs."

通常认为，工人一般对管理事务并不关心。这种观点即使不是错误的，至少也是过时的：最近公布的一项调查显示，在回应问卷调查的近1200名工人中，有79%的人表示对公司重组以及重新设计福利项目这两个问题很感兴趣。

In this argument, the author concludes that workers are not apathetic about management issues. The author's chain of reasoning is that since 79 percent of the 1200 workers who responded to a recently published survey expressed interest in the topics of corporate restructuring and redesign of benefits programs, the notion that workers are apathetic about management issues is incorrect. However, as discussed below, close scrutiny of the survey reveals that it accomplishes little toward supporting the author's conclusion.

The major problem with the argument is that it is based on a problematic survey. For one thing, the statistics cited in the editorial may be misleading because the total number of workers employed by the corporation is not specified. For example, if the corporation employs 1800 workers, the fact that 79 percent of the nearly 1200 respondents showed interest in these topics provides strong support for the conclusion. On the other hand, if the corporation employs 100, 000 workers, the conclusion drawn from the survey will be seriously undermined. For another, the respondents' views are not necessarily representative of the views of the work force in general. Due to the fact that the survey has to do with apathy, it makes sense that only less apathetic workers would respond to it, thereby distorting the overall picture of apathy among the work force. Without knowing how the survey was conducted, it is impossible to assess whether or not this might be the case.

Another problem with the argument is that the author makes a hasty generalization about the results of the survey. The survey asks specifically about the worker's interest in corporate restructuring and redesign of benefits programs. While corporate restructuring often implies promotions and layoffs, redesign of benefits programs is closely related to workers' salaries. It makes sense that workers would be interested in corporate restructuring and the redesign of benefits programs, since these issues affect them directly. Therefore, it is unreasonable to assume that workers would be similarly interested in other management issues—ones that do not affect them or affect them less.

To sum up, the conclusion about workers' interest in management issues cannot be reasonably drawn from the survey's information. To strengthen it, the author must provide evidence that the respondents account for a significant and representative portion of all workers. To better assess the argument, I would need to know whether workers are interested in other management topics—not just those that affect them directly.

"On average, middle-aged consumers devote 39 percent of their retail expenditure to department store products and services, while for younger consumers the average is only 25 percent. Since

一般而言，中年消费者的零用消费支出中有39%的钱花在百货商店和服务项目上，而在年轻的消费者中这一比例

the number of middle-aged people will increase dramatically within the next decade, department stores can expect retail sales to increase significantly during that period. Furthermore, to take advantage of the trend, these stores should begin to replace some of those products intended to attract the younger consumer with products intended to attract the middle-aged consumer."

平均只有25％。由于中年消费者的数量在接下来的10年中将急剧增长，百货商店有望在此期间实现零售销售额的大幅增长。另外，为了更好地利用这一趋势，百货商店应该开始把一些原来以年轻人为销售对象的商品替换成吸引中年消费者的商品。

In this argument, the author asserts that department store sales will increase significantly over the next few years because the number of middle-aged people is expected to increase over the next decade. The author reasons that since statistics show that middle-aged people devote a much higher percentage of their retail expenditure to department-store services and products than younger consumers, the dramatic increase in the number of middle-aged people within the next decade is bound to significantly raise department stores' sales. To capitalize on this trend, the author further recommends that department stores increase their inventory aimed at middle-aged consumers and decrease their inventory of products aimed at younger consumers. This argument is critically flawed in several respects.

First of all, the author assumes that an increase in the number of middle-aged people portends an overall increase in department-store sales. This assumption, however, is problematic. It depends on the further assumption that other population groups, likes or dislikes, will remain relatively constant. However, it is not necessarily the case. If the expected increase in the number of middle-aged people is offset by an equally significant decrease in the number of younger people, there will be little or no net gain in sales.

Secondly, the author recommends that department stores should replace products intended to attract younger consumers with products more suitable to middle-aged consumers. This recommendation is not persuasive in two respects. For one thing, it relies on the assumption that the number of younger consumers will not increase. Since a sizable increase in the population of younger consumers could conceivably offset the difference in the retail expenditure patterns of younger and middle-aged consumers, it would be unwise to make the recommended inventory adjustment. For another, the author ignores the retail expenditure middle-aged and younger consumers devote to department store products and services. Although younger consumers spend a smaller percentage of their retail expenditure on department store products than middle-aged consumers, they might spend more in terms of the actual amount.

Even if middle-aged consumers are spending more than younger ones in department stores, this argument ignores the possibility that the trend may change within the next decade. Younger consumers might prefer to shop in department stores instead of other types of stores, and middle-aged consumers might turn to different kinds of stores, too. This will lead to a higher expenditure by younger consumers in department stores, compared to that of middle-aged consumers.

In sum, the argument is unconvincing as it stands. To strengthen the argument the author must provide concrete evidence that the population of younger consumers will remain relatively constant and their spending habits will not change over the next decade. To buttress the argument, the author must also provide evidence that the middle-aged consumers will continue to spend more money in department stores than younger consumers during the next decade.

19 The following appeared in the editorial section of a local newspaper.
下面内容摘自一份地方报纸的社论部分：

"This past winter, 200 students from Waymarsh State College traveled to the state capitol building to protest against

去年冬天，Waymarsh州立大学有200名学生前往州议会大厦，抗议对各项

proposed cuts in funding for various state college programs. The other 12, 000 Waymarsh students evidently weren't so concerned about their education: they either stayed on campus or left for winter break. Since the group who did not protest is far more numerous, it is more representative of the state's college students than are the protesters. Therefore the state legislature need not heed the appeals of the protesting students."

州立大学项目基金进行削减的提案。另外12000名Waymarsh的学生显然对他们的教育不太关心：他们不是待在校园里，就是出去过寒假了。由于未参与抗议的人数远多于抗议者，所以他们比抗议者更能代表本州立大学生的意见。因此，州立法机构不必理会抗议学生的呼吁。

In this editorial, the author concludes that the state legislature does not have to consider the views of protesting students. To support this conclusion, the author points out that only 200 of the 12, 000 students traveled to the state capitol to protest the cuts in college programs. Since an overwhelming majority of the students did not take part in this protest, the author assumes that they are not interested in this issue. I find this argument logically unconvincing in several critical respects.

To begin with, the author assumes that 200 students' views are not representative of the entire student body. However, the only evidence to support this assumption is that only one-sixtieth of the students took part in the protest. If it turns out, for example, that the protesting students were randomly selected from the entire student body, their views would reflect the views of the entire college. Without information regarding the way in which the protesting students were selected, it is presumptuous to conclude that their opinions fail to reflect the opinions of their colleagues.

Secondly, the author cites the fact that the other 12, 000 students stayed on campus or left for winter break to demonstrate that they are not concerned about education cuts. One obvious retort to this line of reasoning is that the students who did not participate did so with the knowledge that their concerns would be expressed by the protesting students. In fact, if the protest was staged during the winter break, it suggests a great inconvenience for students to enter the protest against cuts because most students may have returned home in remote places. A low turnout does not suggest a low level of interest, but instead implies a high level of organizational opposition since students had to be recruited during their vacation time. In any case, the author has failed to demonstrate a logical connection between the students' alleged lack of concern and the fact that they either stayed on campus or left for winter break. Without this connection, the conclusion drawn by the author that the other 12, 000 students are not concerned about their education is unconvincing.

In conclusion, the author fails to convince me that the state legislature need not consider the appeals of the protesting students. To strengthen the argument, the author would have to demonstrate that the protesting students had some characteristic in common that biases their views, thereby nullifying their protest as representative of the entire college.

14 The following appeared as part of a newspaper editorial.
下面内容摘自某家报纸的社论：

"Two years ago Nova High School began to use interactive computer instruction in three academic subjects. The school dropout rate declined immediately, and last year's graduates have reported some impressive achieve-ments in college. In future budgets the school board should use a greater portion of the available funds to buy more computers, and all schools in the district should adopt interactive computer instruction throughout the curriculum."

两年前，Nova高中开始在三门学科中使用互动式计算机教学。该学校的退学率立刻下降，而且去年的毕业生报告说他们在大学取得了很好的成绩。在未来的预算中，校董事会应该在能得到的资金中拨出更多资金用来购买更多的计算机，而且该地区的所有学校都应该在全部课程中使用互动式计算机教学。

In this editorial, the author concludes that Nova High's school board should buy more computers and all schools in the district should adopt interactive computer instruction throughout the curriculum. To support this, the author points out that the introduction of interactive computer instruction in three academic subjects immediately led to a decline in the school's dropout rate. The author also mentions that last year's graduates experienced impressive achievements in college. However, careful examination of this sup-porting evidence reveals that it lends little credible support to the author's argument.

To begin with, the author attributes the decline in dropouts and the achievements of last year's graduates to the introduction of interactive computer instruction. However, it is not necessarily the case. The mere fact that the introduction of interactive computer instruction preceded the impressive performance of recent graduates and the decline in the dropout rate is insufficient to conclude that it caused these events. Many other factors could bring about these same results. For example, achievements could have been made in subjects other than the ones with interactive computer instruction. It is also possible that last year's graduates who did not receive interactive computer instruction benefited from the introduction of programs preparing students for college. In addition, the decline in dropout may be ascribed to stricter discipline applied during the last year. Without solid evidence linking the decline in dropout and achievements of the recent graduates to the interactive instruction, it is presumptuous to suggest that the computer instruction was in some way responsible for these results.

Secondly, even supposing the Nova High School's falling dropout rate and last year's graduates' achievements benefit directly from the use of interactive computer instruction, the success of the instruction in only three subjects does not guarantee a similar sweeping success if computer instruction is adopted in the curriculum of all the schools in the district. On the one hand, some subjects may have less pertinence to computers, therefore, adopting computers in these subjects may distract students from learning what should be learned. On the other, if schools use a greater portion of the available funds to buy more computers, they will have less funds to spend on other crucial items, and education quality will be compromised. Besides, it is possible that some schools can not afford to provide computer instruction on all subjects for all students.

In sum, the recommendation for adopting interactive computer instruction throughout the curriculum of all schools in the district is not well supported. The editorial might have been strengthened by making it clear that the decline of the dropout rate and the achievements of the graduates are the direct result of interactive computer instruction, and that the instruction is also applicable to other schools in the district, and that all schools in the district can afford this kind of instruction.

> **20 The following appeared in an article in a health and fitness magazine.**
> 下面内容摘自某健康健身杂志上的一篇文章：

"Laboratory studies show that Saluda Natural Spring Water contains several of the minerals necessary for good health and that it is completely free of bacteria. Residents of Saluda, the small town where the water is bottled, are hospitalized less frequently than the national average. Even though Saluda Natural Spring Water may seem expensive, drinking it instead of tap water is a wise investment in good health."

实验室的研究表明，Saluda天然泉水含有多种健康必需的矿物质，且完全无菌。在灌装此水的Saluda小镇，居民患病就医的频率低于全国的平均水平。尽管Saluda天然泉水的价格看似不菲，但用它来代替自来水作饮用水是一项有益健康的明智投资。

In this argument the author concludes that drinking Saluda Natural Spring Water instead of tap water is a wise investment in good health. The author's chain of reasoning is that since Saluda Natural Spring Water contains several necessary minerals for good health, and it is completely free of bacteria, residents of Saluda—the town where it is bottled—are hospitalized less frequently than the national average. However, the author's argument relies on several poor assumptions, and is therefore unpersuasive as it stands.

To begin with, the argument is based on the assumption that tap water does not contain the minerals in question and is not completely free of bacteria. However, the author provides no evidence to support this assumption. It is entirely possible that tap water contains the same minerals and is free of bacteria. If so, the author's conclusion that Saluda Natural Spring Water is superior to tap water is substantially undermined.

Secondly, the author fails to provide any concrete evidence that the water residents of Saluda drink is the same as Saluda Natural Spring Water. Lacking evidence to the contrary, it is possible that the source of Saluda Natural Spring Water is limited in Saluda, and the local residents usually drink tap water. It is also possible that Saluda is not the source of the bottled water but is merely the place where Saluda Natural Spring Water is bottled. As no evidence is offered in the argument to dispute these possibilities, the author's claim that residents of Saluda usually drink Saluda Natural Spring Water is open to doubt.

Thirdly, the author assumes that Saluda Natural Spring Water is the major reason why residents of Saluda are hospitalized less frequently than the national average. However, there is little evidence that this water is the only difference between this place and the rest of the country. Perhaps the residents are hospitalized less frequently because they are younger than the national average, or they are all vegetarians, or they exercise daily, or because their climate is more conducive to leading a healthy life. That is, there might be other reasons than the one cited to account for this disparity.

Finally, even if the Saluda Natural Spring Water is the main reason why the residents of Saluda are hospitalized less, the author fails to consider that there is more than one way to keep drinking water free from bacteria or take supplemental minerals necessary for a healthy diet good. For instance, to keep drinking water free from bacteria, the most common practice is to boil water up to 100 Celsius and keep it at that temperature for more than 5 minutes. By eating various foods, we can also take in enough minerals for good health. Obviously, in order to stay healthy, drinking Saluda Natural Spring Water is not the only choice. Lacking credible evidence and cost-effective analysis, the author can not convince me that drinking Saluda Natural Spring Water instead of tap water is a wise investment.

In sum, the speaker's argument is weak because it depends on a series of doubtful assumptions. To strengthen the argument, the author must provide evidence that tap water does not contain the minerals in question and is not completely free of bacteria. Moreover, the author must demonstrate that the residents of Saluda regularly drink Saluda Natural Spring Water and that this is why they are hospitalized less frequently than the national average. To make a better argument, the author should also provide a cost-effective analysis showing that drinking Saluda Natural Spring Water instead of tap water is a wise investment in good health.

28 The following appeared in the editorial section of a local newspaper.
下面内容摘自某地方报纸的社论部分：

"Commuter use of the new subway train is exceeding the transit company's projections. However, commuter use of the shuttle buses that transport people to the subway stations is below the projected volume. If the transit company expects commuters to ride the shuttle buses to the subway rather than drive there, it must either reduce the shuttle bus fares or increase the price of parking at the subway stations."

上下班的人对新地铁的使用超出了运输公司的设计方案。但是，上下班的人对运送他们去地铁站的往返公交车的使用则低于设计容量。如果运输公司希望上下班的人乘公交车而不是开车去地铁站，就必须下调公交车的票价或者提高地铁站停车场的停车费。

The author's conclusion is that in order to make more commuters ride shuttle buses to the subway rather than drive there, the transit company must either reduce the shuttle bus fares or increase parking fees at the subway stations. The reasons offered to support this conclusion are that commuter use of the new subway train is exceeding projections, while commuter use of the shuttle buses is below expectations. As it stands, the argument rests on a series of dubious assumptions, and is therefore unconvincing.

First of all, the argument is based on the assumption that the bus fares and the parking fees are the only two reasons that caused the limited use of shuttle buses. However, this is not necessarily the case. The author fails to consider and rule out the possibility that other factors, such as shuttle routing, scheduling, safety, service, or carpools may have a negative effect on shuttle use. Lacking credible evidence that the bus fares and the parking fees are the only two factors that lead to limited use of shuttle buses, the author can not convince me that adjusting fares or parking fees would solve the problem.

Secondly, even assuming that bus fares and parking fees are the only two factors that affect the shuttle use, the argument rests on the further assumption that reducing shuttle fees and increasing parking fees are mutually exclusive alternatives. The author fails to provide justifiable reason for imposing this either-or choice. It is highly possible that the company could take the two actions simultaneously, leading to better results. Furthermore, if the author is wrong in the assumption that bus fares and parking fees are the only two possible causes of the problem, then the most effective solution might include other useful measures, such as rescheduling, providing better service on the buses and repairing the shuttles to get better security condition.

In sum, the argument is not persuasive because the author oversimplifies both the problem and its possible solutions. To strengthen it, the author must provide credible evidence that (1) the problem is actually caused by shuttle bus fares and the parking fees at the subway station; (2) the company could only choose one solution between reducing bus fares and raising price of parking at the station; (3) there is no other solution to the problem other than the two discussed above. In addition, the author should consider which combination of possible solutions would bring about the greatest increase in the use of shuttle buses.

31 **The following appeared as part of the business plan of an investment and financial consulting firm.**
下面内容摘自一家投资理财公司的商业计划：

"Studies suggest that an average coffee drinker's consumption of coffee increases with age, from age 10 through age 60. Even after age 60, coffee consumption remains high. The average cola drinker's consumption of cola, however, declines with increasing age. Both of these trends have remained stable for the past 40 years. Given that the number of older adults will significantly increase as the population ages over the next 20 years, it follows that the demand for coffee will increase and the demand for cola will decrease during this period. We should, therefore, consider transferr-ing our investments from Cola Loca to Early Bird Coffee."

研究表明，咖啡饮用者的平均咖啡消费量会随着年龄的增长（从10岁到60岁）而增长。即使到60岁以后，这些人的咖啡消费量仍然会居高不下。然而，可乐饮用者的平均可乐消费量则随着年龄的增长而下降。在过去的40年中这两种趋势都保持稳定。由于在未来的20年内老年人口将显著增加，所以，这一时期内人们对咖啡的需求量会增长而对可乐的需求量会降低。因此我们应该考虑将我们的投资从Loca可乐转向Early Bird咖啡。

In this argument, the author recommends transfering investment from Cola Loca to Early Bird Coffee. To support this recommendation, the author points out that the number of older adults will significantly increase over the next 20 years. The author also cites studies indicating that coffee consumption increases with age while cola consumption declines with increasing age. Based on this evidence, the author concludes that coffee demand will increase while cola demand will decrease during the next 20 years. Therefore, it is advisable to transfer investments from Cola Loca to Early Bird Coffee. Careful scrutiny of the argument reveals various statistical and other logical problems which render it unconvincing.

First of all, although trends cited in the studies have remained stable for the past 40 years, there is no guarantee that the same trends will continue over the next 20 years. The research results can only reflect the habits of the last generation under study. If the drinking habits of this generation change as time changes, the study's results can hardly be used to predict the future. Perhaps as the whole population ages, people in their 60's will feel they are still young and want to show off their energy and vigor by continuing to drink cola. If that is the case, the credibility of the arguer's assumption is called into question.

Moreover, the mere fact that the number of older adults will significantly increase over the next 20 years is not sufficient to support the conclusion that the demand for cola will decrease while demand for coffee increases. The author fails to consider and rule out other factors that might account for the changes in demand. The supply and cost of cola and coffee beans, as well as other costs of doing business as a producer of coffee or cola, may fluctuate over a long time period. These factors may affect comparative prices of coffee and cola, which in turn may affect comparative demand for coffee and cola. In addition, although demand for cola by the older group of customers might decrease, the youth sector's consumption of cola might rise. As a result, increase in the demand from young people may offset the decrease from the old people, and boost sales of cola as a whole.

Finally, even if the trends given in the argument will be true over the next 20 years, it does not necessarily indicate that investing in Early Bird Coffee will be more profitable than investing in Cola Loca. The author unfairly applies the general trend in the whole industry to specific companies. It is entirely possible that Cola Loca employs the right advertising strategy and will enlarge its share of the cola market. Also it might cut down its costs to a large degree. Either of these scenarios, if true, would still render Cola Loca a profitable business. Conversely, although sales for the whole coffee industry may increase, Early Bird Coffee might be losing its customers if it is not able to compete with other companies. Therefore, it is unwise to transfer investments without investigating the specific conditions of the two businesses.

In conclusion, it is imprudent for the author to draw his conclusion simply on the basis of the evidence presented. To make a truly wise investment, the author would have to take into account other factors that might affect consumer trends in the future. To strengthen the argument, the author should also investigate the individual businesses before he applies the general trend in the industry to specific companies.

39 The following appeared in an Avia Airlines departmental memorandum.
下面内容摘自 **Avia** 航空公司的部门备忘录：

"On average, 9 out of every 1, 000 passengers who traveled on Avia Airlines last year filed a complaint about our baggage-handling procedures. This means that although some 1 percent of our passengers were unhappy with those procedures, the overwhelming majority were quite satisfied with them; thus it would appear that a review of the procedures is not important to our goal of maintaining or increasing the number of Avia's passengers."

去年乘坐 Avia 航空公司航班的乘客中有千分之九的人对我们的行李托运流程作出了投诉。这表明，尽管有近百分之一的乘客对这一流程表示不满，绝大多数的乘客还是相当满意的。由此可见，审查行李托运流程对我们保持或增加客流量这一目标并不重要。

The author's conclusion is that a review of the baggage-handling procedures is not important to the company's goal of maintaining or increasing the number of Avia's passengers. To support this conclusion, the author asserts that the great majority of Avia passengers are happy with baggage handling at the airline because only one percent of their passengers during the last year filed a complaint about Avia's baggage-handling procedures. This argument contains several critical flaws which render it unpersuasive.

To begin with, the argument depends on the assumption that the passengers who did not complain were satisfied with the airline's baggage-handling procedures. However, that is not necessarily the case. The fact that on average 9 out of 1,000 passengers took the time and effort to formally complain indicates nothing about the experiences or attitudes of the remaining 991. Perhaps many passengers were displeased but too busy to formally complain. It is also highly possible that some passengers express their displeasure by not taking Avia Airlines in the future instead of making formal complaints. Lacking more sufficient information about passengers' attitudes, the author cannot assume that the great majority of passengers were happy with the baggage-handling procedures.

Secondly, even if only 1 percent of passengers were unhappy with the procedures, the author's prediction that the company could maintain or increase the number of Avia's passenger is still open to doubt. For one thing, the statistics cited in the argument might distort the seriousness of the problem. Given that most modern aircraft carry as many as 300 to 500 passengers, it is possible that Avia received as many as 4 or 5 complaints per flight. Ignoring these numbers trivializes the record. Moreover, without complete information about customers' attitudes toward other competitive companies' baggage-handling procedures, it is entirely possible that there are fewer or even no passengers who complain about the procedures at other companies. Therefore, Aviva's one percent complaint rate might be significant enough to motivate customers to switch to another airline, and the author's prediction about the Aviva's market is seriously undermined.

To sum up, the author fails to convince me that a review of the baggage-handling procedures at Avian Airlines is unnecessary to maintain or increase the number of Aviva's passengers. To strengthen the argument, the author should provide evidence that the passengers who did not complain are actually pleased with baggage-handling procedures. To better assess the argument, I would need more information about the numbers of Avian passengers per flight last year and about the baggage-handling records of Aviva's competitors.

> **47 The following appeared as part of an article in the business section of a local newspaper.**
> 下面内容摘自某地方报纸中商业版面上的一篇文章：

"The owners of the Cumquat Café evidently made a good business decision in moving to a new location, as can be seen from the fact that the Café will soon celebrate its second anniversary there. Moreover, it appears that businesses are not likely to succeed at the old location: since the Café's move, three different businesses—a tanning salon, an antique emporium, and a pet-grooming shop—have occupied its former spot."

乔迁新址对Cumquat餐馆的业主而言，无疑是一项明智的商业举措，这可以从该餐馆很快就要在新址举行两周年店庆这一事实中看出。此外，在Cumquat餐馆旧址经营的企业看起来都不太可能取得成功，自从该餐馆搬走后，该处已经换了三家不同的企业：一家日光浴沙龙，一家古董店和一个宠物美容店。

写作提纲：

1. 在新地址庆祝第二个周年纪念日这一事实只能说明咖啡店搬到新地址之后存活了下来，但作者并没有给出足够的证据证明它是不是比原来好了。
2. 地点并不一定是导致另外三家店无法在原咖啡店地点经营下去的唯一因素。
3. 就算那个地点不适合开那三种店，也并没有证据证明该地点不适合开咖啡店。

In this argument, the author concludes that moving to the new location was a good choice for the owners of Cumquat Café. To substantiate this conclusion, the author points out that while the Cafe has been in business for two years at its new location, three businesses have failed at its previous location. The author believes that the cause of the three businesses going out of business is the fact that they all occupied the same location, inferring that the old location is not a good place for a business. I find this argument problematic in several respects.

In the first place, the argument rests on the assumption that the second anniversary in the new location is a sign of success. However, it is not necessarily the case. Lacking specific information about the operating condition of the Café, I have good reasons to doubt whether it can attract enough customers and maintain stable revenue in the new location. That is to say, by itself, the mere fact that the Café has remained in business in the new location for nearly two years, is not sufficient evidence to support the assumption that the Café has achieved success there.

Secondly, the author assumes that the three businesses' failure was caused by their location. However, the author provides no proof to support this assumption. While location is an important contributing factor to a business' success or failure, it is certainly not the only factor. Many other factors, such as a shortage of working capital, scarcity of qualified employees, poor business practices, lack of advertising, or poor customer service could just as likely lead to the failure of these three businesses. Without a detailed analysis of the reasons these businesses failed, it would be unreasonable to ascribe their failure to their location.

Finally, even if those three businesses failed because they are at the old location, the author still commits a fallacy of false analogy by simply equating the Cumquat Café with the other three businesses. In fact, it is highly possible that near the old location there are many customers who frequent a Cafés but seldom go to tanning salons, antique emporiums, or pet-grooming shops. For example, a pet-grooming shop or a tanning salon located in a downtown metropolitan business district is unlikely to succeed simply because this type of business is obviously unsuitable for the location. On the other hand, a Café in the same location might be extremely successful simply because of its suitability to the location. In short, without credible evidence showing enough similarities between the Café and these three businesses, it is unwarranted to assume that if the Café didn't relocate, it would have suffered the same fate as these three businesses.

To summarize, the argument is unconvincing as it stands. If the author wants to strengthen the conclusion, he or she must provide evidence that the Cumquat Café's revenue has increased or at least remained stable during the two years since it moved to the new location. To better evaluate the argument, the author should also provide evidence that the failure of the three businesses is only due to their location, and that the Cumquat Café shares enough similarities with these three businesses to suffer the same fate.

52 The following editorial appeared in the Elm City paper.
下面社论摘自Elm市报：

"The construction last year of a shopping mall in downtown Oak City was a mistake. Since the mall has opened, a number of local businesses have closed, and the downtown area suffers from an acute parking shortage, and arrests for crime and vagrancy have increased in the nearby Oak City Park. Elm City should pay attention to the example of the Oak City mall and deny the application to build a shopping mall in Elm City."

去年在Oak市中心修建购物中心是个错误的举动。自从该购物中心开业以来，有大量的本地企业倒闭了，市中心受到停车位严重缺乏的困扰，并且在附近的Oak市公园拘捕的罪犯和流浪汉的数量也有所增加。Elm市应该以Oak市为戒，杜绝在Elm市建设购物中心。

写作提纲

1. 作者列出的所有问题和购物中心的建设只是在时间上存在先后关系，而没有给出证据显示它们之间存在任何因果关系。
2. 作者只给出该购物中心可能给Oak市带来不良影响，而没有考虑它对本市的发展所起的推动作用。因此，权衡利弊之后我们有可能会发现建设该购物中心的举动是明智的。
3. 即使如作者所说在Oak市中心修建购物中心是不可取的，我们也不能由此得出在另外一个城市——Elm的其它地方建购物中心肯定会遭到失败这一结论。

In this editorial, the author asserts that Elm City should deny the application to build a shopping mall in the city. To support this assertion, the author states that since the shopping mall has opened in downtown Oak City, the city has suffered a series of serious problems—the closure of local businesses, lack of parking in the downtown area, and the high incidence of crime and vagrancy in the nearby Oak City Park. On several grounds, this evidence lends little credible support to the author's conclusion.

To begin with, the author unfairly assumes that the addition of the new mall is the cause of the various problems cited. The sequence of these events, by themselves, is not sufficient to demonstrate that the former caused the later because a chronological relationship is only one of the indicators of a causal relationship between two events. Perhaps the techniques of local businesses are out of date, or Oak City has suffered an economic depression ever since the new mall opened. Moreover, the rise in arrests for crime and vagrancy does not necessarily indicate that the number of people who commit crimes or vagrancy has increased. It is highly possible that the increase in arrests resulted from stricter law enforcement policies. No additional evidence linking the new mall's opening and the problems is offered in the argument, making for the possibility that the two events are not causally related but merely coincident.

Secondly, the author has only considered the mall's negative effects in the city. A more detailed analysis of the situation might reveal that the positive benefits for the city far outweigh the problems on which the author focuses. For example, new jobs might have been created for the residents of Oak City, and tax revenues might have increased. Lacking a more comprehensive analysis of the impact of the mall in Oak City, it is presumptuous on the part of the author to assert that Oak City's decision to allow the mall to be built was impolitic.

Finally, even if the shopping mall did cause the closing of local businesses and increasing crime and vagrancy in Oak City, the author's assumption that Elm City will suffer from the same fate as Oak City is still open to doubt. Without better evidence showing any similarity between the two cities, it is unwarranted to conclude that a shopping mall will lead to the same results in Elm City. Perhaps, Elm City does not have enough shopping malls to meet the needs of its citizens. Also, it is possible that the local businesses in Elm City have great competitive advantages and will not be forced to close by the shopping mall, and that the police in Elm City are efficient in impeding crime and vagrancy. If so, these differences may seriously undermine a conclusion based on the analogy between the two cities.

In sum, the editorial's conclusion is not well supported. Before I can accept it, the author must demonstrate that (1) the construction of the mall caused the various problems mentioned in Oak City, (2) the negative effects of the project outweighed the positive effects, and (3) Oak City and Elm City share enough similarities to suffer from the same fate.

---

70 The following appeared in a memorandum from the president of a company that makes shampoo.
下面内容摘自某洗发香波公司总裁的一份备忘录：

"A widely publicized study claims that HR2, a chemical compound in our shampoo, can contribute to hair loss after prolonged use. This study, however, involved only 500 subjects. Furthermore, we have received no complaints from our customers during the past year, and some of our competitors actually use more HR2 per bottle of shampoo than we do. Therefore, we do not need to consider replacing the HR2 in our shampoo with a more expensive alternative."

一项广泛宣扬的研究声称，我们的洗发香波里所含的一种化合物HR2，长期使用后可能导致脱发。但是，这项研究只涉及了500个接受实验者。此外，过去的一年里我们并未从我们的顾客那里接到投诉，而且我们的一些竞争者在一瓶香波里使用的HR2量比我们还要多。因此，我们不必考虑用更贵的物质来替代我们香波里的HR2。

In this memorandum, the president of the company concludes that they do not need to replace the HR2 in their shampoo with a more expensive alternative even though a scientific study claims that prolonged use of HR2 can cause hair loss. To support this conclusion, the president writes that since the scientific study involved only 500 subjects, it can be disregarded. The president also points out that none of their customers have complained of problems during the past year and some of their competitors use more HR2 per bottle than their company. However, close scrutiny of this evidence and of the president's line of reasoning reveals that they provide little credible support for the conclusion.

First, lacking more information about the scientific study, it is unfair to deny the statistical reliability of the widely publicized study since it only involved 500 subjects. If the subjects for the study were randomly chosen and represent a diverse cross section of shampoo users, the results from 500 subjects will be sufficient to draw a convincing conclusion about the harm to hair caused by HR2. Consequently, the president's conclusion will be seriously undermined.

Secondly, the argument is based on the assumption that because there have been no complaints from the company's customers, its shampoo will not lead to hair loss after prolonged use. This assumption is flawed in two critical respects. For one thing, the fact that none of the company's customers complained about the negative effect of the shampoo does not necessarily indicate that all of them were happy with the shampoo containing HR2. It is entirely possible that customers express their displeasure simply by not purchasing the company's shampoo. The greater percentage of such people, the weaker the argument's evidence is as a sign of customer's satisfaction with the shampoo. For another, while "prolonged use" was not defined in the memorandum, the fact that none of the company's customers have complained about any problems during the past year is not a reliable reason to believe that problems will not arise in the future.

Finally, the fact that other companies use more HR2 in their products than the company in question does is irrelevant to the question of whether the company should remove HR2 from its product. Lacking information about the sales of its competitors, I have good reason to suspect customers have already stopped buying shampoo produced by those companies, leading to a sharp decrease in their revenues. If so, the company could gain an edge over its competitors by removing the compound HR2 from its products. Therefore, it is impolitic for the president to refuse to replace the HR2 in their shampoo with a more expensive alternative.

To sum up, the memorandum is logically flawed and therefore unpersuasive as it stands. To strengthen the argument, the president should provide better evidence that 500 subjects are not a sufficient number of people in a study to draw a reliable conclusion about the negative effect of HR2, and that the customers who did not complain about the shampoo were actually satisfied with it. To better assess the memorandum, I would need to know whether the sales of the company's competitors producing shampoo with more HR2 have declined or not.

---

106 The following appeared as part of an article in the book section of a newspaper.
下面内容摘自某份报纸读书栏目中的一篇文章：

"Currently more and more books are becoming available in electronic form—either free-of-charge on the Internet or for a very low price-per-book on compact disc.* Thus literary classics are likely to be read more widely than ever before. People who couldn't have purchased these works at bookstore prices will now be able to read them for little or no money; similarly, people who find it inconvenient to visit libraries and wait for books to be returned by other patrons will now have access to whatever classic they choose from their home or work computers. This

现在越来越多的书有了电子版，或者放在网上免费下载，或者压缩在光盘上以很低的价格出售。因此文学经典可以得到比以前更广泛的阅读。不能以书店价格购买这些书的人现在可以用很少的钱或者不花钱阅读他们。类似的，不方便去图书馆或者等待其他人还书的人现在可以通过家里或者工作场所的电脑得到他想

increase in access to literary classics will radically affect the public taste in reading, creating a far more sophisticated and learned reading audience than has ever existed before."

要的任何名著。这种接触文学名著的机会增多，将从根本上影响公众的阅读品味，塑造比以前更成熟更博学的读者。

*A compact disc is a small portable disc capable of storing relatively large amounts of data that can be read by a computer.

In this article, the author asserts that people will become more sophisticated and learned than ever before. The author's line of reasoning is that the availability of books in electronic form and access to books via the Internet will facilitate people's access to literacy classics. As a result, literary classics are likely to be read more widely than ever before, and people will become more cultured and learned. Careful examination of this supporting evidence, however, reveals that it lends little credible support to the author's assertion.

To begin with, the conclusion is based on the assumption that the higher price of books and the inconvenience of visiting libraries are the only two reasons why people have read fewer classics in the past. While this is a tempting assumption, it is not obviously true. The author fails to consider and rule out other reasons affecting the number of literary classics people read. It is entirely possible that people prefer popular books or mystery novels to literary classics, or that people have switched their interests from reading books to watching television, surfing the internet or indulging in other entertainments such as computer video games or mobile phone games. If so, the conclusion that lower price and convenience can lead to the popularity of reading literary classics would be seriously undermined.

Secondly, the mere fact that more and more books are becoming available in electronic form is not sufficient to support the assumption that literary classics are now more available in that form. On the face of it, this assumption seems innocuous. However, lacking specific information about literary classics, I have good reasons to doubt whether literary classics can also be uploaded to the Internet. It is highly possible that the copyright rules affecting literary classics does not permit their reproduction in electronic form. So probably people will still have to pay as much money for literary classics or borrow them from library. Therefore, I can hardly be convinced that these changes in the form of common books also apply to literary classics. Furthermore, even assuming that access to literary classics at affordable prices has increased, it does not necessarily mean that people's desire to read literary classics will increase accordingly. Besides, reading literary classics alone will not necessarily guarantee a far more sophisticated and learned reading audience.

To sum up, the conclusion that people will become more sophisticated and learned is not well supported. To strengthen the argument, the author would have to provide evidence for the assumption that the higher price of purchasing books and the inconvenience of visiting libraries are the only two factors preventing people from reading more literary classics. To strengthen the argument, the author must also provide direct evidence that literary classics are just as available in electronic form as other kinds of books are.

109 The following appeared as part of a business plan created by the management of the Take Heart Fitness Center.

下面内容摘自Take Heart健身中心管理者起草的一份商业计划：

"After opening the new swimming pool early last summer, Take Heart saw a 12 percent increase in the use of the center by members. Therefore, in order to increase the number of our members and thus our revenues, which depend on membership fees, we should continue to add new recreational facilities in subsequent years: for example, a multipurpose game room, a

去年夏初开了新的游泳池以后，Take Heart发现会员对该中心的利用率增加了12％。因此，为了增加我们的会员数量和依赖于会员费的收入，我们应该在以后几年中继续增加新的娱乐设施：比如，一个多功能游戏室，一个网球场，一

tennis court, and a miniature golf course. Being the only center in the area offering this range of activities would give us a competitive advantage in the health and recreation market."

个迷你高尔夫球场。作为本地唯一一家提供各种活动的健身中心，我们将在健身和娱乐市场的竞争中保持优势。

In this article, the author recommends that the Take Heart Fitness Center should add new recreational facilities in subsequent years. The author's line of reasoning is that Take Heart experienced a 12 percent increase in member usage after opening a new swimming pool last summer. Therefore, the practice of adding more recreational facilities in coming years is bound to increase membership and thus revenues at Take heart. However, the argument is problematic in several critical respects.

The major problem with the argument is that the author provides no credible evidence to support the assumption that an increase in member usage portends an increase in membership. The only evidence cited by the author to support this assumption is a 12 percent increase in member usage. However, it is highly possible that some members would like to visit the fitness center to inspect and try out the new swimming pool. This would account for the increase. Moreover, as the author provides no evidence that this new rate of usage was sustained, the abrupt increase provides little evidence that the addition of facilities such as the pool will attract new members.

The second problem with the argument is that it is based on another assumption that the swimming pool was responsible for the increase in member usage. The sequence of these events, by itself, is not sufficient to prove that the former caused the later. No additional evidence linking the two events is offered in the argument, thus opening up the possibility that the more frequent use of the center by members is caused by other factors. For example, it is entirely possible that the center repaired other facilities or began to provide better service. It is also possible that the climate is very pleasant or some members happened to have more leisure time last month. Without additional information, it is impossible to know if the addition of the pool was related to the increased usage that the author claims in his argument.

Furthermore, even if the swimming pool was responsible for the increase in the Fitness Center's popularity, the author's prediction that other recreational facilities would cause the same result is open to doubt. Lacking better evidence showing enough similarities between the swimming pool and other recreational facilities, the author can not reasonably assume that a multipurpose game room or a tennis court will achieve the same results. Maybe, the residents in this city only enjoy swimming in the fitness center and have little interest in other recreational activities. Unless the author can rule out this and other possibilities, the analogy between the swimming pool and other facilities is dubious at best.

Finally, the author fails to make a case for the claim that Take Heart will be the only center in the area to offer a wide range of activities to its members and thus have a competitive advantage in the fitness market.

In conclusion, based on the reasons discussed above, the argument is logically flawed and therefore unwarranted as it stands. To strengthen the argument, the author must provide specific evidence that the swimming pool is the primary reason accounting for the increased use of the center, and that the member usage is reliable indicator of new membership. To better evaluate the argument, the author should also provide evidence that the members would enjoy other facilities at least as much as they do the swimming pool.

112 The following appeared in a memo to the Saluda town council from the town's business manager.

以下内容摘自Saluda镇的商务经理递交给镇委员会的一份备忘录：

"Research indicates that those who exercise regularly are hospitalized less than half as often as those who don't exercise. By providing a well-equipped gym for Saluda's municipal employees,

研究显示，规律锻炼的人生病的概率比不锻炼的人要小一半。给Saluda的市政员工提供一个设备良

we should be able to reduce the cost of our group health insurance coverage by approximately 50% and thereby achieve a balanced town budget."

好的体育馆，应该可以减少大约50%的健康保险支出，从而使镇预算保持平衡。

In this argument, the business manager suggests that the Saluda town council should provide a well-equipped gym for its municipal employees as a means of balancing the town's budget. The manager's line of reasoning is that since studies show that people who exercise regularly are hospitalized less than half as often than those who don't, Saluda could save approximately 50% on the cost of its group health insurance coverage by providing its municipal employees with a well-equipped gym. Consequently, the savings on insurance coverage would balance Saluda's budget. The argument relies on several doubtful and unsupported assumptions, and is therefore unconvincing.

First and foremost, the argument is based on the assumption that Saluda's employees will exercise regularly if a well-equipped facility is provided for them. This assumption may hold true in some cases. However, it is not necessarily the case. The mere fact that a gym is made available for use by employees is no guarantee that they will avail themselves to it at all, let alone on a regular basis. It is possible that the employees would not exercise even if the town establishes a well-equipped gym. Probably, many municipal employees in the town are entirely tied to work and have no time to go to the gym.

Secondly, the argument depends on another assumption that Saluda's employees do not exercise regularly. However, the manager provides no evidence to support this critical assumption. Perhaps there are many well-equipped gyms which have already met the exercise needs of Saluda's municipal employees, and all of the employees already engage in daily exercise. If so, the hospitalization rate will be unaffected by equipping an exercise facility and no savings will be realized on group health insurance.

Furthermore, even with the assumption discussed above, the manager's further claim that the town would be able to reduce its insurance cost is still open to doubt. The manager unfairly equates the frequency that the employees go to the hospital with the cost of insurance. Without sufficient information, I have good reason to doubt if those employees who are hospitalized most have only minor medical problems that cost the town relatively little in insurance premiums. On the other hand, it is equally possible that those employees who go to hospital infrequently will generally have serious illnesses and cost the town a lot of money. Therefore, the reduction of the cost of group health insurance coverage expected by the manager is not guaranteed.

Finally, even if the gym will contribute to reducing the insurance costs, the town may still be unable to achieve a balanced budget, since profit is a factor of both revenue and cost. It is highly possible that the additional cost of the gym cannot be covered by the reduced revenue and will therefore lead to a net loss in the total budget. If so, the manager's plan is totally unacceptable.

Based on the reasons I have listed above, the argument is logically flawed and therefore unwarranted as it stands. To strengthen the argument, the manager should provide evidence that（1）the new gym would surely attract more people to exercise regularly,（2）those people who exercise regularly are less likely to suffer from serious illnesses, and（3）the cost of building a well-equipped exercise facility will not negate the savings realized on the group health insurance.

---

129 The following appeared in a memorandum from a regional supervisor of post office operations.
以下内容摘自邮局运营部一位地区总监的一份备忘录：

"During a two-week study of postal operations, the Presto City post office handled about twice as many items as the Lento

为期两周的邮政运营研究发现，虽然Presto和Lento这两个城市的规模差不

City post office, even though the cities are about the same size. Moreover, customer satisfaction appears to be higher in Presto City, since the study found fewer complaints regarding the Presto City post office. Therefore, the postmasters at these two offices should exchange assignments: the Presto City postmaster will solve the problems of inefficiency and customer dissatisfaction at the Lento City office while the Lento City postmaster learns firsthand the superior methods of Presto City."

多，但前者处理的邮政业务是后者的两倍。而且，看起来Presto市的顾客满意度更高，因为研究结果表明人们对Presto市邮局的投诉比较少。因此，两个邮局的局长应该交换位置。Presto市的局长将会解决Lento市邮局的低效和顾客不满意问题，而Lento市的局长可以从Presto市学习第一手的先进管理方法。

In this memorandum, the author recommends that the postmasters of the two city post offices should exchange assignments to solve the problems of inefficiency and customer dissatisfaction in the Lento post office. This recommendation is based on the evidence that the Presto post office handled much more items and received fewer complaints than the Lento post office did during a two-week study. The recommendation advanced in the memorandum is questionable for three reasons.

To begin with, the mere fact that the Presto post office handled about twice as many items as the Lento post office during the two-week study period is not sufficient to demonstrate that the Presto post office is more efficient than the Lento post office. Although the two cities are about the same size, there is no guarantee that people in these two cities use the postal service with equal frequency. Perhaps citizens in Presto prefer to write letters in traditional ways while citizens in the Lento prefer to email. Therefore, the Lento post office simply did not have as many items to handle as the Presto post office. Likewise, a study period of two weeks is too short to reveal the actual conditions at the two post offices. Perhaps during this period, most of the staff members at the Lento office were on their vacation. The inefficiency there could be attributed to temporary lack of staff rather than long term inefficiency.

Similarly, fewer complaints regarding the Presto post office does not necessarily mean that the Presto post office provides better service than the Lento post office. It is entirely possible that postal service in Presto has been poor for so long that customers lost interest in complaining, since they understood that complaints did not cause any changes. Moreover, it could also be the specific study period that caused fewer complaints about the Presto post office. Perhaps in a whole year, the number of complaints about the Presto's postal service was the same as that of the Lento post office. However, during the study period, the Lento post office might have received more complaints than usual.

Finally, in order to solve Lento post office's problem, the author recommend that the postmasters at the two city post offices exchange assignments. However, the feasibility of such a recommendation is open to doubt because the author fails to point out the real reason behind the inefficiencies and customer dissatisfaction at the Lento City office. One rebuttal to this argument could be that employees at Lento post office are generally inexperienced and lack training. Consequently, since poor service has little to do with management, the mere change of leaders would do little to improve service at the Lento office. Moreover, the proposed exchange of postmasters may cause unexpected results to both post offices since neither of them is familiar with the other city's situation.

In conclusion, it is imprudent for the author to suggest exchanging postmasters solely on the basis of the evidence presented. To strengthen the argument, the author would have to provide additional evidence to demonstrate that postal service at the Lento post office is indeed inferior to that at Presto and that an exchange of postmasters can effectively improve the current situation.

"Last year, the city contracted with Flower Power to plant a variety of flowers in big decorative pots on Main Street and to water them each week. By midsummer many of the plants were wilted. This year the city should either contract for two waterings a week or save money by planting artificial flowers in the pots. According to Flower Power, the initial cost for artificial flowers would be twice as much as for real plants, but after two years, we would save money. Public reaction certainly supports this position: in a recent survey, over 1, 200 Gazette readers said that the city wastes money and should find ways to reduce spending."

去年，本市和Flower Power签订合同，让其在主大道上的大装饰花瓶内种植多种花卉并每周浇水一次。还没到仲夏，许多植物都枯萎了。今年，本市要么约定让他们每周浇水两次，要么在花瓶内插上假花以节省费用。据Flower Power称，假花的初始费用为真花的两倍，但两年后，我们将会开始省钱。公众显然会支持这种解决方式：在最近的调查中，超过1200名本报读者表示本市浪费资金，应该设法减少开支。

In this editorial, the author recommends that it is cost-effective to replace real flowers with artificial flowers in the big decorative pots on Main Street. The author reasons that although artificial flowers are more expensive than real ones, their maintenance cost is much less because they do not need watering. Therefore, planting artificial flowers on Main Street will save money in the long run. Moreover, as a recent survey indicates that most people expressed their dissatisfaction with the fiscal performance of the city council and the hope for a reduction in public spending, the author concludes that the public will agree with the idea of planting artificial flowers on Main Street. In several respects, however, the evidence lends little credible support to the argument.

To begin with, the author assumes that two waterings a week will prevent flowers in big decorative pots on Main Street from wilting. However, he provides no evidence to support this assumption. It is highly possible that some of the plants may need more than two waterings a week to keep them alive. It is equally possible that some plants may prefer drier conditions, and two waterings a week will possibly cause their death. Unless the author can establish a causal correlation between the survival of the plants and more watering, the assumption that two waterings a week will stop the plants from wilting is open to doubt.

Secondly, the argument is based on the assumption that planting artificial flowers can reduce public expenditure in the long run. However, that is not necessarily the case. The author may emphasize the merits of artificial flowers since they do not need water to survive and grow, but he fails to notice that over time the appearance of artificial flowers inevitably deteriorates, weakening their decorative function. Then people will have to wash them with considerable amount of water. Furthermore, the artificial flowers will be damaged or even destroyed by bad weather. Therefore, the city will have to spend additional money on replacing the old or damaged ones. In this case, the author's assertion that installing plastic flowers will save the city money is open to doubt.

Thirdly, even if planting artificial flowers can save money for the city, the argument depends on the further assumption that the public will be happy with the artificial flowers. However, this assumption is unwarranted as it is based on a dubious survey. Obviously, the results of the survey are questionable because the argument does not indicate that the readers who participated in the survey were representative of the general public or that a sufficient number were included in the surveys to warrant the claim that the city wastes money and should find ways to reduce spending.

Finally, even assuming that the results of the survey are reliable, it is still imprudent to assert that the general public would support the idea of using artificial flowers as substitutes for real ones. Although the public favors thrift, they have not specified that replacing real flowers with artificial ones should be one way to reduce public expenses. The public may call for changes in other public work and services other than the replacement of real flowers. As far as I know, lots of people have inherent preferences for real flowers, due to their particular features. When real flowers are blossoming, fragrant smell spreads over a large area. Compared with artificial flowers, real flowers change their appearance through the seasons.

In sum, the argument relies on several doubtful assumptions that render it unconvincing. To strengthen the argument, the author should provide more direct evidence indicating that placing plastic plants in the pots will be more cost-effective than planting real flowers. To better assess the argument, the author should also provide concrete evidence that the public have a strong interest in artificial flowers, and will not mind replacing the real flowers with the artificial ones on Main Street.

142 The following appeared in a memorandum from the development director of the Largo Piano Company.

以下内容摘自Largo钢琴公司开发经理的一份备忘录：

"The Largo Piano Company has long been known for producing carefully handcrafted, expensive pianos used by leading concert pianists. During the past few years, however, our revenues have declined; meanwhile, the Allegro Musical Instrument Company introduced a line of inexpensive digital pianos and then saw its revenues increase. In order to increase Largo's sales and in fact outsell Allegro, we should introduce a line of digital pianos in a variety of price ranges. Our digital pianos would be likely to find instant acceptance with customers, since they would be associated with the prestigious Largo name."

Largo钢琴公司在为主流音乐会钢琴家精心手工制作昂贵钢琴这一领域久负盛名。然而在过去的几年中，我们的收入下降了。同时，Allegro乐器公司推出了便宜的数码钢琴，接着就发现它的收入增加了。为了增加Largo的销售额，实际上是为了卖得比Allegro多，我们应该推出不同价位的数码钢琴。我们的数码钢琴很有可能会立刻被顾客接受，因为人们会把它们与声望很高的Largo这个名字联系在一起。

In this memorandum, the Largo's development director recommends that Largo should introduce a line of digital piano as a means of increasing sales and outselling Allegro. The director reasons that since Allegro experienced an increase in revenues after it introduced a line of inexpensive digital pianos, Largo could also enlarge its sales by adopting the same method. The director also points out that Largo's digital pianos will be very popular with customers because these pianos would be associated with the prestigious Largo name. However, the memorandum relies on a series of unsubstantiated assumptions, which render it unconvincing.

To begin with, the director assumes that the Allegro's introduction of a line of inexpensive digital pianos is responsible for its increase in revenues. However, the author provides no credible evidence to support this assumption. While temporal precedence is one of the conditions required to establish a causal relationship between two events, by itself it is not a sufficient condition. It is entirely possible that the increase of revenues coincides with the sale of inexpensive digital pianos, while the two actually had no causal connection. Moreover, the author fails to consider and rule out other factors affecting the sale of pianos, such as piano prices, marketing strategy, advertising effectiveness, availability of the products and so forth. Therefore, it is just as possible that Allegro's increase in revenues can be attributed to these factors rather than the introduction of digital pianos.

Secondly, even if Allegro's increase in revenues is largely due to the introduction of inexpensive digital pianos, the argument depends on the further assumption that the same strategy can also successfully increase the revenues of Largo. However, that is not necessarily the case. It is entirely possible that Allegro has long been known for producing inexpensive and fashionable pianos and therefore can easily achieve higher revenues from digital pianos. On the other hand, it is also possible that Largo will lose the loyalty of old customers by introducing inexpensive digital pianos, since doing so is generally regarded as a sign of compromised quality. Without specific evidence showing enough similarities between the two companies, it is unwarranted to assert that Largo will achieve the same result as Allegro after introducing a line of digital pianos.

Finally, Largo's high reputation among pianists can not guarantee that its digital pianos will be likely to find instant acceptance with customers. While Largo has long been known for producing handcrafted pianos, Allegro may be famous for its digital pianos. Common customers may prefer Allegro's digital pianos to Largo's digital pianos. If so, the director may even find digital pianos manufactured by Largo unmarketable. Therefore, the assertion that Largo's digital pianos will find instant acceptance with customers would be seriously undermined.

To sum up, the argument is logically flawed and therefore unconvincing as it stands. To strengthen it, the author should provide evidence that (1) Allegro's increased revenues were due to the introduction of inexpensive digital pianos, and (2) Largo and Allegro share enough similarities to achieve the same business success through adopting the same strategy. To better assess the argument, I would also need to know whether the digital pianos manufactured by Largo are more appealing and cost-effective than those manufactured by Allegro.

PART **3**

Argument题库考题
翻译与写作提纲

众所周知，GMAT写作考试中考生遇到的每一题都是从网上公布的题库中抽取的。为了取得高分，最好能把所有的题目都准备一遍。然而，多达179道题的Argument题库，几乎没有人有能力或精力把所有的题都做一遍。比较折衷的方法是写提纲，而写179道题的提纲对大多数考生来说还是难以做到，因为考生都很忙，根本没有那么多的时间投入到写作的准备上来。另一方面，准确理解题目的意思是做好每一道题的前提。鉴于以上两点，本书列出了题库中179道Argument题的翻译及提纲，希望对考生的复习备考有所帮助。

为了方便考生复习备考，本书的题目按照网上广为流传的方式编号：即按照Official Guide(第十版)的顺序编排，删去的题目(54，56，69，71，90，98，99，103)保持其原来的序号。

虽然在2006年10月公布的题库中，删除了所有2005年新增的题目，但仔细分析后就会发现这部分题目有相当一部分与最新题库中的某些题比较相似；另一方面，某些题目在考试中仍会出现，所以本书保留了这部分题目，供考生参考。

目前的题库(共179题)由三部分组成：

1) The Official Guide （10th Edition）题库，编号1～139，删去了8道（54，56，69，71，90，98，99，103），共131道题；

2) 2005年增加34题，编号140～173；

3) 2006年又增加了14题，编号174～187。

---

① The following appeared as part of an annual report sent to stockholders by Olympic Foods, a processor of frozen foods.

下文摘自一家奥林匹克食品公司(一家冷冻食品公司)提交给股东的年度报告。

"Over time, the costs of processing go down because as organizations learn how to do things better, they become more efficient. In color film processing, for example, the cost of a 3-by-5-inch print fell from 50 cents for five-day service in 1970 to 20 cents for one-day service in 1984. The same principle applies to the processing of food. And since Olympic Foods will soon celebrate its twenty-fifth birthday, we can expect that our long experience will enable us to minimize costs and thus maximize profits."

Discuss how well reasoned you find this argument. In your discussion be sure to analyze the line of reasoning and the use of evidence in the argument. For example, you may need to consider what questionable assumptions underlie the thinking and what alternative explanations or counterexamples might weaken the conclusion. You can also discuss what sort of evidence would strengthen or refute the argument, what changes in the argument would make it more logically sound, and what, if anything, would help you better evaluate its conclusion.

随着时间的推移，企业学会了更好的工作方法，从而提高了效率，因此加工成本逐步下降。以彩色胶卷为例，冲印一张3×5英寸照片的成本从1970年的50美分并耗时5天降至1984年的20美分，且只需1天就可完成。同样的规律也适用于食品加工业。由于奥林匹克食品公司马上就要举办25周年庆典大会了，我们可以凭借长期的从业经历来实现成本的最小化，从而达到利润最大化的目标。

你觉得这个论证的推理怎么样？请在你的论述中分析这个论证的推理过程以及它所使用的论据。比如，你需要考虑支持作者观点的假设是否可疑，有没有其他解释或者反例可以削弱这一结论。你也可以讨论什么样的论据可以加强或者反驳这个论证，对该论证做出怎么样的改变才能使它更加符合逻辑，以及哪些东西可以帮助你更好地评价这个结论。

（A）Gratuitous assumption: The conclusion of the argument is based on a gratuitous assumption that the company can minimize costs and maximize profits because the company has been in operation for 25 years. The author fails to cite any evidence to support that the long experience of Olympic Foods will guarantee minimal costs and maximum profits.

(B) False analogy: The food processing industry is not analogous to the color film processing industry. Differences between the two industries clearly outweigh the similarities, thus making the analogy highly invalid.

(C) Causal oversimplification: Other factors that may contribute to the reduced cost of color film processing should be considered and ruled out.

② The following appeared in a memorandum from the business department of the Apogee Company.
下文摘自Apogee公司业务部的一份备忘录。

"When the Apogee Company had all its operations in one location, it was more profitable than it is today. Therefore, the Apogee Company should close down its field offices and conduct all its operations from a single location. Such centralization would improve profitability by cutting costs and helping the company maintain better supervision of all employees."

当Apogee公司的所有业务集中于一个地方时，它的赢利水平要比现在高。因此，Apogee公司应该关闭在其他地方开设的办事处，把业务集中到一个地方。这样不但可以降低成本，而且有助于公司更有效地监控员工，从面提高公司的盈利能力。

(A) Gratuitous assumption: The author assumes that centralization would improve profitability by cutting costs and streamlining supervision of employees. This assumption is not supported by any data or projections.

(B) Causal oversimplification: The author unfairly assumes that centralization was the only factor that led to Apogee's greater past profitability. Furthermore, it is also imprudent to conclude that the establishment of the field offices is the only reason for the declining profits.

(C) All things are equal: Even if Apogee succeeded in the past by centralization, this strategy would not necessarily guarantee a similar success today.

③ The following appeared in a memorandum issued by a large city's council on the arts.
下文摘自一个大城市艺术委员会发行的备忘录。

"In a recent citywide poll, fifteen percent more residents said that they watch television programs about the visual arts than was the case in a poll conducted five years ago. During these past five years, the number of people visiting our city's art museums has increased by a similar percentage. Since the corporate funding that supports public television, where most of the visual arts programs appear, is now being threatened with severe cuts, we can expect that attendance at our city's art museums will also start to decrease. Thus some of the city's funds for supporting the arts should be reallocated to public television."

在最近开展的一项全市民意测验中，回答自己收看视觉艺术类电视节目的居民比5年前调查时高出了15个百分点。在过去的5年中，参观市艺术博物馆的人数也增加了相似的百分点。鉴于由公司赞助的公共电视台——即大多数视觉艺术节目播放的地方——目前所收到的赞助有可能会大幅削减，我们可以预计，参观市艺术博物馆的人数也会开始减少。因此，应该从市艺术基金中拨出一部分资金给公共电视台。

(A) Causal oversimplification: It is groundless to say that increased exposure to the visual arts on television has caused a similar increase in local art museum attendance only because the latter occurred concurrently with the former. Without any knowledge of the exact number of arts television program viewers and art museum patrons, it is difficult to evaluate the relevance of art television programs. Furthermore, perhaps there are other factors relevant to the increased the interest in the local art museum.

（B）Gratuitous assumption one: The author's argument is based on a gratuitous assumption that the funding which supports public television should not be reduced because the attendance of the art museums will decrease.

（C）Gratuitous assumption two: The author's argument is based on another gratuitous assumption that severe cuts in corporate funding which supports public television will lead to the reduction of the visual arts programs.

> **4 The following appeared in a report presented for discussion at a meeting of the directors of a company that manufactures parts for heavy machinery.**
> 下文摘自一份重型机械部件生产公司董事会的讨论报告。

"The falling revenues that the company is experiencing coincide with delays in manufacturing. These delays, in turn, are due in large part to poor planning in purchasing metals. Consider further that the manager of the department that handles purchasing of raw materials has an excellent background in general business, psychology, and sociology, but knows little about the properties of metals. The company should, therefore, move the purchasing manager to the sales department and bring in a scientist from the research division to be manager of the purchasing department."

公司收入的减少和生产的延误是同时出现的。而延误的主要原因是采购金属材料的计划很糟糕。考虑到负责原料采购的部门经理虽然具有深厚的商业背景和丰富的心理学、社会学知识，但是对金属材料的性质却知之甚少，公司应该将采购经理调到销售部门，并从研究部门调一位研究员来担任采购部门经理一职。

（A）Causal oversimplification: The report fails to establish a causal connection between the falling revenues of the company and delays in manufacturing. The mere fact that falling revenues coincide with delays in manufacturing is insufficient to conclude that the delays caused the decline in revenue.

（B）Gratuitous assumption: No evidence is stated in the report to support that knowledge of the properties of metals is necessary and sufficient for planning metal purchasing.

> **5 The following appeared in an announcement issued by the publisher of *The Mercury*, a weekly newspaper.**
> 下文摘自*The Mercury*周刊出版商发表的公告。

"Since a competing lower-priced newspaper, *The Bugle*, was started five years ago, *The Mercury's* circulation has declined by 10, 000 readers. The best way to get more people to read *The Mercury* is to reduce its price below that of *The Bugle*, at least until circulation increases to former levels. The increased circulation of *The Mercury* will attract more businesses to buy advertising space in the paper."

自从5年前*The Bugle*这份竞争力强、价格低廉的报纸问世以来，*The Mercury*的发行量下降了一万份。使更多人订阅*The Mercury*的最好方法是把它的价格降到*The Bugle*之下，并且降价至少要持续到发行量恢复以前的水平为止。随着发行量的增加，*The Mercury*会吸引更多的企业来订购该报纸的广告版面。

（A）Gratuitous assumption: The publisher assumes that price is the only factor that caused the decline in readership. But no evidence is given to support this claim. In fact, there are many other factors that might account for a decline in *The Mercury's* popularity.

（B）Oversimplified assumption: It is not obvious that lowering the subscription price is the most effective way to gain new readers. Furthermore, higher circulation should not be the ultimate goal of the newspaper.

6 **The following appeared as part of an article in a magazine devoted to regional life.**
下文摘自一份区域生活类杂志上的一篇文章。

"Corporations should look to the city of Helios when seeking new business opportunities or a new location. Even in the recent recession, Helios's unemployment rate was lower than the regional average. It is the industrial center of the region, and historically it has provided more than its share of the region's manufacturing jobs. In addition, Helios is attempting to expand its economic base by attracting companies that focus on research and development of innovative technologies."

企业在寻找新的商机或者新的办事处时，应该关注Helios市。即使在最近的经济萧条时期，Helios市的失业率也比地区平均水平低。它是该地区的工业中心，以前也曾为本地区创造了非常多的制造业就业机会。另外，Helios正试图通过吸引那些专注于新技术研发的公司来拓展自己的经济基础。

（A） In the first place, it is questionable whether the available labor pool in Hlios could support all types of corporations. Given that Helios has attracted mainly industrial and manufacturing companies in the past, it is unlikely that the local pool of prospective employees would be suitable for corporations of other types.

（B） In the next place, the size of the available work force may not be able to meet the need of the prospective corporations. Because the unemployment rate is lower than average in Helios, corporations that require large numbers of workers would not find Helios attractive.

7 **The following appeared in the health section of a magazine on trends and lifestyles.**
下文摘自一份流行和时尚杂志的健康栏目。

"People who use the artificial sweetener aspartame are better off consuming sugar, since aspartame can actually contribute to weight gain rather than weight loss. For example, high levels of aspartame have been shown to trigger a craving for food by depleting the brain of a chemical that registers satiety, or the sense of being full. Furthermore, studies suggest that sugars, if consumed after at least 45 minutes of continuous exercise, actually enhance the body's ability to burn fat. Consequently, those who drink aspartame-sweetened juices after exercise will also lose this calorie-burning benefit. Thus it appears that people consuming aspartame rather than sugar are unlikely to achieve their dietary goals."

食用人造甜味剂糖精的人最好直接食用天然糖，因为糖精不但不能减少体重，反而会导致体重增加。比如，高浓度的糖精可以耗尽大脑中某种让人感觉对食物恢足的化学物质，从而引起人们对食物的渴望。另外，研究显示，如果在连续运动超过45分钟后食用天然糖，将会切实提高人体燃烧脂肪的能力。因此，运动后饮用含糖精的饮料，人体就会失去耗散热量的益处。由此看来，食用糖精而非天然糖的人很难达到节食的目标。

（A） To begin with, the author's conclusion is based on an unfair assumption that all aspartame users consume high levels of the artificial sweetener.

（B） Another problem with the author's generalization is that not all dieters use sugar after long periods of exercise.

8 **The following appeared in the editorial section of a corporate newsletter.**
以下内容摘自公司简报的社论部分。

"The common notion that workers are generally apathetic about management issues is false, or at least outdated: a

通常认为，工人一般对管理事务并不关心。这种观点即使不是错误的，至少

recently published survey indicates that 79 percent of the nearly 1,200 workers who responded to survey questionnaires expressed a high level of interest in the topics of corporate restructuring and redesign of benefits programs."

也是过时的：最近公布的一项调查显示，在回应问卷调查的近1200名工人中，有79%的人表示对公司重组以及重新设计福利项目这两个问题很感兴趣。

（A）Insufficient sample one: The statistics cited in the editorial may be misleading because the total number of workers employed by the corporation is not specified.

（B）Insufficient sample two: The respondents' views are not necessarily representative of the views of the work force in general. It makes sense that only less apathetic workers would respond to it.

（C）Hasty generalization: workers may be interested in corporate restructuring and redesign of benefits programs. However, it is unfair to assume that workers would be similarly interested in other management issues.

9 The following appeared in the opinion column of a financial magazine.
以下内容摘自某财经杂志的意见栏。

"On average, middle-aged consumers devote 39 percent of their retail expenditure to department store products and services, while for younger consumers the average is only 25 percent. Since the number of middle-aged people will increase dramatically within the next decade, department stores can expect retail sales to increase significantly during that period. Furthermore, to take advantage of the trend, these stores should begin to replace some of those products intended to attract the younger consumer with products intended to attract the middle-aged consumer."

一般而言，中年消费者的零用消费支出中有39％的钱花在百货商店和服务项目上，而在年轻的消费者中这一比例平均只有25％。由于中年消费者的数量在接下来的10年中将急剧增长，百货商店有望在此期间实现零售销售额的大幅增涨。另外，为了更好地利用这一趋势，百货商店应该开始把一些原来以年轻人为购买对象的商品替换成吸引中年消费者的商品。

Outline 1

（A）First, the argument omits the assumption that the business volumes of both the middle-aged consumers and the younger consumers are the same.

（B）An increase in the number of middle-aged people does not necessarily portend an overall increase in department-store sales.

（C）The author unfairly assumes that profits from selling different goods are the same. As younger consumers may not buy the same products as middle-aged consumers, more sales don't necessarily mean more profits.

（D）The author's conclusion is based on an unfounded assumption that the number of younger consumers will not increase in the next decade.

Outline 2

（A）In the first place, the argument ignores the actual amount of retail expenditure of both middle-aged and younger consumers devoted to department store products and services.

（B）In the second place, the author bases his conclusion on the unfounded assumption that the trend of middle-aged consumers spending more than younger ones in department stores will not change within the next decade.

（C）Finally, the argument never addresses the population difference between middle-aged consumers and younger ones.

"This past winter, 200 students from Waymarsh State College traveled to the state capitol building to protest against proposed cuts in funding for various state college programs. The other 12, 000 Waymarsh students evidently weren't so concerned about their education: they either stayed on campus or left for winter break. Since the group who did not protest is far more numerous, it is more representative of the state's college students than are the protesters. Therefore the state legislature need not heed the appeals of the protesting students."

去年冬天，Waymarsh州立大学有200名学生前往州议会大厦，抗议对各项州立大学项目基金进行削减的提案。另外1.2万名Waymarsh的学生显然对他们的教育不太关心：他们不是呆在校园里，就是出去过寒假了。由于未参与抗议的人数远多于抗议者，所以他们比抗议者更能代表本州州立大学生的意见。因此，州立法机构不必理会抗议学生的呼吁。

（A）To begin with, the author's assumption that the one-sixtieth of the students who took part in the protest cannot represent the entire student body is unwarranted. Without information regarding the way in which the protesting students were selected, it is presumptuous to conclude that their opinions fail to reflect the opinions of their colleagues.

（B）Another problem with this argument is that the author fails to provide any evidence that the remaining 12,000 students who stayed on campus or left for winter break are not concerned about their education.

"In the first four years that Montoya has served as mayor of the city of San Perdito, the population has decreased and the unemployment rate has increased. Two businesses have closed for each new business that has opened. Under Varro, who served as mayor for four years before Montoya, the unemployment rate decreased and the population increased. Clearly, the residents of San Perdito would be best served if they voted Montoya out of office and reelected Varro."

在Montoya担任San Perdito市市长的前4年里，该市人口减少而失业率上升。每新开一家公司就有两家公司倒闭。而在Montoya之前Varro担任市长的4年间，失业率下降，人口增长。显然，如果投票让Montoya下台，重新选Varro担任该市的市长，San Perdito市的市民将会得到更好的服务。

（A）To begin with, the author fails to establish a causal relationship between Motoya's administration and the problems of unemployment in San Perdito, as well as its population loss.

（B）Secondly, the argument at hand might have been intentionally oversimplified for the specific purpose of angering citizens of San Perdito, and thereby turning them against the incumbent mayor.

（C）Furthermore, the unemployment rate and the population's decrease are not the only factors in evaluating the performance of the mayor of a city.

"Advertising the reduced price of selected grocery items in the *Daily Gazette* will help you increase your sales. Consider

在*Gazette Daily*上刊登选定商品的降价广告有助于提高销售额。不妨参考上个

the results of a study conducted last month. Thirty sale items from a store in downtown Marston were advertised in the Gazette for four days. Each time one or more of the 30 items was purchased, clerks asked whether the shopper had read the ad. Two-thirds of the 200 shoppers asked answered in the affirmative. Furthermore, more than half the customers who answered in the affirmative spent over $100 at the store."

月开展的一项研究的结果。Marston中心区的一家商店连续4天在Gazette日报上刊登30种降价商品的广告。每当有人购买这些降价商品时，售货员就问他们有没有看过这则广告。在接受访问的200名顾客中有三分之二的人回答说看过。并且回答看过广告的顾客中有超过一半的人在该店消费一百美元以上。

(A) First of all, the author fails to establish a general causal relationship between reading the ad and purchasing sale items as well as non-sale items.

(B) Secondly, the author assumes that the poll indicates that advertising certain sales will cause a general increase in sales. But the poll does not even address the issue of increased overall sales.

(C) Finally, the fact that the *Daily Guzette* has an obvious vested interest in these advertisements may well discredit the argument.

---

⑬ The following appeared as part of a campaign to sell advertising time on a local radio station to local businesses.
以下内容摘自一份地方电台向当地企业推销广告业务的宣传资料。

"The Cumquat Cafe began advertising on our local radio station this year and was delighted to see its business increase by 10 percent over last year's totals. Their success shows you how you can use radio advertising to make your business more profitable."

Cumquat餐馆今年开始在我们本地电台播放广告，结果可喜地看到它的业务比去年的总量增长了10%。他们的成功向您展示了如何利用电台广告使您的企业获利更多。

(A) The author overlooks a number of other factors that might have contributed to the Cumquat's success.

(B) Furthermore, granting that radio advertising is responsible for the Cumquat's success, we cannot safely assume that because a small restaurant has benefited from radio advertising, any and all local businesses will similarly benefit.

---

⑭ The following appeared as part of a newspaper editorial.
以下内容摘自某家报纸的社论。

"Two years ago Nova High School began to use interactive computer instruction in three academic subjects. The school dropout rate declined immediately, and last year's graduates have reported some impressive achievements in college. In future budgets the school board should use a greater portion of the available funds to buy more computers, and all schools in the district should adopt interactive computer instruction throughout the curriculum."

两年前，Nova高中开始在三门学科中使用互动式计算机教学。该学校的退学率立刻下降，而且去年的毕业生报告说他们在大学取得了很好的成绩。在未来的预算中，校董事会应该在能得到的资金中拨出更多资金用来购买更多的计算机，而且该地区的所有学校都应该在所有课程中使用互动式计算机教学。

(A) Firstly, this argument is a classic instance of "after this, therefore because of this" reasoning. The mere fact that the introduction of interactive computer instruction preceded the impressive performance of recent graduates and the decline in the dropout rate is insufficient to conclude that it was the cause of these events.

(B) Even supposing the Nova High School's declining dropout rate and last year's graduates' achievements benefit directly from the usage of interactive computer instruction, the success of the instruction in only three subjects would not guarantee a similar sweeping success in adopting computer instruction throughout the curriculum of all schools in the district.

"Re-elect Adams, and you will be voting for proven leadership in improving the state's economy. Over the past year alone, seventy percent of the state's workers have had increases in their wages, five thousand new jobs have been created, and six corporations have located their headquarters here. Most of the respondents in a recent poll said they believed that the economy is likely to continue to improve if Adams is reelected. Adams's opponent, Zebulon, would lead our state in the wrong direction, because Zebulon disagrees with many of Adams's economic policies."

再次选举Adams，并向他投票吧！相关事实已经证明他具有改善本州经济的领导能力。仅仅在过去一年的时间内，本州有70％的工人工资上涨，新增了5000个工作岗位，另外还有6个公司将他们的总部设在了这里。在最近的一次民意测验中，大部分回答者表示，如果Adams再次当选，他们相信经济将会持续发展。Adams的对手Zebulon会让我们州的经济误入歧途，因为Zebulon在很多经济政策问题上和Adams唱反调。

(A) In the first place, the statistics cited in the argument are intended to support the main claim that the state is economically better off with Adams as governor. But these statistics are vague and oversimplified, and thus may distort the state's overall economic picture.

(B) Secondly, as the author does not indicate who conducted the poll, who responded, or how the poll was conducted, the survey results cited by the author are of little worth as evidence for public opinion about Adams or his economic policies.

(C) Thirdly, the author fails to establish a casual relationship between Adams's administration and the state's economic boom.

(D) Finally, the author provides no evidence at all to support the assumption that the state would be worse off with Zebulon in office.

"Throughout the last two decades, those who earned graduate degrees found it very difficult to get jobs teaching their academic specialties at the college level. Those with graduate degrees from Waymarsh University had an especially hard time finding such jobs. But better times are coming in the next decade for all academic job seekers, including those from Waymarsh. Demographic trends indicate that an increasing number of people will be reaching college age over the next ten years; consequently, we can expect that the job market will improve dramatically for people seeking college-level teaching positions in their fields."

在过去20年间，获得学位的研究生们发现在大学里找到一份教授他们学术专长的工作是很困难的。那些从Waymarsh大学获得研究生学位的人要找到这类工作尤其困难。但在接下来的10年中，寻找学术职位的人就业形势会大有好转，包括Waymarsh大学的毕业生。人口统计反映的趋势表明适龄上大学的人数在未来10年将增加。因此我们可预计，对那些在自身领域内寻找大学教学工作的人来说，就业市场将会大有改观。

（A）To begin with, the author assumes that an increase in the number of college-aged people over the next decade will result in an increase in the number of people who attend college during this period. However, this assumption is problematic; other factors may nullify this expectation.

（B）Secondly, the author unfairly assumes that increased university enrollments will lead to an increase in teaching positions in all fields.

（C）Finally, lacking information about the reasons why Waymarsh graduates had an especially difficult time finding teaching jobs, it is difficult to assess their prospects for the future.

---

17 The following appeared in an article in a consumer-products magazine.
以上内容摘自某消费者产品杂志上的一篇文章。

"Two of today's best-selling brands of full-strength prescription medication for the relief of excess stomach acid, Acid-Ease and Pepticaid, are now available in milder nonprescription forms. Doctors have written 76 million more prescriptions for full-strength Acid-Ease than for full-strength Pepticaid. So people who need an effective but milder nonprescription medication for the relief of excess stomach acid should choose Acid-Ease."

Acid-Ease 和 Pepticaid 是如今最畅销的两种用于缓解胃酸过多的强力处方药，目前它们可以作为轻度非处方药出售。医生开出的强力 Acid-Ease 药方要比强力 Pepticaid 药方多出 7,600 万张。所以需要有效但较温和的非处方药来治疗胃酸过多的人应该选择 Acid-Ease。

（A）Firstly, as the author does not indicate that the comparison between the number of prescriptions is based on the same period, the assumption that the prescription form of Acid-Ease is more popular among doctors is problematic.

（B）Secondly, the author assumes that doctors prefer the prescription form of Acid-Ease for the reason that it is more effective at relieving excess stomach acid. However, doctors may have preferred Acid-Ease for reasons other than its effectiveness.

（C）Finally, the author unfairly assumes that the milder non-prescription forms of Acid-Ease and Pepticaid will be analogous to their full-strength prescription versions.

---

18 The following is an excerpt from a memo written by the head of a governmental department.
以下内容摘自政府某部门领导所写的备忘录。

"Neither stronger ethics regulations nor stronger enforcement mechanisms are necessary to ensure ethical behavior by companies doing business with this department. We already have a code of ethics that companies doing business with this department are urged to abide by, and virtually all of these companies have agreed to follow it. We also know that the code is relevant to the current business environment because it was approved within the last year, and in direct response to specific violations committed by companies with which we were then working—not in abstract anticipation of potential violations, as so many such codes are."

我们既不需要严格的道德规范，也不需要强化执行机制来确保和本部门做生意的公司在行为上合乎道德。我们已经有了和本部门做生意的公司必须遵守的道德准则，事实上所有这些公司也同意遵循这些准则。我们也知道该准则和当前的经济环境吻合，因为它是去年被批准的，而且针对的是当时与本部门办事时公司违规的实例。和其他准则有所不同，我们的准则并非抽象地估计可能会出现的违规行为。

（A）To begin with, the author fails to provide sufficient evidence to support the claim that stronger enforcement mechanisms are unnecessary. The fact that companies agreed to follow an existing code of ethics does not mean that they will always follow it.

（B）Secondly, the author unfairly assumes that the code of ethics that was approved last year will be representative of all the ethics problems that concern the department.

19 The following appeared as part of an article in the travel section of a newspaper.
以下内容摘自某报旅游版上的一篇文章。

"Over the past decade, the restaurant industry in the country of Spiessa has experienced unprecedented growth. This surge can be expected to continue in the coming years, fueled by recent social changes: personal incomes are rising, more leisure time is available, single-person households are more common, and people have a greater interest in gourmet food, as evidenced by a proliferation of publications on the subject."

在过去的10年中，Spiessa国的餐饮业经历了前所未有的增长。该增长有望继续保持下去，其动力是最近的一些社会变化：个人收入增加，人们的休闲时间增加，单身家庭越来越普遍，人们对美食更感兴趣——这从美食类出版物的大量发行中可以看得出来。

（A）In the first place, the argument is based on the dubious assumption that the number of restaurants in Spiessa will continue to expand at the same rate as in the recent past.

（B）Also, the author unfairly assumes that the economic and social circumstances cited will actually result in more people eating out at restaurants.

（C）Finally, the author's conclusion is drawn from an unwarranted assumption that no extrinsic factors will restrain people in Spiessa from choosing to spend more time and money eating out.

20 The following appeared in an article in a health and fitness magazine.
以下内容摘自某健康健身杂志上的一篇文章。

"Laboratory studies show that Saluda Natural Spring Water contains several of the minerals necessary for good health and that it is completely free of bacteria. Residents of Saluda, the small town where the water is bottled, are hospitalized less frequently than the national average. Even though Saluda Natural Spring Water may seem expensive, drinking it instead of tap water is a wise investment in good health."

实验室研究表明，Saluda天然泉水含有多种健康必须的矿物质，且完全无菌。在灌装此水的Saluda小镇，居民患病就医的频率低于全国的平均水平。尽管Saluda天然泉水看似价格不菲，但用它来代替自来水作饮用水是一项有益健康的明智投资。

（A）Firstly, the argument is based on the questionable assumption that tap water does not contain the minerals in question and is not completely free of bacteria.

（B）Secondly, the author fails to provide any concrete evidence that the water residents of Saluda drink is the same as Saluda Natural Spring Water.

（C）Finally, it is assumed that the reason Saluda's residents are hospitalized less frequently than the national average is because they drink Saluda Natural Spring Water.

21 **The following appeared as part of an editorial in an industry newsletter.**
以下内容摘自某行业简报的社论部分。

"While trucking companies that deliver goods pay only a portion of highway maintenance costs and no property tax on the highways they use, railways spend billions per year maintaining and upgrading their facilities. The government should lower the railroad companies' property taxes, since sending goods by rail is clearly a more appropriate mode of ground transportation than highway shipping. For one thing, trains consume only a third of the fuel a truck would use to carry the same load, making them a more cost-effective and environmentally sound mode of transport. Furthermore, since rail lines already exist, increases in rail traffic would not require building new lines at the expense of taxpaying citizens."

货车运输公司只需缴纳一部分高速公路养路费，不必为他们使用的公路缴纳财产税，但铁路公司每年得花几十亿来保养和更新铁路设施。政府应该降低铁路公司的财产税，因为在陆路运输方面，铁路货运比公路货运更合适。运送相同的货物时火车所用燃料相当于货运汽车的三分之一，这一点就使它成为更高效更环保的运输方式。此外，由于铁道线路已经存在，增加铁路交通不需要耗费纳税者的钱。

（A）First of all, the argument depends upon a misleading comparison between railroad and truck company expenditures.

（B）Additionally, the author assumes that property taxes should be structured to provide incentives for cost-effective and environmentally beneficial business practices. This assumption is questionable because property taxes are normally structured to reflect the value of property.

（C）Furthermore, the environmental soundness of a practice might be relevant in determining tax structuring, but society does not compensate a business for its cost-efficiency.

（D）Finally, the author unfairly assumes that sending goods by rail is clearly a more appropriate mode of ground transportation than highway shipping.

22 **The following appeared in the editorial section of a newspaper.**
以下内容摘自某报纸的社论部分。

"As public concern over drug abuse has increased, authorities have become more vigilant in their efforts to prevent illegal drugs from entering the country. Many drug traffickers have consequently switched from marijuana, which is bulky, or heroin, which has a market too small to justify the risk of severe punishment, to cocaine. Thus enforcement efforts have ironically resulted in an observed increase in the illegal use of cocaine."

随着公众对吸毒问题越来越关注，当权者在防止非法毒品进入国内这方面提高了警惕。许多毒贩子已经从贩卖大麻和海洛因转向贩卖可卡因，因为大麻体积太大，而海洛因市场太小，冒风险不合算。这样一来，具有讽刺意味的是，当权者大力加强对毒品的监管力度反而导致了可卡因的非法使用者明显增多。

（A）In the first place, the author has engaged in "after this, therefore because of this" reasoning. The only reason offered for the assertion that the increased vigilance caused the increase in cocaine use is the fact that the former preceded the latter.

（B）Secondly, the author assumes that an increase in the supply of cocaine is sufficient to bring about an increase in its use. While this is a tempting assumption, it is a problematic one.

The following appeared in a speech delivered by a member of the city council.
以下内容摘自市议会某成员的演讲。

"Twenty years ago, only half of the students who graduated from Einstein High School went on to attend a college or university. Today, two thirds of the students who graduate from Einstein do so. Clearly, Einstein has improved its educational effectiveness over the past two decades. This improvement has occurred despite the fact that the school's funding, when adjusted for inflation, is about the same as it was twenty years ago. Therefore, we do not need to make any substantial increase in the school's funding at this time."

20年前，Einstein高中的毕业生只有一半上大学继续深造，现在，该中学的毕业生中有三分之二的人可以上大学。显然，这20年来，Einstein高中的教学质量提高了。尽管除去通货膨胀因素后，学校现有经费和20年前几乎持平，但该校还是提高了教学质量。因此，目前看来，我们无需大幅度增加学校的经费。

(A) To begin with, the author unjustifiably presumes that educational efficiency is synonymous with students going to college after graduation.

(B) Additionally, the author unfairly presumes that the number of students going to college after graduation has increased because Einstein is doing a better job of educating its students.

(C) Finally, even if Einstein has improved its education quality, this factor alone is not a compelling reason to deny Einstein additional funding.

24 **The following appeared in a memo from the customer service division to the manager of Mammon Savings and Loan.**
以下内容摘自客服部门递交给Mammon借贷银行经理的备忘录。

"We believe that improved customer service is the best way for us to differentiate ourselves from competitors and attract new customers. We can offer our customers better service by reducing waiting time in teller lines from an average of six minutes to an average of three. By opening for business at 8:30 instead of 9:00, and by remaining open for an additional hour beyond our current closing time, we will be better able to accommodate the busy schedules of our customers. These changes will enhance our bank's image as the most customer-friendly bank in town and give us the edge over our competition."

我们相信提高客服质量是我们有别于竞争对手，并吸引新客户的最佳方法。我们可以把顾客在出纳台前排队等待的时间从平均6分钟缩短到3分钟，从而为顾客提供更加完善的服务。如果营业网点的开门时间从9点提前到8点半，停止营业的时间向后推迟一小时，我们就能更好地为工作日程繁忙的顾客提供服务。这些改革举措能够提升我们银行的形象，从而成为本市对顾客最友好的银行，在竞争里脱颖而出。

(A) In the first place, the author unfairly assumes that Mammon's competitors are similar to Mammon in all respects other than the ones listed.

(B) Additionally, the author assumes that the proposed improvements will sufficiently distinguish Mammon from its competitors. This is not necessarily the case.

(C) Moreover, the conclusion is based on the unfounded assumption that Mammon's customers are only concerned with the amount of time it takes them to do their banking.

(D) Finally, the author unjustifiably assumes that Mammon can offer these improved services without sacrificing other current features that attract customers.

25 **The following appeared as part of an article in a magazine on lifestyles.**
以下内容摘自生活方式类杂志上的一篇文章。

"Two years ago, City L was listed 14th in an annual survey that ranks cities according to the quality of life that can be enjoyed by those living in them. This information will enable people who are moving to the state in which City L is located to confidently identify one place, at least, where schools are good, housing is affordable, people are friendly, the environment is safe, and the arts flourish."

两年前，L市在城市居民生活质量的年度调查中排名14。这一信息有助于移居到L市所在州的人们放心地找到一个居处，那里至少有好的学校，买得起的住房，市民友善，环境安全，并且艺术繁荣。

（A）One major problem with this argument is that the author fails to indicate what individual characteristics of cities were used for the ranking's criteria.

（B）Another problem with this argument is that the author provides no indication of how each characteristic was weighed in the ranking.

（C）Furthermore, the author's conclusion depends on the questionable assumption that the conditions listed by the author have remained unchanged in City L since the survey was conducted two years ago.

（D）Finally, the author fails to indicate how many cities were included in the survey.

26 **The following appeared in a memorandum from a member of a financial management and consulting firm.**
以下内容摘自某家财务管理咨询公司一名成员的一篇备忘录。

"We have learned from an employee of Windfall, Ltd., that its accounting department, by checking about ten percent of the last month's purchasing invoices for errors and inconsistencies, saved the company some $10, 000 in overpayments. In order to help our clients increase their net gains, we should advise each of them to institute a policy of checking all purchasing invoices for errors. Such a recommendation could also help us get the Windfall account by demonstrating to Windfall the rigorousness of our methods."

我们从Windfall有限公司的一位员工那里得知，该公司的会计部门对上个月10%的采购发票进行了纰漏检查，结果把公司多付的一万美元追了回来。为了帮助我们的客户提高他们的净收入，我们应该建议他们形成一个检查所有采购发票是否存在错漏的制度。同时，根据该建议，向Windfall公司展示我们方法的严格性会有助于我们赢得Windfall公司成为我们的客户。

（A）To begin with, the conclusion of this argument is based upon insufficient evidence. The evidence drawn from Windfall's experience is insufficient to support the conclusion that all purchasing invoices are subject to similar errors.

（B）Secondly, the argument unfairly assumes that instituting a policy of checking all purchasing invoices will help find errors and inconsistencies.

（C）Finally, even supposing the checking does save money for the company, the argument ignores the fact that the checking itself costs the company money. If the cost is more than what is gained from correcting the errors, the company will lose money.

The following appeared in a newspaper editorial.
以下内容摘自某报纸的社论。

"As violence in movies increases, so do crime rates in our cities. To combat this problem we must establish a board to censor certain movies, or we must limit admission to persons over 21 years of age. Apparently our legislators are not concerned about this issue since a bill calling for such actions recently failed to receive a majority vote."

随着电影中暴力镜头的增加，本市的犯罪率也在上升。为了解决这个问题，我们必须成立一个委员会来审查特定的电影，或者将这些电影的入场资格限制在21岁以上。显然我们的立法者并不关心这件事，因为最近一个要求采取这种行动的提案没有得到多数立法者的赞成。

（A）The main problem with the argument is that the author fails to establish a causal relationship between portrayals of violence in movies and urban crime.

（B）Another problem with the argument is that the author's solution unfairly assumes that only persons under the age of 21 are adversely affected by movie violence.

（C）Finally, the author fails to establish a causal relationship between the fact that the proposed bill failed to receive a majority vote and the assumption that the legislators are not concerned about the issue of rising crime rates.

28 **The following appeared in the editorial section of a local newspaper.**
以下内容摘自某地方报纸的社论部分。

"Commuter use of the new subway train is exceeding the transit company's projections. However, commuter use of the shuttle buses that transport people to the subway stations is below the projected volume. If the transit company expects commuters to ride the shuttle buses to the subway rather than drive there, it must either reduce the shuttle bus fares or increase the price of parking at the subway stations."

上下班的人对新地铁的使用超出了运输公司的设计方案。但是，上下班的人对运送他们去地铁站的往返公交车的使用则低于设计容量。如果运输公司希望上下班的人乘公交车而不是开车去地铁站，就必须下调公交车的票价或者提高地铁站停车场的停车费。

（A）In the first place, the author unfairly assumes that reducing shuttle fares and increasing parking fees are the only solutions available to the problem of limited shuttle use.

（B）Secondly, the author assumes that reducing shuttle fees and increasing parking fees are mutually exclusive. However, this assumption is unwarranted.

29 **The following was excerpted from the speech of a spokesperson for Synthetic Farm Products, Inc.**
以下内容摘自合成农产品公司的某位发言人的讲话。

"Many farmers who invested in the equipment needed to make the switch from synthetic to organic fertilizers and pesticides feel that it would be too expensive to resume synthetic farming at this point. But studies of farmers who switched to organic farming last year indicate that their current crop yields are lower. Hence their purchase of organic farming equipment, a

许多投资购买了从合成肥料转向有机肥料和杀虫剂所需设备的农民觉得现阶段恢复合成型农业的费用过高。但是对去年转向有机农业的农民的研究表明，他们现在的农作物产量变低了。因此他们对有机农业设备的购买费用与连续减产

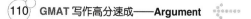

relatively minor investment compared to the losses that would result from continued lower crop yields, cannot justify persisting on an unwise course. And the choice to farm organically is financially unwise, given that it was motivated by environmental rather than economic concerns."

所蒙受的损失相比只是一小笔投资，不能作为一个坚持不明智选择的理由。另外，开展有机农业主要是出于对环境保护的考虑，而不是经济利益，所以从经济利益方面考虑，选择有机农业是不明智的。

（A）The major problem with this argument is that the author fails to provide sufficient information regarding the comparative reasoning and how the studies were conducted.

（B）Additionally, the author provides no evidence to support the assumption that the low crop yields for first-time organic farmers last year are representative of their overall crop yields.

（C）Finally, the author unfairly assumes that a practice cannot be both environmentally and economically beneficial.

---

30 **The following appeared in a newspaper story giving advice about investments.**
以下的内容摘自某份报纸上一篇提供投资建议的文章。

"As overall life expectancy continues to rise, the population of our country is growing increasingly older. For example, over twenty percent of the residents of one of our more populated regions are now at least 65 years old, and occupancy rates at resort hotels in that region declined significantly during the past six months. Because of these two related trends, a prudent investor would be well advised to sell interest in hotels and invest in hospitals and nursing homes instead."

随着人们生命期望值的持续增长，我国的人口趋向于老龄化。比如，在我国一个人口密度较大的地区有超过20%的居民是65岁以上的老人，而过去6个月以来该地区度假旅馆的入住率大幅下降。鉴于这两种趋势，一个谨慎的投资者最好卖出酒店的股份，而把投资转向医院和老人护理院。

（A）In the first place, the author provides no evidence to support the claim that the population as a whole is aging and that the hotel occupancy rate in general is declining.

（B）Also, the author fails to provide any evidence to support the claim that the aging of the population has caused the decline in hotel occupancy.

（C）Finally, the author assumes that investing in hospitals and nursing homes will be profitable. However, this assumption is unwarranted.

---

31 **The following appeared as part of the business plan of an investment and financial consulting firm.**
以下内容摘自一家投资理财公司的商业计划。

"Studies suggest that an average coffee drinker's consumption of coffee increases with age, from age 10 through age 60. Even after age 60, coffee consumption remains high. The average cola drinker's consumption of cola, however, declines with increasing age. Both of these trends have remained stable for the past 40 years. Given that the number of older adults will significantly increase as the population ages over the next 20 years, it follows that the demand for coffee will increase and the demand for cola will decrease during this period. We should,

研究表明，咖啡饮用者的平均咖啡消费量会随着年龄的增长（从10岁到60岁）而增长。即使到60岁以后，这些人的咖啡消费量仍然会居高不下。然而，可乐饮用者的平均可乐消费量则随着年龄的增长而下降。过去40年中这两种趋势都保持稳定。由于在未来的20年内老年人口将显著增加，所以，这一时期内人们对咖啡的需求量会增长而对可乐的需求量

therefore, consider transferring our investments from Cola Loca to Early Bird Coffee."

会降低。因此我们应该考虑将投资从Loca可乐转向Early Bird咖啡。

（A）First, without any basis, the author assumes that relative supply conditions will remain unchanged over the next twenty years.

（B）Secondly, the argument fails to account for the timing of the increase in coffee consumption.

（C）Thirdly, the firm unjustifiably relies on studies that correlate coffee and cola consumption with age. The firm does not provide evidence to confirm the reliability of these studies.

（D）Finally, the author fails to establish a causal relationship between the increasing number of coffee consumers and a corresponding increase in profits in the coffee industry.

---

32 The following appeared in the editorial section of a West Cambria newspaper.
以下内容摘自West Cambria报纸的社论部分。

"A recent review of the West Cambria volunteer ambu-lance service revealed a longer average response time to accidents than was reported by a commercial ambulance squad located in East Cambria. In order to provide better patient care for accident victims and to raise revenue for our town by collecting service fees for ambulance use, we should disband our volunteer service and hire a commercial ambulance service."

最近一篇针对West Cambria志愿救护队的评论指出，该救护队对事故的平均反应时间要比East Cambria商业救护队长。为了给事故受害者提供更好的护理，也为了能通过收取救护费来提高本镇的收入，我们应当解散志愿救护队并雇用商业救护队。

（A）The main problem with the argument is that the author's belief that better patient care would be provided by a commercial ambulance service than by a volunteer service is based on insufficient evidence. The author unjustifiably presumes that response time to an accident is the only factor that influences patient care.

（B）Another problem with the argument is that the author's plan for raising revenue for West Cambria is questionable. It is unlikely that significant revenues will be raised by charging a fee for ambulance use.

（C）Finally, the author neglects other factors that might account for the longer average response times revealed by the recent review.

---

33 The following is part of a business plan being discussed at a board meeting of the Perks Company.
以下内容摘自Perks公司董事会正在讨论的一份商业计划。

"It is no longer cost-effective for the Perks Company to continue offering its employees a generous package of benefits and incentives year after year. In periods when national unemployment rates are low, Perks may need to offer such a package in order to attract and keep good employees, but since national unemployment rates are now high, Perks does not need to offer the same benefits and incentives. The money thus saved could be better used to replace the existing plant machinery with more technologically sophisticated equipment, or even to build an additional plant."

继续年复一年地给员工提供丰厚福利和激励措施对于Perks公司来说不再划算。当全国的失业率较低时，Perks可能需要用丰厚的待遇来吸引并留住优秀的员工。但由于现在全国的失业率较高，Perks无需死守原来的优厚待遇和激励措施不放。从中省出的钱有更好的用途，可以用来购买先进的设备，换掉现在的机器设备，或者构建一个新的车间。

 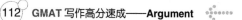

（A）In the first place, the argument relies on the questionable reasoning that it is unnecessary for any company to pay relatively high wages during periods of high unemployment because the market will supply good employees at lower rates of pay.

（B）In the second place, the argument relies on the assumption that the cost-effectiveness of a wage policy is determined solely by whatever wages a market can currently bear. This assumption overlooks the peripheral costs of reducing or eliminating benefits.

（C）Finally, the author fails to provide evidence to support the claim that it is necessary for Perks to introduce more technologically sophisticated equipment or to build an additional plant.

---

34 **The following appeared as part of a plan proposed by an executive of the Easy Credit Company to the president.**

以下内容摘自Easy Credit公司某个经营主管向总裁提交的一份计划书。

"The Easy Credit Company would gain an advantage over competing credit card services if we were to donate a portion of the proceeds from the use of our cards to a well-known environmental organization in exchange for the use of its symbol or logo on our card. Since a recent poll shows that a large percentage of the public is concerned about environmental issues, this policy would attract new customers, increase use among existing customers, and enable us to charge interest rates that are higher than the lowest ones available."

如果我们公司从信用卡业务收入中拿出一部分钱捐给一家知名的环保机构，以换取在我们的信用卡上使用他们的标识的权利，那么我们公司在信用卡业务的竞争中就会占取优势。因为最近一次民意调查显示，大部分群众都关注环保问题，所以这种策略能吸引新客户，增加现有客户信用卡的使用率，使我们收取的利率高于现有的最低利率。

（A）To begin with, the author unfairly assumes that the environmental organization whose logo is sought is concerned with the same environmental issues that the poll shows there is widespread concern about on the public's part.

（B）Secondly, the author's conclusion is based on the unfounded assumption that the public's concern about environmental issues will result in a desire to use the Easy Credit Company credit card.

（C）Finally, the author unfairly assumes that the raised interest rates of the Easy Credit Company as a result of its use of symbol or logo of the environmental organization will not exert a negative effect on the card's attractiveness to consumers.

---

35 **The following appeared as part of a recommendation from the financial planning office to the administration of Fern Valley University.**

以下内容摘自Fern Valley大学财务规划办公室提交给学校管理部门的建议书。

"In the past few years, Fern Valley University has suffered from a decline in both enrollments and admissions applications. The reason can be discovered from our students, who most often cite poor teaching and inadequate library resources as their chief sources of dissatisfaction with Fern Valley. Therefore, in order to increase the number of students attending our university, and hence to regain our position as the most prestigious university in the greater Fern Valley metropolitan area, it is necessary to initiate a fund-raising campaign among the alumni that will enable us to expand the range

在过去的几年里，Fern Valley大学的录取人数和申请入学人数都有所下降。原因可以从我们学校的学生那里找到：他们经常把对本校不满的主要原因归结为教学水平差和图书馆资料不全。因此，为了增加我们学校的学生人数，恢复本校在Fern Valley地区最知名学府的地位，有必要在校友中发起一场资金募集活动，

of subjects we teach and to increase the size of our library facilities."

用筹集的资金来扩展学科范围，改善图书馆设施。

(A) The main problem with the argument is that the proposal unfairly assumes that the recent enrollment and application decline was caused by the poor teaching and the inadequate library resources.

(B) Next, this argument depends on the questionable assumption that providing a greater range of subjects and a larger library will alleviate the students' chief sources of dissatisfaction.

(C) Finally, the author provides no support for the claim that students are dissatisfied with the teaching and library resources at Fern Valley.

---

36 The following appeared in an article in a college departmental newsletter.
以下内容摘自某个大学院系简报上的一篇文章。

"Professor Taylor of Jones University is promoting a model of foreign language instruction in which students receive ten weeks of intensive training, then go abroad to live with families for ten weeks. The superiority of the model, Professor Taylor contends, is proved by the results of a study in which foreign language tests given to students at 25 other colleges show that first-year foreign language students at Jones speak more fluently after only ten to twenty weeks in the program than do nine out of ten foreign language majors elsewhere at the time of their graduation."

Jones大学的Taylor教授推出了一种全新的外语教学方案：先让学生接受10周的强化培训，然后把他们送到国外和当地家庭合住10周的时间。Taylor教授认为该教学方案的优越性已被某项研究结果证实。该项研究对另外25所大学的学生进行了外语测试，其结果表明，Jones大学一年级外语系学生在参加该教学方案仅10周或者20周后，其口语的流利程度就超过了其他学校90%的外语系学生毕业时的水平。

(A) First, the author fails to provide enough information regarding the procedure of the study, the size of the sample and the content of the test.

(B) Secondly, we cannot tell from this article whether the universities in the study, or their students, are comparable in other ways.

(C) Finally, the author unfairly presumes that speaking fluently equals proficiency in a foreign language.

---

37 The following appeared as part of an article in the business section of a local newspaper.
以下内容摘自某地方报纸商业版上的一篇文章。

"Motorcycle X has been manufactured in the United States for over 70 years. Although one foreign company has copied the motorcycle and is selling it for less, the company has failed to attract motorcycle X customers—some say because its product lacks the exceptionally loud noise made by motorcycle X. But there must be some other explanation. After all, foreign cars tend to be quieter than similar American-made cars, but they sell at least as well. Also, television advertisements for motorcycle X highlight its durability and sleek lines, not its noisiness, and the ads typically have voice-overs or rock music rather than engineroar on the sound track."

X摩托车在美国已有70多年的生产历史。尽管一家外国公司仿造了这种摩托车并低价出售，该公司却不能吸引X摩托车的客户——有人说这是因为它的产品不像X摩托车那样，骑行时会发出非常响亮的轰鸣声。但这应该不是唯一的原因。毕竟，外国汽车一般比类似的美国汽车噪音小，但是这些外国汽车的销路非常好，至少是和美国汽车一样好。再者，X摩托车的电视广告强调的是该车的经久耐用和流线型设计，而不是它所发出的噪音大小，而且广告的音轨上通常出现的是画外音或者摇滚音乐，而非引擎的轰鸣声。

（A） The main problem with the argument is that the argument rests on the assumption that what automobile customers find appealing is analogous to what motorcycle customers find appealing.

（B） Another problem with the reasoning in the argument is the claim that engine noise is not an important selling feature of Motorcycle X because it is not explicitly touted in advertisements.

38 The following appeared in the editorial section of a campus newspaper.
以下内容摘自某校报的社论部分。

"Because occupancy rates for campus housing fell during the last academic year, so did housing revenues. To solve the problem, campus housing officials should reduce the number of available housing units, thereby increasing the occupancy rates. Also, to keep students from choosing to live off-campus, housing officials should lower the rents, thereby increasing demand."

因为上学年校园公寓的入住率有所下降，所以住房收入也相应减少。为了解决这个问题，学校公寓管理者应该减少可供入住的公寓数量，以提高入住率。此外，公寓管理者还应通过降低房租来吸引学生，减少校外租房的学生数量，从而扩大校内的租房需求。

（A） In the first place, the author unfairly assumes that boosting occupancy rates for campus housing will improve revenues.

（B） Secondly, the argument is based on an unwarranted assumption that lowering rents will lead to higher revenues by increasing demand.

（C） Finally, the author fails to establish a causal relationship between current rental rates and low demand.

39 The following appeared in an Avia Airlines departmental memorandum.
以下内容摘自Avia航空公司的部门备忘录。

"On average, 9 out of every 1, 000 passengers who traveled on Avia Airlines last year filed a complaint about our baggage-handling procedures. This means that although some 1 percent of our passengers were unhappy with those procedures, the overwhelming majority were quite satisfied with them; thus it would appear that a review of the procedures is not important to our goal of maintaining or increasing the number of Avia's passengers."

去年Avia航空公司航班的乘客中有千分之九就行李托运流程向我们提出了投诉。这表明，尽管有近百分之一的乘客对这一流程表示不满，绝大多数的乘客还是相当满意的。由此可见，审查行李托运流程对我们保持或增加客流量这一目标并不重要。

（A） To begin with, the author provides no evidence to support the assumption that the 99 percent of Avia passengers who did not complain were happy with the airline's baggage-handling procedures.

（B） Secondly, lacking any information about the number of passengers per flight and about the complaint records of competing airlines, the statistics presented in the memorandum might distort the seriousness of the problem.

40 The following appeared as part of an article in a weekly newsmagazine.
以下内容摘自某新闻周刊上的一篇文章。

"The country of Sacchar can best solve its current trade deficit problem by lowering the price of sugar, its primary export. Such an action would make Sacchar better able to compete for

Sacchar国解决贸易赤字的最好方法是降低其主要出口物——糖的价格。这一举动将使Sacchar国在与其他糖出口国的

markets with other sugar-exporting countries. The sale of Sacchar's sugar abroad would increase, and this increase would substantially reduce Sacchar's trade deficit."

竞争中取得更好的市场。Sacchar国的糖在国外的销量将会增加，这将使Sacchar国的贸易赤字大幅下降。

(A) In the first place, this argument is based on an oversimplified analysis of the trade deficit problem Sacchar currently faces.

(B) In the second place, the author's argument is based on a questionable assumption that increasing sales by lowering the price of sugar will yield an increase in income and substantially reduce Sacchar's trade deficit.

41 The following appeared as part of an article in a trade publication.
以下内容摘自某贸易刊物中的一篇文章。

"Stronger laws are needed to protect new kinds of home-security systems from being copied and sold by imitators. With such protection, manufacturers will naturally invest in the development of new home-security products and production technologies. Without stronger laws, therefore, manufacturers will cut back on investment. From this will follow a corresponding decline not only in product quality and marketability, but also in production efficiency, and thus ultimately a loss of manufacturing jobs in the industry."

我们需要更有力的法律来保护新型住宅安全系统不被仿效者仿造并销售。有了这种保护，生产商自然就会投资研发新型的住宅安全产品和生产技术。没有严厉的法律，生产商将会削减投入。这将导致产品质量、可销售性及至生产效率的滑坡，最后会造成该行业生产性工作岗位的减少。

(A) First, the argument depends on an unfounded assumption that existing copyright, patent and trade secret laws are inadequate to protect home-security system design.

(B) Secondly, the author unfairly assumes that stronger legal protection will encourage manufacturers to invest in home security-system production, while the absence of strong legal protection will have the opposite effect.

(C) Finally, the author fails to establish a causal relationship between imposing stronger laws and what happens in the marketplace.

42 The following appeared in the opinion section of a national newsmagazine.
以下内容摘自某全国性新闻杂志的观点栏目。

"To reverse the deterioration of the postal service, the government should raise the price of postage stamps. This solution will no doubt prove effective, since the price increase will generate larger revenues and will also reduce the volume of mail, thereby eliminating the strain on the existing system and contributing to improved morale."

为了扭转邮政业务越来越不景气的局面，政府应该提高邮票的价格。这种解决方法毫无疑问将是有效的。因为价格提升会产生更大的收益，而且会减少邮件数量，从而缓解目前系统中存在的紧张局面，并有助于提高员工的士气。

(A) To begin with, the argument is based on a mistaken assumption that eliminating strain on the system and improving employee morale are mutually achievable by way of an increase in stamp prices.

(B) Furthermore, the author's conclusion that the proposed price increase is necessary to reduce deterioration of the postal service relies on the unwarranted assumption that no other action would achieve the same result.

(C) Thirdly, the author unfairly assumes that reducing mail volume and increasing revenues will improve employee morale.

（D）Finally, the author provides no evidence to support the assumption that a price increase will reduce the volume of mail.

---

43 The following appeared in an article in the health section of a newspaper.
以下内容摘自某报纸健康版面上的一篇文章。

"There is a common misconception that university hospitals are better than community or private hospitals. This notion is unfounded, however: the university hospitals in our region employ 15 percent fewer doctors, have a 20 percent lower success rate in treating patients, make far less overall profit, and pay their medical staff considerably less than do private hospitals. Furthermore, many doctors at university hospitals typically divide their time among teaching, conducting research, and treating patients. From this it seems clear that the quality of care at university hospitals is lower than that at other kinds of hospitals."

一种普遍的错误观念认为，大学附属医院比社区医院或私立医院要好。但这种观念是毫无根据的：我们地区的大学附属医院和私立医院相比，医生人数少15%，患者的治愈率低20%，总体利润要少得多，给医务人员的待遇也低得多。另外，大学附属医院的医生大多身兼数职：教学、科研以及治疗。由此可见，大学附属医院的医疗质量显然要比其他医院低。

（A）The main problem with the argument is that the author provides no evidence to demonstrate that university hospitals in this region are representative of all university hospitals.

（B）Secondly, the fact that university hospitals have a lower success rate in treating patients is not sufficient to support the claim that the quality of care is lower in university hospitals than it is at other hospitals.

（C）Finally, the author fails to establish a causal link between the various factors cited in the comparison and the quality of care delivered to patients.

---

44 The following is part of a business plan created by the management of the Megamart grocery store.
以下内容摘自Megamart杂货店管理层制定的一份商业计划。

"Our total sales have increased this year by 20 percent since we added a pharmacy section to our grocery store. Clearly, the customer's main concern is the convenience afforded by one-stop shopping. The surest way to increase our profits over the next couple of years, therefore, is to add a clothing department along with an automotive supplies and repair shop. We should also plan to continue adding new departments and services, such as a restaurant and a garden shop, in subsequent years. Being the only store in the area that offers such a range of services will give us a competitive advantage over other local stores."

自从我们在杂货店内增加了药品部后，本年度我们的销售总额增加了20%。显然，顾客主要关注的是一次性购物的便利性。因此，在以后的两三年内，提高利润最稳妥的办法是增加一个服装部和一个汽车配件及维修店。我们还要计划在以后的年份里继续增加新的部门和服务，比如餐馆和园艺商店。成为本地唯一一家拥有如此广泛服务的商店会使我们比本地其他的杂货店更具竞争力。

（A）To begin with, the management unfairly assumes that the increase in total sales was due to the addition of the pharmacy section.

（B）Secondly, granted that the increase in total sales was due to the addition of the pharmacy section, this fact alone is insufficient to support the claim that additional departments will increase sales even further.

45 The following appeared as part of a column in a popular entertainment magazine.
以下内容摘自一份流行娱乐杂志上的某个专栏。

"The producers of the forthcoming movie 3003 will be most likely to maximize their profits if they are willing to pay Robin Good several million dollars to star in it—even though that amount is far more than any other person involved with the movie will make. After all, Robin has in the past been paid a similar amount to work in several films that were very financially successful."

即将开拍的电影《3003》的制片人如果愿意花几百万美元邀请Robin Good来主演这部电影，最有可能使他们的利润最大化，尽管Robin Good的片酬要比其他演员的高得多。毕竟，过去也有一些影片开出相同的片酬聘请Robin Good，结果这些电影全都成功地赚了很多钱。

（A）In the first place, the author offers no evidence to support the assumption that the financial success of several other films was due entirely to Robin Good's participation.

（B）Secondly, even if it were the case that Robin's participation had brought about financial success of several other films, there is no guarantee that Robin's participation in the movie 3003 will maximize its profits.

46 The following appeared in a memorandum from the directors of a security and safety consulting service.
以下内容摘自某安全保险咨询公司董事会的备忘录。

"Our research indicates that over the past six years no incidents of employee theft have been reported within ten of the companies that have been our clients. In analyzing the security practices of these ten companies, we have further learned that each of them requires its employees to wear photo identification badges while at work. In the future, therefore, we should recommend the use of such identification badges to all of our clients."

我们的研究指出，过去6年间我们的10家客户公司中没有员工内盗的记录。我们对这10家公司的安全措施进行了分析，进一步发现它们全都要求员工在上班期间佩戴有照片的工作徽章。因此，我们将向所有的客户推荐使用这种工作徽章。

（A）The main problem with the argument is that the author fails to establish a causal connection between wearing identification badges and the absence of employee theft.

（B）Secondly, the directors unfairly assume that employee theft is a problem that is common among their clients and about which their clients are equally concerned.

（C）Finally, even if it is the case that the use of such identification badges is effective in preventing employee from thieving in the ten companies in question, there is no guarantee that the same method would work just as well for all the other clients of the consulting firm.

47 The following appeared as part of an article in the business section of a local newspaper.
以下内容摘自某地方报纸商业版面上的一篇文章。

"The owners of the Cumquat Café evidently made a good business decision in moving to a new location, as can be seen from the fact that the Café will soon celebrate its second anniversary there. Moreover, it appears that businesses are not likely to succeed at the old location: since the Café's move,

乔迁新址对Cumquat餐馆的业主而言，无疑是一项明智的商业举措，这可以从该餐馆很快就要在新址举行两周年店庆这一事实中看出。此外，在Cumquat餐馆旧址经营的企业看起来都不太可能取得

three different businesses—a tanning salon, an antique emporium, and a pet-grooming shop—have occupied its former spot."

成功。自从餐馆搬走后，该地已经换了三家不同的企业：一家日光浴沙龙，一家古董店和一家宠物美容店。

(A) In the first place, the author fails to offer sufficient evidence to support the conclusion that Cumquat Café made a good business decision in moving to a new location.

(B) Secondly, the author provides no evidence to support the assumption that the reason for the failure of the three businesses was their location.

---

48 **The following appeared in the editorial section of a local newspaper.**
以下内容摘自某地方报纸的社论。

"The profitability of Croesus Company, recently restored to private ownership, is a clear indication that businesses fare better under private ownership than under public ownership."

最近交给私人经营的Croesus公司，其盈利能力表明，企业在私人拥有产权的条件下要比在公有产权条件下运营得好。

(A) To begin with, the argument makes an unfounded assumption that Croesus Company is representative of all companies that have converted from public to private ownership.

(B) Secondly, the author unfairly assumes that the reason for Croesus's profitability was its conversion from public to private ownership.

---

49 **The following appeared in the editorial section of a local newspaper.**
以下内容摘自某地方报纸的社论。

"If the paper from every morning edition of the nation's largest newspaper were collected and rendered into paper pulp that the newspaper could reuse, about 5 million trees would be saved each year. This kind of recycling is unnecessary, however, since the newspaper maintains its own forests to ensure an uninterrupted supply of paper."

如果能将全国发行量最大的报纸早间版所用的纸全部回收并化成纸浆供该报纸重新使用，每年就可以少砍500万棵树。然而，这种回收是不必要的，因为该报拥有它自己的森林，以确保纸张源源不断的供应。

(A) In the first place, the argument depends on a problematic assumption that the only reason to recycle the newspaper is to ensure a continuous supply of paper.

(B) Also, the author unfairly assumes that only the newspaper would have an interest in the pulp processed from its recycled morning edition.

---

50 **The following appeared as part of a business plan recommended by the new manager of a musical rock group called Zapped.**
以下内容摘自一个名为Zapped的摇滚乐队的新经纪人推荐的商业计划。

"To succeed financially, Zapped needs greater name recognition. It should therefore diversify its commercial enterprises. The rock group Zonked plays the same type of music that Zapped plays, but it is much better known than Zapped because in addition to its concert tours and four

要想在经济上取得成功，Zapped必须有更高的知名度。因此，它应该使自身的商业运作多元化。摇滚乐队Zonked的音乐风格与Zapped类似，但其知名度却比Zapped高，这是因为Zonked不但举办巡回演出会并出了

albums, Zonked has a series of posters, a line of clothing and accessories, and a contract with a major advertising agency to endorse a number of different products."

四张专辑，还发布了一系列海报，设计了系列服装及相关装饰，并和一家大型广告公司签约代言多种不同的商品。

（A） The main problem with this argument involves the author's assumption that the only relevant difference between Zapped and Zonked is that Zonked has greater name recognition than Zapped.

（B） Additionally, the author unfairly assumes that name recognition is all that is required for financial success.

---

51 The following appeared in a magazine article on trends and lifestyles.
以下内容摘某流行和时尚杂志上的一篇文章。

"In general, people are not as concerned as they were a decade ago about regulating their intake of red meat and fatty cheeses. Walk into the Heart's Delight, a store that started selling organic fruits and vegetables and whole-grain flours in the 1960's, and you will also find a wide selection of cheeses made with high butterfat content. Next door, the owners of the Good Earth Café, an old vegetarian restaurant, are still making a modest living, but the owners of the new House of Beef across the street are millionaires."

一般而言，人们已经不像10年前那样关心他们的肉类和高脂奶酪的摄入量。走进Heart's Delight杂货店———一家从60年代开始就出售绿色水果和蔬菜以及无公害面粉的商店，你会看到品种丰富的富含乳脂的奶酪。隔壁的Good Earth餐馆是一家老式素菜馆，它的业主们仍然过着朴素的生活，而街对面新开的一家牛肉店的业主们都已经是百万富翁了。

（A） In the first place, the argument relies on the unfounded assumption that the dietary habits and attitudes of customers at these three businesses reflect those of the general population.

（B） Secondly, trends at these three businesses do not necessarily reflect the dietary habits and attitudes of their customers in the way the author claims.

（C） Finally, the author unfairly assumes that the different financial conditions of the two restaurants were caused by their respective menu items—vegetarian food at the former and red meat as well as fatty cheeses at the latter.

---

52 The following editorial appeared in the Elm City paper.
以下社论摘自Elm市报。

"The construction last year of a shopping mall in downtown Oak City was a mistake. Since the mall has opened, a number of local businesses have closed, and the downtown area suffers from an acute parking shortage, and arrests for crime and vagrancy have increased in the nearby Oak City Park. Elm City should pay attention to the example of the Oak City mall and deny the application to build a shopping mall in Elm City."

去年在Oak市中心修建购物中心是个错误的举动。自从该购物中心开业以来，大量的本地企业倒闭了，市中心受到停车位严重缺乏的困扰，并且在附近的Oak市公园拘捕的罪犯和流浪汉的数量也有所增加。Elm市应该以Oak市为戒，杜绝在Elm市建设购物中心。

（A） To begin with, the author unfairly assumes that the construction of the new mall is the cause of the various problems cited.

（B） Secondly, the author has focused only on the negative effects the mall has had on the city.

（C） Finally, granted that it is the construction of a shopping mall in downtown Oak City last year that might have caused the various problems cited, building another shopping mall in Elm City will not necessarily lead to all these problems.

53 **The following appeared as part of an editorial in a weekly newsmagazine.**
以下内容摘自某新闻周刊上的一篇社论。

"Historically, most of this country's engineers have come from our universities; recently, however, our university-age population has begun to shrink, and decreasing enrollments in our high schools clearly show that this drop in numbers will continue throughout the remainder of the decade. Consequently, our nation will soon be facing a shortage of trained engineers. If we are to remain economically competitive in the world marketplace, then, we must increase funding for education—and quickly."

历史上，我国的大多数工程师都接受过大学教育。然而，最近我们的大学适龄人口开始缩减，而高中的注册人数减少清楚地表明大学生数量下降这一趋势将在这十年剩下的几年里继续下去。因此，我们国家很快会就面临缺乏训练有素的工程师的局面。如果要在国际市场中保持经济上的竞争力，我们就必须尽快增加教育基金。

（A） In the first place, the argument is based on an unfounded assumption that because our university-age population is shrinking, university enrollments will likewise shrink.

（B） Secondly, decreases in overall enrollments do not necessarily result in proportional enrollment decreases in each field of study.

（C） Thirdly, the author fails to establish a causal relationship between economic competitiveness in the world market and the number of engineers coming out of universities.

（D） Finally, the author provides no evidence to support the assumption that increased funding for education will solve the problem of the decline in the university-age population as well as the shortage of trained engineers.

54 已被ETS删除。

55 **The following appeared in an Excelsior Company memorandum.**
以下内容摘自Excelsior公司的备忘录。

"The Excelsior Company plans to introduce its own brand of coffee. Since coffee is an expensive food item, and since there are already many established brands of coffee, the best way to gain customers for the Excelsior brand is to do what Superior, the leading coffee company, did when it introduced the newest brand in its line of coffees: conduct a temporary sales promotion that offers free samples, price reductions, and discount coupons for the new brand."

Excelsior公司计划推出自己的咖啡品牌。因为咖啡是一种奢侈食品，而且已经有很多知名的咖啡品牌，所以Excelsior品牌赢得顾客的最好方法是仿照Superior——一家主流咖啡公司——在其系列产品中加入最新品牌时的做法：通过临时派发免费样品、降价以及发放优惠卷的方法来进行新品牌的促销。

（A） First, the argument depends on the unwarranted assumption that a promotional strategy that works for one company will work for another.

（B） Secondly, the argument is based on the unfounded assumption that Excelsior can afford a promotional plan similar to Superior's.

（C） Finally, the author provides no evidence to support the assumption that Superior's promotional campaign for its newest coffee was successful.

56 已被ETS删除。

57 **The following appeared as part of an article in a popular arts and leisure magazine.**
以下内容摘自某份流行艺术与休闲杂志上的一篇文章。

"The safety codes governing the construction of public buildings are becoming far too strict. The surest way for architects and builders to prove that they have met the minimum requirements established by these codes is to construct buildings by using the same materials and methods that are currently allowed. But doing so means that there will be very little significant technological innovation within the industry, and hence little evolution of architectural styles and design—merely because of the strictness of these safety codes."

建设公共建筑物的安全条例已经变得过于严格了。对建筑师和施工者来说，证明他们已经达到这些安全条例所规定的最低要求最可靠的方法是采用当前允许使用的材料和技术来构建公共建筑物。然而，这样做就意味着在建筑业内将会鲜有技术革新，从而也不会有建筑风格和设计的进步——而这些都是由安全条例过于严格引起的。

（A）In the first place, the evidence cited pertains only to the construction of public buildings, yet the author draws a conclusion about the whole building industry.

（B）Secondly, the author fails to provide any concrete evidence to prove that the strict safety codes governing public buildings will have the effects predicted.

58 **The following is from a campaign by Big Boards, Inc., to convince companies in River City that their sales will increase if they use Big Boards billboards for advertising their locally manufactured products.**
以下内容摘自Big Boards有限公司的一份广告计划，旨在使位于River市的公司相信如果他们使用Big Boards的广告牌来宣传他们在本地制造的产品，那么他们的销售额就会上升。

"The potential of Big Boards to increase sales of your products can be seen from an experiment we conducted last year. We increased public awareness of the name of the current national women's marathon champion by publishing her picture and her name on billboards in River City for a period of three months. Before this time, although the champion had just won her title and was receiving extensive national publicity, only five percent of 15,000 randomly surveyed residents of River City could correctly name the champion when shown her picture; after the three-month advertising experiment, 35 percent of respondents from a second survey could supply her name."

Big Boards使你的产品销售额上升的潜在能力可以从去年我们做的一个试验中看出。我们把当前全国女子马拉松冠军的照片和名字印在River市的广告牌上并保持3个月的时间，从而提高了她的知名度。在这之前，尽管冠军刚刚得到她的头衔而且得到了全国人民的广泛关注，但在随机抽取的1.5万名River市居民中只有5%的人可以在看到照片时准确叫出她的名字。3个月的广告宣传之后，第二次调查中有35%的应答者可以叫出她的名字。

（A）The main problem with the argument is that it relies on a false analogy. Name recognition of an athlete is not analogous to the sales of products.

（B）Another problem with the argument is that the author ignores other possible factors that might have contributed to the popularity of the current national women's marathon champion.

（C）Finally, the conclusion of the argument depends on a questionable survey.

59 **The following appeared as part of an article on government funding of environmental regulatory agencies.**

以下内容摘自关于政府为环境管理机构筹资的一篇文章。

"When scientists finally learn how to create large amounts of copper from other chemical elements, the regulation of copper mining will become unnecessary. For one thing, since the amount of potentially available copper will no longer be limited by the quantity of actual copper deposits, the problem of overmining will quickly be eliminated altogether. For another, manufacturers will not need to use synthetic copper substitutes, the production of which creates pollutants. Thus, since two problems will be settled—overmining and pollution—it makes good sense to reduce funding for mining regulation and either save the money or reallocate it where it is needed more."

当科学家们最终得知如何用其他化学元素大量生产铜以后，对铜矿开采进行管理就显得不必要了。首先，由于可获得的铜的产量不再受限于铜矿的实际蕴藏量，过度开采的问题很快就会完全地清除。另外，合成的铜替代品将不再需要，生产这种物质会对环境造成污染。由于这两个问题——过度开采和环境污染——都得到了解决，所以减少采矿治理的基金，将之节约下来或用到更需要的地方是非常合理的。

（A）In the first place, the conclusion is based on a hasty generalization. Advances in copper synthesis technology will in all likelihood have no bearing on whether regulation of other kinds of mining should be changed.

（B）Secondly, the argument rests on an unwarranted assumption that copper mining will slow down and manufacturers will stop using synthetic copper substitutes once copper can be chemically synthesized.

（C）Finally, the author provides no evidence to substantiate the assumption that synthesizing copper will not create the same kind of pollution problems as those resulting from the synthesis of copper substitutes.

60 **The following appeared as part of an article in a popular science magazine.**

以下内容摘自某通俗科学杂志上的一篇文章。

"Scientists must typically work 60 to 80 hours a week if they hope to further their careers; consequently, good and affordable all-day child care must be made available to both male and female scientists if they are to advance in their fields. Moreover, requirements for career advancement must be made more flexible so that preschool-age children can spend a significant portion of each day with a parent."

科学家如果希望在事业上有所发展，那么他们每周必须工作60到80个小时。因此，服务周到且价格合理的全天儿童看护对希望在自身领域有所发展的男性和女性科学家来说是必不可少的。而且，为有所建树而做的所有研究工作必须灵活安排，以便学龄前儿童每天都能和父母中的一位一起度过足够长的时间。

（A）To begin with, the main problem with this argument is that it is self-contradictory in recommending both putting scientists' children in all-day child care facilities and their spending a significant amount of time each day with children.

（B）Secondly, the recommendations rest on the unwarranted assumption that all, or at least most, scientists have young or preschool-age children.

61

The following appeared as part of a recommendation by one of the directors of the Beta Company.

以下内容摘自Beta公司某经理人的一份建议书。

"The Alpha Company has just reduced its workforce by laying off fifteen percent of its employees in all divisions and at all levels, and it is encouraging early retirement for other employees. As you know, the Beta Company manufactures some products similar to Alpha's, but our profits have fallen over the last few years. To improve Beta's competitive position, we should try to hire a significant number of Alpha's former workers, since these experienced workers can provide valuable information about Alpha's successful methods, will require little training, and will be particularly motivated to compete against Alpha."

Alpha公司刚刚通过在所有部门所有层次减15%的员工这一举措减少了员工人数，同时还鼓励其他员工提前退休。众所周知，Beta公司生产的某些产品与Alpha公司相类似，但我们的利润在过去几年内下降了。为了提高Beta的竞争力，我们应该设法大量雇用Alpha的前雇员，因为这些有经验的工人能提供关于Alpha成功方法的有用信息，基本不需要培训，并且能够很容易激起他们与Alpha竞争的热情。

(A) For one thing, the argument presupposes that Alpha's methods are successful. This is not necessarily the case.

(B) For another, the author unfairly assumes that the former Alpha employees hired by Beta will be well-trained and valuable.

(C) In addition, the argument depends on a problematic assumption that Alpha and Beta are sufficiently similar and that former Alpha employees could be of special value to Beta.

(D) Finally, the assertion that former Alpha employees would be motivated to compete against Alpha is partially unwarranted.

62

The following appeared in the letters-to-the-editor section of a local newspaper.

以下内容摘自某地方报纸上的编辑信箱版块。

"Muscle Monthly, a fitness magazine that regularly features pictures of body builders using state-of-the-art exercise machines, frequently sells out, according to the owner of Skyview Newsstand. To help maximize fitness levels in our town's residents, we should, therefore, equip our new community fitness center with such machines."

根据Skyview报摊摊主所述，Muscle Monthly杂志经常会销售一空。这是一份健康杂志，它定期刊登使用最好训练器械的健美运动员的特写照片。因此，为了提高我镇居民的健康水平，我们应该给新社区健身中心装备这样的器械。

(A) In the first place, the argument is based on the questionable assumption that the bodybuilders pictured using the machines in Muscle Monthly magazine reached their state of fitness as a result of using these machines.

(B) Secondly, the author unfairly assumes that machines that are suitable for bodybuilding will also be suitable to help maximize the fitness levels of the town's residents.

(C) Finally, even if it were the case that such machines can help maximize fitness levels, equipping the new community fitness center with such machines can not guarantee that the residents will use them.

63 **The following appeared as part of an article in the business section of a local newspaper.**
以下内容摘自某地方报纸商业版的一篇文章。

"The Cumquat Café made a mistake in moving to a new location. After one year at the new spot, it is doing about the same volume of business as before, but the owners of the RoboWrench plumbing supply wholesale outlet that took over its old location are apparently doing better: RoboWrench is planning to open a store in a neighboring city."

Cumquat咖啡店搬到新地址是个错误。到新址一年以后，它的营业额和以前基本一样。但在它原址开业的RoboWrench管道设备批发商店的店主显然做得更好：RoboWrench正计划在附近某个城市再开一家商店。

（A）First, the argument is based on a meaningless comparison between two businesses which are totally different from each other.

（B）Secondly, the argument provides no concrete evidence to demonstrate that RoboWrench is doing better since it took over Cumquat's old location.

（C）Finally, the claim that Cumquat made a mistake in moving may be too hasty, since the conclusion is based on only one year's business at the new location.

64 **The following appeared in a memorandum from the Director of Human Resources to the executive officers of Company X.**
以下内容摘自X公司人力资源经理递交给该公司行政官员的备忘录。

"Last year, we surveyed our employees on improvements needed at Company X by having them rank, in order of importance, the issues presented in a list of possible improvements. Improved communications between employees and management was consistently ranked as the issue of highest importance by the employees who responded to the survey. As you know, we have since instituted regular commun-ications sessions conducted by high-level management, which the employees can attend on a voluntary basis. Therefore, it is likely that most employees at Company X now feel that the improvement most needed at the company has been made."

去年，我们就X公司需要哪些改进这个问题对员工展开了调查，让他们把调查表中所列出的可能需要改进的问题按照重要性排序。根据参与调查的员工反应，"加强员工和管理层的沟通"这一问题被一致认为最具重要性。如你所知，自那以后我们建立了由高层管理人员组织、雇员可以自愿参加的定期交流会。因此，X公司大多数员工现在会认为最应该改进的问题已经解决了。

（A）In the first place, the argument rests on a doubtful survey. In the absence of information about the number of employees surveyed and the number of respondents, it is impossible to assess the validity of the survey results.

（B）Secondly, the author fails to provide any evidence to substantiate the assumption that the list in the survey included all the important issues the employees are most concerned about.

（C）Finally, granted that improved communications between employees and management is the issue with which the employees are most concerned, regular communication sessions will not necessarily address the problem.

65 **The following appeared in a memorandum from the vice president of Road Food, an international chain of fast-food restaurants.**

以下内容摘自Road Food———一家国际快餐连锁店副总的备忘录。

"This past year, we spent almost as much on advertising as did our main competitor, Street Eats, which has fewer restaurants than we do. Although it appeared at first that our advertising agency had created a campaign along the lines we suggested, in fact our total profits were lower than those of Street Eats. In order to motivate our advertising agency to perform better, we should start basing the amount that we pay it on how much total profit we make each year."

过去的一年中，我们和我们的主要竞争者Street Eats在广告上的花费差不多。他们的餐馆比我们少。虽然表面上看起来我们的广告代理商依据我们的规划开展了活动，实际上我们的总利润比Street Eats低。为了促使我们的广告商做得更好，我们应该开始根据每年获得的总利润来给报酬。

（A）To begin with, the author unfairly assumes that it was the advertising campaign that caused the Road Food's low profits.

（B）Secondly, the author suggests that the advertising agency failed to carry out Road Food's guidelines, and that this failure was the reason for its disappointing profits.

（C）Thirdly, the author's comparison between Road Food and Street Eats is less pertinent than a comparison between Road Food's own profits prior to its latest advertising campaign and its profits during this campaign.

（D）Finally, the author unfairly assumes that the advertising agency will be more motivated if its fee is based on Road Food profits.

66 **The following appeared in the promotional literature for Cerberus dog food.**

以下内容摘自Cerberus狗食的广告词。

"Obesity is a great problem among pet dogs, just as it is among their human owners. Obesity in humans is typically caused by consuming more calories than the body needs. For humans, a proper diet for losing weight is a reduced-calorie diet that is high in fiber and carbohydrates but low in fat. Therefore, the best way for dog owners to help their dogs lose weight in a healthy way is to restrict the dog's diet to Cerberus reduced-calorie dog food, which is high in fiber and carbohydrates but low in fat."

如同他们的主人一样，肥胖也是宠物狗的一大问题。人类的肥胖主要是由于他们摄入了超过身体所需的热量所致。对人类而言，适宜减肥的饮食是含热量低的食物，即纤维素和碳水化合物含量高但脂肪含量低的食物。因此，狗主人帮助他们的宠物健康减肥的最好方法是只让它吃Cerberus的低热量狗食，这种狗食纤维素及碳水化合物的含量高，但脂肪的含量低。

（A）First, the argument rests on an unfounded assumption that the cause of obesity in dogs is the same as the cause in humans.

（B）Secondly, the author unfairly assumes that treatment that is effective for humans will be equally effective for dogs.

（C）Finally, even if the reduced-calorie diet that is high in fiber and carbohydrates but low in fat can help the dogs lose weight, the Cerberus dog food is not necessarily the best choice for the dogs' owners to deal with their pets' obesity.

67 The following appeared in an article in a travel magazine.

以下内容摘自某份旅游杂志上的一篇文章。

"After the airline industry began requiring airlines to report their on-time rates, Speedee Airlines achieved the number one on-time rate, with over 89 percent of its flights arriving on time each month. And now Speedee is offering more flights to more destinations than ever before. Clearly, Speedee is the best choice for today's business traveler."

航空业开始要求航空公司报告他们的准时率以后，Speedee航空公司以每月89%以上的准时到达率雄居榜首。现在，Speedee提供了更多的航班，可以到达更多地方。显然，Speedee是当今商务旅行者的最好选择。

(A) For one thing, the argument depends on an unwarranted assumption that on-time rates, number of flights, and destination choices are the only features of airlines service that determines how a particular airline ranks overall for a business traveler.

(B) For another, the author's claim that "Speedee now offers more flights to more destinations than ever before" is too vague to be meaningful.

(C) Finally, the argument fails to indicate how long ago the industry began requiring airlines to report on-time rates.

68 The following appeared in a memorandum to the planning department of an investment firm.

以下内容摘自某投资公司企划部的一份备忘录。

"Costs have begun dropping for several types of equipment currently used to convert solar energy into electricity. Moreover, some exciting new technologies for converting solar energy are now being researched and developed. Hence we can expect that solar energy will soon become more cost efficient and attractive than coal or oil as a source of electrical power. We should, therefore, encourage investment in Solario, a new manufacturer of solar-powered products. After all, Solario's chief executive was once on the financial planning team for Ready-to-Ware, a software engineering firm that has shown remarkable growth since its recent incorporation."

目前使用的几种将太阳能转换为电能的设备成本开始下降。并且，一些令人兴奋的太阳能转换的新技术正在研究开发中。因此我们可以预期作为电力来源的太阳能将会比煤和石油更有效益且更吸引人。所以，我们应该鼓励人们对Solario———一家新兴的太阳能设备制造厂投资。毕竟，Solario的首席执行官曾任职于Ready-to-Ware的财务计划部，那家新近成立后就发展迅速的软件工程公司。

(A) In the first place, the author fails to provide any substantial evidence to support the assumption that the current costs of converting solar energy into electricity are lower or at least equal to the costs of using traditional energy sources, and therefore, the new type of energy will be financially and environmentally more attractive to users.

(B) In the second place, even if the cost reduction of the solar energy is immediately accessible, it is still imprudent to say that solar energy is more attractive compared with coal and oil as a source of electrical power.

(C) Finally, the author unfairly assumes that the previous business experience of Solario's chief executive will be an asset in the development of the new company.

69 已被ETS删除。

70 **The following appeared in a memorandum from the president of a company that makes shampoo.**
以下内容摘自某洗发香波公司总裁的一份备忘录。

"A widely publicized study claims that HR2, a chemical compound in our shampoo, can contribute to hair loss after prolonged use. This study, however, involved only 500 subjects. Furthermore, we have received no complaints from our customers during the past year, and some of our competitors actually use more HR2 per bottle of shampoo than we do. Therefore, we do not need to consider replacing the HR2 in our shampoo with a more expensive alternative."

一项广泛宣扬的研究声称,HR2——我们的洗发香波里所含的一种化合物——长期使用后可能导致脱发。但是,这项研究只涉及了500个接受实验者。此外,过去一年里我们并未从顾客那里接到投诉,而且我们的一些竞争者在一瓶香波里使用的HR2量比我们还要多。因此,我们不必考虑用更贵的物质来替代我们香波里的HR2。

（A） In the first place, the fact that the scientific study on HR2 involved only 500 subjects is insufficient grounds to disregard the results of the study.

（B） In the next place, the fact that none of the company's customers have complained of problems during the past year is not a reliable reason to believe that problems will not arise in the future.

（C） Finally, the fact that other companies use more HR2 in their products than the company in question is irrelevant to the question of whether the company should remove HR2 from its product.

71 已被ETS删除。

72 **The following appeared as part of a recommendation from the business manager of a department store.**
以下内容摘自某百货公司业务经理的一份备忘录。

"Local clothing stores reported that their profits decreased, on average, for the three-month period between August 1 and October 31. Stores that sell products for the home reported that, on average, their profits increased during this same period. Clearly, consumers are choosing to buy products for their homes instead of clothing. To take advantage of this trend, we should reduce the size of our clothing departments and enlarge our home furnishings and household products departments."

本地服装店报告说,从8月1号到10月31号这3个月里,他们的平均利润下降了。销售家庭用品的商店同期的平均利润却上升了。很明显,顾客正选择为他们的家购买用品而不是为自己买衣物。为了利用这个趋势,我们应该缩减我们服装部的规模,而扩大家庭装饰和家用产品部的规模。

（A） First, data gathered from a three-month period is insufficient to draw a general conclusion of the overall trend.

（B） Secondly, it is possible that the sales trend in a particular location is not representative of sales in other regions.

（C） Finally, the author fails to explain what actually caused an increase in profits for stores that sell household products and a decrease in profits for clothing stores.

73 **The following appeared in a letter to the editor of a regional newspaper.**
以下内容摘自写给某地区报纸编辑的一封信。

"In response to petitions from the many farmers and rural landowners throughout our region, the legislature has spent valuable time and effort enacting severe laws to deter motorists from picking fruit off the trees, trampling through the fields, and stealing samples of foliage. But how can our local lawmakers occupy themselves with such petty vandalism when crime and violence plague the nation's cities? The fate of apples and leaves is simply too trivial to merit their attention."

根据本地很多农民和荒地拥有者的请求，立法机构花费了很多宝贵的时间和精力制定法律以制止开车的人从树上摘水果、从田地中穿过、偷摘植物样本。但是我们的立法者怎么能在城市中犯罪和暴力泛滥时为这样一个小小的破坏行为耗费他们的时间呢？苹果和叶子的命运太微不足道了，不值得他们去注意。

（A）In the first place, the author is presenting a false dilemma by imposing an either-or choice between two courses of action that need not be mutually exclusive. It is equally possible that legislators can address both areas of concern concurrently.

（B）In the next place, the author unfairly trivializes the severity of rural crime by comparing it with urban crime.

（C）Moreover, the argument rests on the assumption that the legislators in question have the opportunity to address urban crime problems.

（D）The degree of severity of the illegal problems in the rural areas is irrelevant to the argument of the author. The legislation's responsibility is to establish laws to solve the emerging problems regardless of the level of the severity.

74 **The following appeared as part of an editorial in a campus newspaper.**
以下内容摘自某校报上的一篇社论。

"With an increasing demand for highly skilled workers, this nation will soon face a serious labor shortage. New positions in technical and professional occupations are increasing rapidly, while at the same time the total labor force is growing slowly. Moreover, the government is proposing to cut funds for aid to education in the near future."

随着对高度熟练工人需求的增加，这个国家很快就会面临劳动力严重短缺的局面。在技术和专业领域的新职位增长迅速，与此同时总的劳动力增长缓慢。此外，政府正计划在近期削减用于教育的投资。

（A）First of all, the increasing demand for highly skilled workers does not represent the overall situation.

（B）Secondly, the author's prediction is based on an unwarranted assumption that the current labor force is less than or at least equal to the demand.

（C）Thirdly, the author unfairly assumes that the present labor force is immobile and that the demand for highly skilled workers will have to be met by workers who are entering the labor market for the first time.

（D）Finally, the argument relies on a gratuitous assumption that the government proposal to cut funds for aid to education will prevent the nation from training more competent workers needed for the new positions in technical and professional occupations.

The following appeared as part of a memorandum from a government agency.
以下内容摘自某政府机构的一份备忘录。

"Given the limited funding available for the building and repair of roads and bridges, the government should not spend any money this year on fixing the bridge that crosses the Styx River. This bridge is located near a city with a weakening economy, so it is not as important as other bridges; moreover, the city population is small and thus unlikely to contribute a significant enough tax revenue to justify the effort of fixing the bridge."

在只得到有限资金用于建筑和修复路桥的情况下，政府今年不应该把任何资金投到对Styx河桥的修整上去。这座桥靠近一个经济正在衰退的城市，所以重要性不如其他的桥。而且，这个城市人口很少，看来不太可能创造很多的税收来证明修桥的努力是适当的。

（A）For one thing, the author fails to provide any evidence that other bridges are more important than the Styx River Bridge.

（B）For another, the author unfairly assumes that the importance of a bridge is determined solely by the economic condition of nearby cities.

（C）Moreover, the fact that the nearby city has a small population and a weakening economy does not prove that the city will not contribute significantly to tax revenues.

（D）Finally, the argument is based on an unwarranted assumption that a city should receive government services proportional to the tax dollars it contributes.

The following appeared as part of an article in an entertainment magazine.
以下内容摘自某娱乐杂志上的一篇文章。

"A series of books based on the characters of a popular movie are consistently bestsellers in local bookstores. Seeking to capitalize on the books' success, Vista Studios is planning to produce a movie sequel based on the books. Due to the success of the books and the original movie, the sequel will undoubtedly be profitable."

一系列关于一部流行电影中角色的书籍持续雄居本地书店的销售榜榜首。为了从书籍的成功中获利，Vista Studios 计划根据这些书拍摄电影续集。由于书籍和原电影的成功，续集将毫无疑问地获利。

（A）The major problem with the argument is that the success of the original movie and the books based on it does not necessitate the profitability of a movie sequel based on the books.

（B）Another problem with the argument is that the success of a series books in local bookstores tells little about their popularity nationwide or even worldwide.

The following appeared in a letter to the editor of a popular science and technology magazine.
以下内容摘自写给通俗科学技术杂志编辑的一封信。

"It is a popular myth that consumers are really benefiting from advances in agricultural technology. Granted—consumers are, on the average, spending a decreasing proportion of their income on food. But consider that the demand for food does not rise in proportion with real income.

一个流行的荒诞说法声称，消费者确实可以从农业技术的提高中获利。诚然，人们的饮食消费支出占他们收入的比例越来越小。但是，考虑到人们对食物的需求不会随着他们收入的增加而增长，所以随着实际收

As real income rises, therefore, consumers can be expected to spend a decreasing proportion of their income on food. Yet agricultural technology is credited with having made our lives better."

入的增加，消费者们就可以指望他们花在食物上的钱占收入的比例下降。而农业技术却据此被说成是让我们生活质量变好的因素。

（A）To begin with, the author provides no evidence to support the allegation that real incomes are rising.

（B）Secondly, the author unfairly assumes that it is the increases in real income that leads to consumers spending a decreasing proportion of their income on food.

（C）Finally, the author ignores other likely benefits of agricultural technology that have contributed to the consumers' quality of life.

---

78 **The following appeared in the editorial section of a local newspaper.**
以下内容摘自某地方报纸的社论部分。

"This city should be able to improve existing services and provide new ones without periodically raising the taxes of the residents. Instead, the city should require that the costs of services be paid for by developers who seek approval for their large new building projects. After all, these projects can be highly profitable to the developers, but they can also raise a city's expenses and increase the demand for its services."

这个城市不必周期性地提高居民税收就可以改善现有的服务，并提供新的服务。相反，城市应该要求为新的大型建筑项目申请许可的发展商支付服务成本。毕竟，这些项目给发展商带来了丰厚的利润，但他们也会提高一个城市的支出并增加对服务的需求。

（A）In the first place, the fact that developers can make large profits from building projects is not a good reason to require them to pay more than their fair share of service costs.

（B）In the second place, the increase in the city's expenses as well as the increase in demand for city services will most likely be offset by the tax revenues these projects generate.

---

79 **The following appeared in the editorial section of a local newspaper.**
以下内容摘自某地方报纸的社论部分。

"In order to avoid the serious health threats associated with many landfills, our municipality should build a plant for burning trash. An incinerator could offer economic as well as ecological advantages over the typical old-fashioned type of landfill: incinerators can be adapted to generate moderate amounts of electricity, and ash residue from some types of trash can be used to condition garden soil."

为了避免掩埋垃圾给健康带来的严重威胁，市政当局应该建立垃圾焚烧场。焚化炉与典型的老式垃圾掩埋法相比具有经济上和环境上的优势：焚化炉经过改造可以用来发电，同时某些类型的垃圾灰烬还可以用来改良花园土壤。

（A）First of all, the author fails to provide any evidence to support the assumption that incinerating trash does not cause any serious health threats.

（B）Secondly, the author's implicit assertion that incinerators are economically advantageous to landfills is poorly supported.

（C）Finally, the author unfairly assumes that discontinuing landfill operations would abate the heath threats they now pose.

The following appeared in the editorial section of a monthly business newsmagazine.
以下内容摘自某商业新闻月刊的社论部分。

"Most companies would agree that as the risk of physical injury occurring on the job increases, the wages paid to employees should also increase. Hence it makes financial sense for employers to make the workplace safer: they could thus reduce their payroll expenses and save money."

大多数公司都同意如果工作时受伤的概率增加，付给雇员的工资也应该增加。因此对雇主来说让工作场所更安全具有经济上的意义：这样他们就可以节省工资开支进而省钱。

(A) First of all, the author unjustifiably assumes that saving money by reducing employee's payroll can offset the expense of making the workplace safer.

(B) Secondly, the argument rests on an unwarranted assumption that companies would agree that as risk decreases wages should also decrease accordingly.

(C) Thirdly, the author unfairly assumes that the only benefit of a safer workplace is the savings employers could realize from lower wages.

81 **The following appeared as part of a company memorandum.**
以下内容摘自某公司的备忘录。

"Adopting an official code of ethics regarding business practices may in the long run do our company more harm than good in the public eye. When one of our competitors received unfavorable publicity for violating its own code of ethics, it got more attention from the media than it would have if it had had no such code. Rather than adopt an official code of ethics, therefore, we should instead conduct a publicity campaign that stresses the importance of protecting the environment and assisting charitable organizations."

采用官方的商业实践道德条例从长远来看对我公司在公众眼中的形象是弊大于利。当我们的一个竞争者由于违反了他自己的道德条例从而受到公众指责时，他会从媒体那里得到比没有这种条例时更多的关注。因此，与其采用官方的道德条例，我们不如开展一场强调保护环境和帮助慈善组织的宣传运动。

(A) In the first place, the author unfairly assumes that the two companies are sufficiently similar to ensure the same consequences of adopting an ethics code for this company as for its competitor.

(B) In the next place, the author unfairly assumes that the competitor was damaged by its code violation and the resulting publicity more than it would have been had it not violated its code.

(C) Finally, the author fails to provide evidence to support the assumption that conducting a publicity campaign is a better choice for the company than adopting the official code of ethics regarding business practices.

82 **The following appeared in the editorial section of a daily newspaper.**
以下内容摘自某日报的社论部分。

"Although forecasts of presidential elections based on opinion polls measure current voter preference, many voters keep changing their minds about whom they prefer until the last few days before the balloting. Some do not even make a final decision until they enter the voting booth. Forecasts based on

虽然，基于民意调查的总统选举预测可以估计当前选民的倾向，但很多选民直到选举前几天还是拿不定主意到底该选谁。一些人甚至在走进投票站之后才能做出最后的决定。因此，基于民意调

opinion polls are therefore little better at predicting election outcomes than a random guess would be."

查的预测和随机猜测相比，在预期选举结果方面好不了多少。

（A） For one thing, in the absence of any information about how many voters change their minds until a few days before the balloting and how many remain undecided until the moment they cast their vote, the author's assertion that opinion polls are little better than random guesses is open to doubt.

（B） For another, not everyone frequently changes his mind or waits until the last moment to decide.

（C） Finally, the author fails to take into account the possibility that opinion polls can be designed in such a way that they allow for preference change.

83 The following appeared in the editorial section of a newspaper in the country of West Cambria.

以下内容摘自West Cambria国某报纸上的社论部分。

"The practice of officially changing speed limits on the highways—whether by increasing or decreasing them—is a dangerous one. Consider what happened over the past decade whenever neighboring East Cambria changed its speed limits: an average of 3 percent more automobile accidents occurred during the week following the change than had occurred during the week preceding it—even when the speed limit was lowered. This statistic shows that the change in speed limit adversely affected the alertness of drivers."

官方改变高速路限速的行为，不论是提速还是降速，都是非常危险的。看看邻国East Cambria过去10年来每次改变限速时发生的事情：改变限速后的一周内交通事故比之前的一周内高出3%，哪怕降低限速也是一样。这个统计说明，改变限速对司机的警戒性产生了不良的影响。

（A） First of all, it is unlikely that the brief one-week periods under comparison are representative of longer time periods.

（B） Secondly, the author fails to take into account possible differences between East and West Cambria that are relevant to how drivers react to speed-limit changes.

（C） Thirdly, the author fails to acknowledge possible differences in the types of accidents occurring before and after the change.

（D） Finally, the author unfairly assumes that the increased 3 percent automobile accidents after the speed limits change was caused by drivers' lack of alertness.

84 The following appeared as part of a memorandum from the vice president of Nostrum, a large pharmaceutical corporation.

以下内容摘自Nostrum（一家大型制药公司）副总的一份备忘录。

"The proposal to increase the health and retirement benefits that our employees receive should not be implemented at this time. An increase in these benefits is not only financially unjustified, since our last year's profits were lower than those of the preceding year, but also unnecessary, since our chief competitor, Panacea, offers its employees lower health and retirement benefits than we currently offer. We can assume that our employees are reasonably satisfied with the health and retirement benefits that

提高我们员工健康和退休福利的提议不应该现在执行。这方面的福利提高不但从经济上讲是不合理的——因为我们去年的利润比之前的年份要少，而且没有必要，因为我们的主要竞争对手Panacea给他们员工的健康和退休福利比我们现在给的还要低。我们可以认为我们的员工对他们现在的

they now have since a recent survey indicated that two-thirds of the respondents viewed them favorably."

健康退休福利都是满意的，因为最近的调查显示，三分之二的应答者对此感到满意。

（A）In the first place, the fact that Nostrum's profits last year were lower than the preceding year does not imply that Nostrum is experiencing financial difficulties that preclude it from increasing employee benefits at this time.

（B）In the next place, the fact that Nostrum's chief competitor provides lower benefits to its employees is not a good reason for Nostrum to deny an increase to its employees.

（C）Finally, the survey upon which the argument rests is too vague to be informative.

---

85 The following appeared as part of an article on trends in television.
以下内容摘自关于电视发展趋势的一篇文章。

"A recent study of viewers' attitudes toward prime-time television programs show that many of the programs that were judged by their viewers to be of high quality appeared on (noncommercial)television networks, and that, on commercial television, the most popular shows are typically sponsored by the best-selling products. Thus, it follows that businesses who use commercial television to promote their products will achieve the greatest advertising success by sponsoring only highly-rated programs—and, ideally, programs resembling the highly-rated noncommercial programs on public channels as much as possible."

最近一项有关观众对黄金时间电视节目态度的研究显示，很多被观众认可的节目出现在非商业电视网上，而商业电视最受欢迎的节目通常由最畅销的商品资助。因此，使用商业电视促销商品的企业可以通过只赞助高收视率的节目——最好是那些与公众电视频道上高收视率节目非常相似的节目——从而获得最大的成功。

（A）First of all, the argument turns on an unfounded assumption that noncommercial public television programs judged by viewers to be of high quality are also popular.

（B）Secondly, the author unfairly assumes that programs resembling highly-rated noncommercial programs on public channels will also be popular on commercial television.

（C）Finally, the argument rests on a problematic assumption that products become best-sellers as a result of their being advertised on popular programs.

---

86 The following appeared as part of an article in the business section of a daily newspaper.
以下内容摘自某日报商业版的一篇文章。

"Company A has a large share of the international market in video-game hardware and software. Company B, the pioneer in these products, was once a $12 billion-a-year giant but collapsed when children became bored with its line of products. Thus Company A can also be expected to fail, especially given the fact that its games are now in so many American homes that the demand for them is nearly exhausted."

A公司在视频游戏的硬件软件方面占有很大的国际市场份额。B公司是这些产品的先驱者，而且曾经一度是年收入120亿元的巨人，但在孩子们厌倦了其系列产品后崩溃了。因此A公司也将失败，特别是考虑到它的产品已经占据了那么多的美国家庭以至于相应的需求已经接近枯竭。

（A）In the first place, the stated similarities between Company A and B are insufficient to support the conclusion that Company A will suffer a fate similar to that of Company B.

（B）In the next place, the author fails to provide evidence to support the assumption that the demand for Company A's products is nearly exhausted.

87 The following appeared as part of an article in a photography magazine.
以下内容摘自某摄影杂志上的一篇文章。

"When choosing whether to work in color or in black-and-white, the photographer who wishes to be successful should keep in mind that because color photographs are more true-to-life, magazines use more color photographs than black-and-white ones, and many newspapers are also starting to use color photographs. The realism of color also accounts for the fact that most portrait studios use more color film than black-and-white film. Furthermore, there are more types of color film than black-and-white film available today. Clearly, photographers who work in color have an advantage over those who work in black-and-white."

选择拍摄彩色照片还是黑白照片时，想要成功的摄影师必须记得：因为彩色照片更真实，杂志选用彩色照片要比黑白的多，而且很多报纸也开始采用彩色照片。彩色照片的真实性还使大多数工作室更多地使用彩色胶卷。此外，如今彩色胶卷的种类也比黑白的多。显然，使用彩色胶卷的摄影师要胜过使用黑白胶卷的摄影师。

（A）To begin with, the author fails to support the assumption that color photographs are in greater demand than black-and-white ones.

（B）Secondly, the author unfairly assumes that a photographer must make an either-or choice between the two types of photography.

（C）Thirdly, the fact that more kinds of color film are available than black-and-white film does not support the conclusion.

（D）Finally, the author ignores other factors—such as initiative, creativity, technical skills, and business judgment—that may be more important than a choice of medium in determining success in photography.

88 The following appeared as part of a letter to the editor of a local newspaper.
以下内容摘自写给某地方报纸编辑的一封信。

"It makes no sense that in most places fifteen year olds are not eligible for their driver's license while people who are far older can retain all of their driving privileges by simply renewing their license. If older drivers can get these renewals, often without having to pass another driving test, then fifteen year olds should be eligible to get a license. Fifteen year olds typically have much better eyesight, especially at night; much better hand-eye coordination; and much quicker reflexes. They are also less likely to feel confused by unexpected developments or disoriented in unfamiliar surroundings, and they recover from injuries more quickly."

在多数地方，15岁的人没有资格拥有驾照，而比他们大很多的人只要更新他们的驾照就能保留他们所有的驾驶特权，这是很不合理的。如果老的驾驶员通常不通过额外的驾驶考试就能更新他们的驾照，那么15岁的人就应该具有获得驾照的资格。15岁的人一般拥有更好的视力，特别是在晚上；他们的手眼协调得更好；他们反应更快。他们不容易被突发情况困扰，也不容易在陌生的环境里迷路，并且他们受伤后恢复的速度也更快。

（A）The major problem with the argument is that the author unfairly assumes that there are no relevant differences between 15-year-olds and older drivers that would justify treating them differently.

（B）Another problem with the argument is that the author unfairly assumes that physical capabilities are the only attributes necessary to operate a motor vehicle.

89 **The following appeared in an ad for a book titled How to Write a Screenplay for a Movie.**
以下内容摘自一则为一本名叫《如何给电影写剧本》的书所做的广告。

"Writers who want to succeed should try to write film screenplays rather than books, since the average film tends to make greater profits than does even a best-selling book. It is true that some books are also made into films. However, our nation's film producers are more likely to produce movies based on original screenplays than to produce films based on books, because in recent years the films that have sold the most tickets have usually been based on original screenplays."

想要成功的作者应该写电影剧本而不是书，因为一般来说，一部普通的电影比一本畅销书挣的钱要多得多。虽然有些书也被改编成电影，但是，我国的制片商更愿意拍摄基于原创剧本而非书籍之上的电影，因为最近几年票房最高的电影都是根据原创剧本拍摄的。

（A） In the first place, the mere fact that ticket sales in recent years for screenplay-based movies have exceeded those for book-based movies is insufficient evidence to conclude that writing screenplays provides a greater financial opportunity for writers.

（B） In the second place, the author unfairly assumes that a writer must make an either-or choice between writing books and writing screenplays.

（C） Thirdly, while the author equates success with movie ticket sales, many writers may define writing success in other terms, such as intellectual or artistic fulfillment.

90 已被ETS删除。

91 **The following appeared in a memorandum from the ElectroWares company's marketing department.**
以下内容摘自ElcetroWares公司市场部的一份备忘录。

"Since our company started manufacturing and marketing a deluxe light bulb six months ago, sales of our economy light bulb—and company profits—have decreased significantly. Although the deluxe light bulb sells for 50 percent more than the economy bulb, it lasts twice as long. Therefore, to increase repeat sales and maximize profits, we should discontinue the deluxe light bulb."

自从我公司6个月前开始制造和销售豪华型电灯泡，我们的经济型电灯泡销售额以及公司利润明显下降。尽管豪华型比经济型贵50％，但它的使用寿命是经济型的2倍。因此，为了提高重复销售并且使利润最大化，我们应该停止生产豪华型电灯泡。

（A） First, the only reason offered for the assumption that the introduction of the deluxe bulb is responsible for both the decline in sales of the economy bulb and the decline in company profits is the fact that the former preceded the latter.

（B） Secondly, the author unfairly assumes that if the company discontinues the deluxe light bulb, consumers will resume buying the economy's light bulb.

（C） Thirdly, the author fails to provide any evidence to support the assumption that the profits from selling the deluxe light bulb can not offset the loss from selling the economy bulb.

92 **The following is taken from an editorial in a local newspaper.**
以下内容摘自某地方报纸上的一篇社论。

"Over the past decade, the price per pound of citrus fruit has increased substantially. Eleven years ago, Megamart charged 5 cents apiece for lemons, but today it commonly charges over 30 cents apiece. In only one of these last eleven years was the weather unfavorable for growing citrus crops. Evidently, then, citrus growers have been responsible for the excessive increase in the price of citrus fruit, and strict pricing regulations are needed to prevent them from continuing to inflate prices."

在过去的10年里，柑橘类水果的价格大幅上升。11年前，Megamart每个柠檬要价5分，现在一般要价为30分一个。过去11年中仅有一年的气候不适宜种植柑橘类农作物。显然，柑橘类农作物的种植者应该对柑橘类水果价格过度上涨负责，我们必须制定严格的价格规范以防他们继续哄抬物价。

（A）To begin with, the example of Megamart is not sufficient to support the assumption that the price per pound of citrus fruit has increased substantially.

（B）Secondly, the author fails to indicate in which year the weather was unfavorable for growing citrus crops.

（C）Thirdly, the author unfairly assumes that the only factor that influences the price of citrus fruit is the weather.

（D）Finally, the author unfairly assumes that the only way to combat increased prices in the citrus fruit market is through government intervention.

93 **The following appeared as part of an article in a local newspaper.**
以下内容摘自某地方报纸上的一篇文章。

"Over the past three years the tartfish industry has changed markedly: fishing technology has improved significantly, and the demand for tartfish has grown in both domestic and foreign markets. As this trend continues, the tartfish industry on Shrimp Island can expect to experience the same over-fishing problems that are already occurring with mainland fishing industries: without restrictions on fishing, fishers see no reason to limit their individual catches. As the catches get bigger, the tartfish population will be dangerously depleted while the surplus of tartfish will devalue the catch for fishers. Government regulation is the only answer: tartfish-fishing should be allowed only during the three-month summer season, when tartfish reproduce and thus are most numerous, rather than throughout the year."

在过去的3年里，tartfish渔业变化很大：捕鱼技术显著提高，国内外市场对tartfish的需求量也在增长。随着这种趋势的扩展，Shrimp岛上的tartfish渔业将会经历和大陆渔业一样的过度捕捞问题：不限制捕鱼，渔夫没有理由限制他们个人的捕捞。当捕捞量增大，tartfish的数目会减少，这很危险，同时，过剩的tartfish会使渔民的捕捞贬值。政府规范是唯一的解决方法：tartfish捕捞只能在夏季的3个月而非全年内进行，那时tartfish正处于繁殖期，因而数量是最多的。

（A）In the first place, the argument rests on an unfounded assumption that fishers are motivated only by greed and that they will increase their catches to maximize profits without regard to the effects over-fishing will have on their livelihood in the future.

（B）In the second place, bigger catches will not necessarily devalue the catch of fish, if the domestic and foreign markets increase dramatically.

（C）Thirdly, while government regulation may be one way to address the problem, it is by no means the only way.

（D）Finally, the author offers no evidence that limiting the season for catching tartfish to three months in the summer will solve the over-fishing problem. Indeed, allowing tartfish-fishing during the reproduction period as the author recommends would actually endanger rather than protect the survival of tartfish.

94 The following appeared in a proposal from the development office at Platonic University.
以下内容摘自Platonic大学发展办公室的一份建议书。

"Because Platonic University has had difficulty in meeting its expenses over the past three years, we need to find new ways to increase revenues. We should consider following the example of Greene University, which recently renamed itself after a donor who gave it $100 million. If Platonic University were to advertise to its alumni and other wealthy people that it will rename either individual buildings or the entire university itself after the donors who give the most money, the amount of donations would undoubtedly increase."

在过去3年中，Plantonic大学入不敷出，所以我们必须找到新的方式来提高收入。我们可以考虑采取Greene大学的方法，它最近用一个1亿美元捐助者的名字重新给自己命名。如果Plantonic大学向它的校友和其他富人宣传说它将按捐助最多者的名字命名一栋独立的建筑或者整个大学，那么捐助的数量毫无疑问会增加。

（A）First of all, the argument depends on an unwarranted assumption that a revenue-producing strategy that works for one university will work for another as well.

（B）Secondly, the author unfairly assumes that the donor for whom Greene University was renamed made the donation because the university offered to name itself after him.

（C）Thirdly, the author fails to provide any evidence to support the assumption that revenues from donations will meet Platonic University's needs.

（D）Finally, the author ignores other ways to solve the problem of a shortage of funds at Platonic University.

95 The following appeared as part of an article in the business section of a local newspaper.
以下内容摘自某地方报纸商业版上的一篇文章。

"Hippocrene Plumbing Supply recently opened a wholesale outlet in the location once occupied by the Cumquat Café Restaurant. Hippocrene has apparently been quite successful there because it is planning to open a large outlet in a nearby city. But the Cumquat Café, one year after moving to its new location, has seen its volume of business drop somewhat from the previous year's. Clearly, the former site is a better business location, and the Cumquat Café has made a mistake in moving to its new address."

Hippocrene管道设备供应商在Cumquat餐馆的旧址开了一家批发店。显然，Hippocrene现在相当成功，因为他们正计划在附近的一个城市再开一家大的批发商店。但是Cumquat餐馆在搬到新地址一年后发现它的业务量比前一年有所下降。很明显，它的前一个地点更适宜做生意，Cumquat餐馆作出的搬迁决定是错误的。

（A）The major problem with the argument is that the two businesses are too dissimilar for a meaningful comparison.

（B）Secondly, the fact that Hippocrene intends to open a new outlet is insufficient to establish the claim that Hippocrene has been successful at Cumquat's previous location.

（C）Thirdly, the author fails to establish a causal relationship between the Comquat Café's move to its new location and the reduction of its business volume.

（D）Finally, the author unfairly assumes that one year's time at the new location is adequate to conclude whether Cumquat made a mistake in moving to that location.

96 The following appeared in a memorandum from the manager of KMTV, a television station.
以下内容摘自KMTV电视台经理的一份备忘录。

"Applications for advertising spots on KMTV, our local cable television channel, decreased last year. Meanwhile a neighboring town's local channel, KOOP, changed its focus to farming issues and reported an increase in advertising applications for the year. To increase applications for advertising spots, KMTV should focus its programming on farming issues as well."

去年，我们的地方有线电视台KMTV广告时段的申请量减少了。而同时附近一个镇子的地方台KOOP把它的重点转向农业问题，据说当年的广告申请量有所增加。为了增加广告时段的申请量，KMTV也应该将其节目重心定位于农业问题。

（A）To begin with, the author unfairly assumes that the towns that KMTV and KOOP serve are sufficiently similar to warrant a conclusion based on an analogy between them.

（B）Additionally, the argument rests on an unfounded assumption that the change in focus to farming issues was the cause of KOOP's increase in advertising applications.

（C）Thirdly, the author provides no evidence to support the assumption that KMTV's decrease in applications for advertising was due to its programming.

97 The following appeared as part of an article in a computer magazine.
以下内容摘自某电脑杂志上的一篇文章。

"A year ago Apex Manufacturing bought its managers computers for their homes and paid for telephone connections so that the managers could access Apex computers and data files from home after normal business hours. Since last year, productivity at Apex has increased by 15 percent. Other companies can learn from the success at Apex: given home computers and access to company resources, employees will work additional hours at home and thereby increase company profits."

一年前，Apex制造公司给它的经理们家里配备了电脑，并为他们支付电话连接费用，这样经理们就可以在工作以外的时间从家里访问Apex的电脑和数据文件。从去年开始，Apex的生产能力增长了15%。其他公司可以借鉴Apex的成功，给员工的家里配备电脑并开通访问公司资源的路径，他们就会在家里加班从而增加公司的利润。

（A）In the first place, the argument suffers from the fallacy of "post hoc, ergo propter hoc". The author fails to establish a causal relationship between Apex's increase in productivity and its equipping its managers with home computers and access to company resources.

（B）In the next place, the author unfairly assumes that Apex and other companies are sufficiently similar to warrant a conclusion based on an analogy between them.

98 已被ETS删除。

99 已被ETS删除。

"Farmers who switched from synthetic to organic farming last year have seen their crop yields decline. Many of these farmers feel that it would be too expensive to resume synthetic farming at this point, given the money that they invested in organic farming supplies and equipment. But their investments will be relatively minor compared to the losses from continued lower crop yields. Organic farmers should switch to synthetic farming rather than persist in an unwise course. And the choice to farm organically is financially unwise, given that it was motivated by environmental rather than economic concerns."
（注：同29题，说法不一样，内容几乎都是一样的。）

去年从合成农业转向有机农业的农民发现他们农作物的产量变低了。他们中有许多人觉得他们已经为有机农业供给品和设备投入了资金，现在再恢复合成农业，付出的代价就太大了。但是他们对有机农业设备的投资比之连续的减产带来的损失只是一笔小钱。从事有机农业的农民应该转向合成农业而不是坚持错误方针。选择有机农业的理由从经济上讲是不明智的，它是基于环保而非经济利益。

（A）The major problem with the argument is that there is no evidence to support the assumption that the first-year yields of farmers who switched to organic farming are representative of their future yields.

（B）Secondly, the argument is based on an unfounded assumption that economic and environmental concerns are mutually exclusive and that only the enterprises motivated by economic concerns are financially rewarding.

"Every person who earned an advanced degree in science or engineering from Olympus University last year received numerous offers of excellent jobs. Typically, many of the Plateau College graduates who want to pursue an advanced degree have gone on to Olympus. Therefore, enrolling as an undergraduate at Plateau College is a wise choice for students who wish to ensure success in their careers."

去年在Olympus大学取得理工科高等学位的毕业生都收到了多家用人单位的聘用邀请，而且职位都很好。一般来说，很多想攻读高等学位的Plateau学院毕业生都去了Olympus。因此，对于渴望事业成功的学生而言，去Plateau学院读本科是一个很明智的选择。

（A）First of all, the author has failed to indicate how many Plateau graduates who pursued advanced degrees at Olympus actually received them.

（B）Secondly, the argument depends upon the unwarranted assumption that the Plateau graduates who have pursued advanced degrees at Olympus University did so in science or engineering.

（C）Finally, the survey about the job prospects of the graduates of Olympus University was based only on last year's statistics. The fact that all students who earned advanced degrees in science or engineering from Olympus University last year received numerous offers of excellent jobs is insufficient to warrant the claim that this pattern will continue in the future.

102 **The following appeared in a memorandum sent by a vice-president of the Nadir Company to the company's human resources department.**

以下内容摘自Nadir公司副总送给公司人力资源部的一份备忘录。

"Nadir does not need to adopt the costly 'family-friendly' programs that have been proposed, such as part-time work, work at home, and job-sharing. When these programs were made available at the Summit Company, the leader in its industry, only a small percentage of employees participated in them. Rather than adversely affecting our profitability by offering these programs, we should concentrate on offering extensive training that will enable employees to increase their productivity."

Nadir不需要采用推荐的昂贵"家庭友好"项目，诸如兼职工作、在家中工作、工作共享等等。当在其行业占据龙头位置的Summit公司采用了这些项目时，它的员工只有一小部分参加了。我们与其采用这些会对我们的利润产生不良影响的项目，不如集中精力给员工提供广泛的培训，使他们能提高自己的生产效率。

（A）To begin with, the fact that only a small percentage of Summit Company's employees participated in these programs when they were offered is not sufficient to support the assumption that Nadir's employees will do likewise.

（B）Secondly, the author fails to provide any evidence to support the assertion that the adoption of "family-friendly" programs will adversely affect Nadir's profitability.

（C）Finally, the author unfairly assumes that "family-friendly" programs will not increase Nadir's productivity.

103 已被ETS删除。

104 **The following appeared as part of an article in a trade magazine for breweries.**

以下内容摘自一份针对酿酒厂的贸易杂志上的一篇文章。

"Magic Hat Brewery recently released the results of a survey of visitors to its tasting room last year. Magic Hat reports that the majority of visitors asked to taste its low-calorie beers. To boost sales, other small breweries should brew low-calorie beers as well."

Magic Hat酒厂最近公布了一份去年对参观其品尝室的人所进行的调查结果。Magic Hat宣布绝大多数参观者要求品尝低热量的啤酒。为了促进销售，其他小酒厂也应该酿造低热量的啤酒。

（A）In the first place, the validity of the survey conducted at Magic Hat Brewery is open to doubt.

（B）In the next place, even if the results of the survey accurately reflect a high level of interest in low-calorie beers among Magic Hat's visitors, this may not be true for other breweries.

（C）Finally, the author fails to make a case for the assumption that visitor interest in tasting low-calorie beers resulted in sales of these beers.

105 **The following appeared in an editorial from a newspaper serving the town of Saluda.**

以下内容摘自一份在Saluda镇发售的报纸上的一篇社论。

"The Saluda Consolidated High School offers over 200 different courses from which its students can choose. A much smaller private school down the street offers a basic curriculum of only 80 different courses, but it consistently sends a higher proportion of its

Saluda公立综合高中提供超过200门不同的课程供学生选择。路那头一所小得多的私立学校提供80种基本课程，但是其毕业生升入大学的

graduating seniors on to college than Consolidated does. By eliminating at least half of the courses offered there and focusing on a basic curriculum, we could improve student performance at Consolidated and also save many tax dollars."

比例始终比公立综合高中要高。去除至少一半的课程而着眼于基本课程，我们可以改善公立综合高中的学生成绩并省下很多税金。

(A) For one thing, the author unfairly assumes that the only relevant difference between Consolidated and the private school is the number of courses offered by each.

(B) For another, the argument rests upon a problematic assumption that the proportion of students who go on to college is an overall measure of student performance.

106 The following appeared as part of an article in the book section of a newspaper.
以下内容摘自某报读书栏目中的一篇文章。

"Currently more and more books are becoming available in electronic form — either free-of-charge on the Internet or for a very low price-per-book on compact disc.* Thus literary classics are likely to be read more widely than ever before. People who couldn't have purchased these works at bookstore prices will now be able to read them for little or no money; similarly, people who find it inconvenient to visit libraries and wait for books to be returned by other patrons will now have access to whatever classic they choose from their home or work computers. This increase in access to literary classics will radically affect the public taste in reading, creating a far more sophisticated and learned reading audience than has ever existed before."

*A compact disc is a small portable disc capable of storing relatively large amounts of data that can be read by a computer.

现在越来越多的书有了电子版，或者放在网上免费下载，或者刻成光盘以很低的价格出售。因此文学经典的读者可以比以前更广泛。不能以书店价格购买这些书的人现在可以用很少的钱或者不花钱来阅读它们。类似的，觉得去图书馆或者等待其他人还书不方便的人现在可以通过家里或者工作场所的电脑得到任何他想要的名著。这种文学名著接触机会的增多将从根本上影响公众的阅读品味，塑造比以前更成熟更博学的读者。

(A) In the first place, the author unfairly assumes that price and lack of convenient access are the primary reasons people fail to read literary classics.

(B) In the second place, while it may be the case that access to books at affordable prices has increased as a result of new technology, the author provides no evidence for the assumption that access to literary classics at affordable prices has increased as well.

(C) Finally, the increase in access to classics cannot ensure improvement or a change in the public's reading tastes. Additionally, reading literary classics alone will not necessarily create a far more sophisticated and learned reading audience.

107 The following appeared as an editorial in a magazine concerned with educational issues.
以下内容摘自一份教育类杂志的一篇社论。

"In our country, the real earnings of men who have only a high-school degree have decreased significantly over the past fifteen years, but those of male college graduates have remained about the same. Therefore, the key to improving the earnings of the next generation of workers is to send all students to college. Our country's most important educational goal, then, should be to

在过去的15年中，我们国家只有高中学历的男性公民实际收入明显下降，而具有大学学历的男性公民的收入基本持平。因此，提高下一代工人收入的关键是把所有学生都送入大学。我们国家最主要的教育目标应该是建

establish enough colleges and universities to accommodate all high school graduates."

立足够多的大学和学院，以容纳所有的高中生。

（A）To begin with, the author fails to take into account the income differences between female high-school and college graduates.

（B）Secondly, the argument relies on a problematic assumption that the primary factor that influences the earnings of workers is their level of education.

（C）Thirdly, if we follow the author's recommendation, the real earnings of college-educated workers may decrease as the supply of college-educated workers will soon outpace the demand for it.

---

108 **The following appeared as part of a business plan created by the management of the Take Heart Fitness Center.**

以下内容摘自Take Heart健身中心管理者起草的一份商业计划。

"After opening the new swimming pool early last summer, Take Heart saw a 12 percent increase in the use of the center by members. Therefore, in order to increase the number of our members and thus our revenues, which depend on membership fees, we should continue to add new recreational facilities in subsequent years: for example, a multipurpose game room, a tennis court, and a miniature golf course. Being the only center in the area offering this range of activities would give us a competitive advantage in the health and recreation market."

去年夏初开了新的游泳池以后，Take Heart会员对本中心的利用率增加了12%。因此，为了增加我们的会员数量和以会员费为主的收入，我们应该在以后几年中继续增加新的娱乐设施：比如，一个多功能游戏室，一个网球场，一个迷你高尔夫球场。作为本地唯一一家提供各种活动设施的健身中心，我们将在健身和娱乐市场的竞争中保持优势。

（A）The major problem with the argument is that the author provides no credible evidence to support the assumption that an increase in member usage portends an increase in membership.

（B）Secondly, the author unfairly assumes that the addition of the swimming pool was responsible for the increase in member usage.

（C）Finally, the author fails to make a case for the claim that Take Heart will be the only center in the area to offer a wide range of activities to its members and thus have a competitive advantage in the fitness market.

---

109 **The following appeared in a letter from a staff member in the office of admissions at Argent University.**

以下内容摘自Argent大学招生办公室一个职员写的一封信。

"The most recent nationwide surveys show that undergraduates choose their major field primarily based on their perception of job prospects in that field. At our university, economics is now the most popular major, so students must perceive this field as having the best job prospects. Therefore, we can increase our enrollment if we focus our advertising and recruiting on publicizing the accomplishments of our best-known economics professors and the success of our economics graduates in finding employment."

最近全国范围的调查显示，本科生选择他们的专业方向主要是基于他们对那个方向工作前途的认识。在我们学校，经济学是目前最热门的专业，因此学生一定认为这个专业的工作前途最好。因此，如果我们做广告和招生时着力宣传我们最出名的经济学教授所取得的成就和我们的经济学毕业生在找工作时所获得的成功，就可以提高我们学校的入学人数。

(A) In the first place, the argument rests on a dubious survey. The author fails to indicate if the students who participated in the surveys were representative of students in general and that a sufficient number were included in the surveys to warrant the claim that the choice of major is dictated by student perception of prospective employment.

(B) In the next place, the argument depends upon an unfounded assumption that students will continue to perceive economics favorably as a source of employment.

(C) Finally, even if we accept the survey results it might be the case that economics is the most popular major at Argent for reasons other than students' perception of job prospects.

110 **The following appeared as part of a memorandum from the loan department of the Frostbite National Bank.**
以下内容摘自Frostbite国家银行借贷部门的一份备忘录。

"We should not approve the business loan application of the local group that wants to open a franchise outlet for the Kool Kone chain of ice cream parlors. Frostbite is known for its cold winters, and cold weather can mean slow ice cream sales. For example, even though Frostbite is a town of 10,000 people, it has only one ice cream spot—the Frigid Cow. Despite the lack of competition, the Frigid Cow's net revenues fell by 10 percent last winter."

我们不应该批准当地某个集团为了在本地开一家Kool Kone冰淇淋连锁店的特许店而提出的借贷申请。Frostbite以其寒冷的冬天而闻名，而寒冷的气候意味着冰淇淋销售不佳。比如，虽然Frostbite是个有一万人的镇子，它却只有一家冰淇淋店——Frigid Cow。尽管竞争小，但Frigid Cow去年冬天的净收入还是下降了10%。

(A) First of all, the fact that Frostbite has cold winters is not sufficient to support the assumption that Kool Kone franchise will not be successful.

(B) Secondly, the loan department unfairly assumes that the Frigid Cow's decline in net revenue last winter was a result of slow sales occasioned by cold weather.

(C) Finally, the fact that Frostbite, a town of 10,000 people, has only one ice cream parlor does not necessarily mean that Frostbite cannot be an ideal location for a Kool Kone ice cream franchise.

111 **The following appeared as part of a letter to the editor of a local newspaper.**
以下内容摘自写给某家地方报纸编辑的一封信。

"Bayview High School is considering whether to require all of its students to wear uniforms while at school. Students attending Acorn Valley Academy, a private school in town, earn higher grades on average than Bayview students and are more likely to go on to college. Moreover, Acorn Valley reports few instances of tardiness, absenteeism, or discipline problems. Since Acorn Valley requires its students to wear uniforms, Bayview High School would do well to follow suit and require its students to wear uniforms as well."

Bayview高中正考虑是不是应该要求它所有的学生在校时都穿校服。Acorn Valley Academy，本镇一所私立学校的学生平均成绩要比Bayview的学生高，也更容易上大学。而且，Acorn Valley基本上没有迟到、旷课和纪律问题。因为Acorn Valley要求学生穿制服，所以Bayview高中也这样做将得到很好的效果。

(A) In the first place, the argument rests upon an unfounded assumption that all of the stated benefits are a result of Acorn's requirement that its students wear uniforms.

（B）In the second place, the author unfairly assumes that the only relevant difference between Bayview and Acorn is the wearing of school uniforms.

（C）Finally, it is unclear whether Bayview suffers from any of the problems the author wishes to correct by mandating its students to wear uniforms.

---

112 The following appeared in a memo to the Saluda town council from the town's business manager.

以下内容摘自Saluda镇事务员递交给镇委员会的一份备忘录。

"Research indicates that those who exercise regularly are hospitalized less than half as often as those who don't exercise. By providing a well-equipped gym for Saluda's municipal employees, we should be able to reduce the cost of our group health insurance coverage by approximately 50% and thereby achieve a balanced town budget."

研究显示，规律锻炼的人生病的概率比不运动的人要小一半。通过给Saluda的市政员工提供一个设备良好的体育馆，我们应该可以减少大约50%的健康保险支出，并从而使镇预算保持平衡。

（A）First of all, the argument is based on an unwarranted assumption that Saluda's municipal employees will exercise regularly if a well-equipped facility is provided for them.

（B）Secondly, the author unfairly assumes that Saluda's employees do not exercise regularly.

（C）Thirdly, the author fails to establish a causal relationship between the hospitalization rate for employees and the cost of their group health insurance.

（D）Finally, the author fails to make a case for the assumption that the cost of building a well-equipped exercise facility will not negate the savings realized on the group health insurance.

---

113 The following appeared in a memorandum written by the assistant manager of a store that sells gourmet food items from various countries.

以下内容摘自销售各国美食的某家商店副经理的一份备忘录。

"An interesting discovery was made last month at a local wine store: the store sold more French than Italian wine on days when recordings of French accordion music were played, but more Italian wine was sold on days when Italian songs were played. Therefore, I recommend that we put food specialties from one particular country on sale for a week at a time and play only music from that country while the sale is going on. By this means we will increase our profits in the same way that the wine store did, and we will be able to predict more precisely what items we should stock at any given time."

本地一家葡萄酒店上个月发现了一个有趣的现象：播放法国的手风琴音乐时，该店卖出的法国酒比意大利酒多；而播放意大利歌曲时，该店卖出的意大利酒比较多。因此，我建议，我们每次用一周的时间来降价促销某一个国家的特定食品，并在促销期内仅播放这个国家的音乐。通过这种方法，我们就能和那家葡萄酒店一样提高我们的利润，并且在任何时候都能更加准确地预测我们该储存哪种货物。

（A）To begin with, the manager fails to establish a causal relationship between the wine sales and the playing of particular national recordings.

（B）Secondly, the manager unfairly assumes that the wine store increased its profits by playing the appropriate music.

（C）Finally, even if it were the case that playing music from a particular country contributed to the sales of wine from the country, it is highly doubtful that the facts drawn from a local wine store are applicable to a store that sells gourmet food items from various countries.

114 **The following appeared in a memorandum from the director of research and development at Ready-to-Ware, a software engineering firm.**

以下内容摘自一家软件工程公司 —— Ready-to-Ware研发部经理的一份备忘录。

"The package of benefits and incentives that Ready-to-Ware offers to professional staff is too costly. Our quarterly profits have declined since the package was introduced two years ago, at the time of our incorporation. Moreover, the package had little positive effect, as we have had only marginal success in recruiting and training high-quality professional staff. To become more profitable again, Ready-to-Ware should, therefore, offer the reduced benefits package that was in place two years ago and use the savings to fund our current research and development initiatives."

Ready-to-Ware给专业人员提供的福利和奖金太多了。自从两年前我们组建公司时引入该福利机制以来，我们的季度利润下降了。而且，这个福利机制几乎没有什么成效，因为我们在招聘和训练高水平专业人员方面只取得了很小的成功。因此，为了获取更多的利润，Ready-to-Ware应该降低两年前制定的福利待遇标准，把省下的钱用于资助当前的研究和开发项目。

（A）In the first place, the director fails to establish a causal relationship between the package of benefits and incentives and the decline of the company's quarterly profits.

（B）In the second place, the director unfairly assumes that the benefits package currently offered is responsible for the marginal success Ready-to-Ware has experienced in recruiting and training new high-quality professionals.

（C）Finally, the director fails to make a case for the assumption that investing savings from the reduced benefits package to current research and development initiatives will make the company more profitable.

115 **The following appeared in a memorandum from the vice-president of the Dolci Candy Company.**

以下内容摘自Dolci糖果公司副总的一份备忘录。

"Given the success of our premium and most expensive line of chocolate candies in a recent taste test and the subsequent increase in sales, we should shift our business focus to producing additional lines of premium candy and discontinuing our lesser-priced, ordinary candies. When the current economic boom ends and consumers can no longer buy major luxury items, such as cars, they will still be able to afford small luxuries, such as expensive candies."

鉴于我们的优质高价巧克力糖果在最近的味道测试中取得成功，以及随之而来的销售增长，我们应该停止生产低价普通糖果，而把工作重点转向生产更多种类的高级糖果。当前经济的快速增长结束时，消费者无力购买主要的奢侈品，如汽车，但他们仍然可以买得起小小的奢侈品，比如昂贵的糖果。

（A）First of all, the fact that the premium line of chocolates met with success in a recent taste test is scant evidence of the claim that this line of candies will continue to be successful in the future.

（B）Secondly, the vice-president fails to establish a causal relationship between the increase in sales experienced after the taste test and sales of the premium candies.

（C）Finally, the vice-president provides no evidence to support the assumption that the economic boom's end will not affect sales of small luxuries such as expensive candies.

116 **The following appeared in a memorandum from the business office of the Lovin' Cupful, a national restaurant chain.**
以下内容摘自全国连锁餐馆Lovin' Cupful业务部的一份备忘录。

"The Lovin' Cupful franchises in our northeast region have begun serving customers Almost, a brand-new powdered instant tea, in place of brewed tea. From what waiters report, it seems that only 2 percent of the customers have complained about the taste and that customers who want refills typically ask for more 'tea'. Apparently, then, about 98 percent of the customers are perfectly happy with the switch, or else they cannot distinguish powdered instant from brewed tea. Therefore, in order to take advantage of the lower price per pound of Almost, all of our restaurants should begin substituting it for brewed tea."

Lovin' Cupful在东北地区的特许店开始给顾客提供一种新的粉末速溶茶Almost,取代了原来的泡茶。侍者报告说只有大约2％的顾客抱怨茶的味道,而想再喝的顾客通常会说再来点"茶"。显然,98％的顾客对这个改换很满意,或者他们无法分辨粉末速溶茶和泡茶。因此,为了利用Almost的低价优势,我们所有的餐馆都应该用它替代泡茶。

（A） To begin with, the fact that 98 percent of the customers have not complained about the taste does not indicate that they are perfectly happy with the switch, or that they cannot distinguish powdered instant from brewed tea.

（B） Secondly, even if it were the case that the overwhelming majority could not currently distinguish between the instant and the brewed tea, it does not guarantee they will not detect a difference in the future.

（C） Finally, the fact that Almost sells well in the northeast region does not ensure that it will also succeed at Lovin' Cupful's other franchises in other parts of the country.

117 **The following appeared in a memorandum from the director of marketing for a pharmaceutical company.**
以下内容摘自某医药公司销售经理的一份备忘录。

"According to a survey of 5, 000 urban residents, the prevalence of stress headaches increases with educational level, so that stress headaches occur most often among people with graduate-school degrees. It is well established that, nationally, higher educational levels usually correspond with higher levels of income. Therefore, in marketing our new pain remedy, Omnilixir, we should send free samples primarily to graduate students and to people with graduate degrees, and we should concentrate on advertising in professional journals rather than in general-interest magazines."

根据对5000名城市居民的调查,人们患紧张性头痛的比率随他们受教育水平的增加而增加,因此紧张性头痛在拥有研究生学历的人中最常发生。很明显,从全国的范围看,高学历通常与高收入相对应。因此,在促销我们的新止痛剂Omnilixir时,我们应该把免费样品主要发送给研究生和具有硕士学位的人,并且应该把广告集中于专业期刊,而不是大众杂志。

（A） For one thing, the results of the survey are questionable as the argument does not indicate who conducted the survey, who responded, or how the survey was conducted.

（B） For another, the fact that people with higher educational levels usually have higher income does not lend support to the assumption that the pharmaceutical company should focus its marketing on the small population of graduate students and people with graduate degrees.

The following appeared as part of an editorial in the Waymarsh City newspaper.
以下内容摘自Waymarsh市报上的一篇社论。

"Last year the parents of first graders in our school district expressed satisfaction with the reading skills their children developed but complained strongly about their children's math skills. To remedy this serious problem and improve our district's elementary education, everyone in the teacher-training program at Waymarsh University should be required to take more courses in mathematics."

去年我们学校所在区的一年级学生家长对他们孩子的阅读能力表示满意，但是对他们孩子的数学能力很不满。为了解决这个严重的问题，提高我们区的基础教育水平，应该要求在Waymarsh大学参加教师培训项目的每一个人都上更多的数学课。

（A）To begin with, it is possible that what the parents expect from their children in mathematics may far outweigh what should be taught in the first grade.

（B）Secondly, the author unfairly assumes that the performance of the first graders in mathematics can represent the elementary education of the district as a whole.

（C）Thirdly, the argument rests upon an unfounded assumption that the poor level of a school's education contributes to the inadequacy of the first graders' math.

（D）Finally, the author provides no evidence to support the assumption that requiring everyone in the teacher-training program at Waymarsh University to take more courses in mathematics will automatically solve the above mentioned problem and further improve the local elementary education in general.

The following is from an editorial that appeared in a River City newspaper.
以下内容摘自River市报上的一篇社论。

"The Clio Development Group wants to build a multilevel parking garage on Dock Street in River City, but the plan should not be approved. Most of the buildings on the block would then have to be demolished. Because these buildings were erected decades ago, they have historic significance and must therefore be preserved as economic assets in the effort to revitalize a restored riverfront area. Recall how Lakesburg has benefited from business increases in its historic downtown center. Moreover, there is plenty of vacant land for a parking lot elsewhere in River City."

Clio发展集团想在River市Dock街修建一个多层停车场，该计划不应该被批准，不然这个街区的大多数建筑将被摧毁。由于这些建筑是几十年前修建的，具有历史意义，所以为了复兴沿河区域，应该把它们当作经济财产保留下来。回想一下Lakesburg是怎样从它古迹中心街区的商业增长中获益的。此外，River城的其他地方有很多空地可以用来修建停车场。

（A）For one thing, the argument depends upon an unwarranted assumption that the success of Lakesburg's historic downtown center portends a similar success for Dock Street in its efforts to revitalize a restored riverfront area.

（B）For another, it is possible that the opening of a multilevel parking garage will boost the economy of Dock Street.

（C）Finally, the author fails to make a case for the assumption that vacant land elsewhere in River City is suitable for building a multilevel parking garage.

120 **The following appeared in a corporate planning memorandum for a company that develops amusement parks.**

以下内容摘自一家游乐园开发公司的一份公司策划备忘录。

"Because travel from our country to foreign countries has increased dramatically in recent years, our next project should be a World Tour theme park with replicas of famous foreign buildings, rides that have international themes, and refreshment stands serving only foods from the country represented by the nearest ride. The best location would be near our capital city, which has large percentages of international residents and of children under the age of 16. Given the advantages of this site and the growing interest in foreign countries, the World Tour theme park should be as successful as our Space Travel theme park, where attendance has increased tenfold over the past decade."

最近几年我国公民出国旅行的人数急剧增加，所以我们的下一个项目应该是开发一个以世界旅行为主题的公园，公园中有外国著名建筑的复制品，充满国际主题的娱乐设施，点心摊位只提供最近那个娱乐设施所代表的国家的食物。最好的地点是在我们的首都附近，那里有大量的各国居民和16岁以下的小孩。有了这个地点优势以及人们对国外兴趣的增长，世界旅行主题公园将会取得如同太空旅行主题公园一样的成功，在过去的10年中，参观太空旅行主题公园的人数增加了10倍。

(A) In the first place, the fact that the number of people traveling abroad has increased dramatically in recent years can not guarantee a corresponding increase in the number of visitors to the World Tour theme park.

(B) In the next place, the author fails to substantiate the assumption that international residents and children under the age of 16 would be most interested in the World Tour theme park.

(C) Finally, the author provides no solid evidence to support the assumption that World Tour theme park would be as successful as the Space Travel theme park.

121 **The following appeared in a memorandum from the publisher to the editorial staff of *The Clarion*, a large metropolitan newspaper.**

以下内容摘自某份大都市报——*The Clarion*的出版商写给编辑人员的一份备忘录。

"During the recent campaign for mayor, a clear majority of city readers who responded to our survey indicated a desire for more news about city government. To increase readership, and thus our profits, we should therefore consistently devote a greater proportion of space in all editions of *The Clarion* to coverage of local news."

在最近的市长竞选中，我市参与调查的读者中绝大多数表示他们希望能够读到更多与市政府相关的新闻。因此，为了增加读者人数，从而提高我们的利润，我们应该持续在*The Clarion*的所有版面中都留出大幅版面来刊登当地新闻。

(A) To begin with, the argument rests upon a dubious survey. There is no detailed information about the survey, including who conducted the survey, who responded, or how the survey was conducted.

(B) Additionally, results from a survey conducted during campaign for mayor is less than representative.

(C) Finally, even if it were the case that readers would have a greater interest in local news after the campaign, it is inadvisable to consistently devote a greater proportion of space in all editions of *The Clarion* to coverage of local news.

The following appeared in a memorandum from the assistant manager of Pageturner Books.

以下内容摘自Pageturner Books副经理的一份备忘录。

"Over the past two years, Pageturner's profits have decreased by five percent, even though we have added a popular café as well as a music section selling CD's and tapes. At the same time, we have experienced an increase in the theft of merchandise. We should therefore follow the example of Thoreau Books, which increased its profits after putting copies of its most frequently stolen books on a high shelf behind the payment counter. By doing likewise with copies of the titles that our staff reported stolen last year, we too can increase profitability."

在过去的两年里，尽管增加了一个大众咖啡馆以及一个出售CD和磁带的音乐部门，但是Pageturner的利润还是下降了5%。同时，我们的商品被偷窃的数量却增加了。因此，我们应该仿照Thoreau书店的做法，它把最容易被偷的书都放在收款台后面一个高高的书架上，然后它的利润就增长了。我们把店员报告的去年被偷的书做同样的处理，也能提高利润。

（A）First of all, the author unfairly assumes that the increase in the theft of merchandise has caused the reduction of Pageturner's profits.

（B）Secondly, the author fails to make a case for the claim that the profit increase of Thoreau Books is due to the mere fact that this bookstore put copies of its most frequently stolen books on a high shelf behind the payment counter.

（C）Thirdly, granted that the method cited in the argument was successful at Thoreau Books, it does not necessarily mean that this method will be effective in solving the problem of the theft at Pageturner Books.

（D）Finally, what was an applicable solution to the theft of merchandise last year is not necessarily practical this year.

The following appeared in a letter to the editor of a River City newspaper.

以下内容摘自写给River市一家报社编辑的一封信。

"The Clio Development Group's plan for a multilevel parking garage on Dock Street should be approved in order to strengthen the economy of the surrounding area. Although most of the buildings on the block would have to be demolished, they are among the oldest in the city and thus of little current economic value. Those who oppose the project should realize that historic preservation cannot be the only consideration: even Athens or Jerusalem will knock down old buildings to put up new ones that improve the local economy."

Clio发展商在Dock街修建多层停车场的计划应该被批准，以便巩固附近地区的经济。虽然这个街区的大多数建筑将被摧毁，但他们是这个城市最老的建筑，因此现在已经没有多少经济价值。那些反对这个项目的人应该认识到，保护历史不能是唯一的考虑因素：即使是雅典和耶路撒冷也会拆除旧建筑来盖新建筑以促进本地经济。

（A）The major problem with the argument is that the author provides no evidence to support the claim that the multilevel parking garage can strengthen the economy of the surrounding area.

（B）Secondly, the author unfairly assumes that historic buildings have little current economic value.

（C）Thirdly, although the historic preservation can not be the only consideration when deciding whether to demolish the historic buildings or not, it is imprudent to ignore historic preservation. A decision should be made after carefully considering all factors.

（D）Finally, the fact that even Athens or Jerusalem will knock down old buildings to put up new ones can not serve as justification to approve the practice of demolishing old buildings on the Dock street.

---

124 **The following appeared in a memorandum from the owner of Carlo's Clothing to the staff.**
以下内容摘自Carlo服饰的老板写给员工的一份备忘录。

"Since Disc Depot, the music store on the next block, began a new radio advertising campaign last year, its business has grown dramatically, as evidenced by the large increase in foot traffic into the store. While the Disc Depot's owners have apparently become wealthy enough to retire, profits at Carlo's Clothing have remained stagnant for the past three years. In order to boost our sales and profits, we should therefore switch from newspaper advertising to frequent radio advertisements like those for Disc Depot."

下一街区的音像店Disc Depot自从去年开始在电台做广告后，业务急剧增长，这可以从商店客流量的大幅增加中看出。当Disc Depot的老板已经富得明显可以不再工作时，Carlo服饰的利润却3年来一直停滞不变。为了促进我们的销售和利润，我们应该像Disc Depot一样从报纸广告转向频繁播送的电台广告。

（A）In the first place, the argument suffers from the fallacy of "post hoc, ergo propter hoc". The author fails to establish a causal relationship between the new advertising campaign and the increase of Disc Depot's business.

（B）In the second place, large increase in foot traffic at Disc Depot is scant evidence to support the claim that its business has grown dramatically.

（C）Finally, the argument commits the fallacy of false analogy. The author unfairly assumes that facts drawn from the music store are applicable to the Carlo's Clothing.

---

125 **The following appeared as part of the business plan of the Capital Idea investment firm.**
以下内容摘自Capital Idea投资公司的商业计划书。

"Across town in the Park Hill district, the Thespian Theater, Pizzazz Pizza, and the Niblick Golf Club have all had business increases within the past two years. Capital Idea should therefore invest in the Roxy Playhouse, the Slice-o'-Pizza, and the Divot Golf Club, three new businesses in the Irongate district. As a condition, we should require them to participate in a special program: Any customer who patronizes two of the businesses will receive a substantial discount at the third. By motivating customers to patronize all three, we will thus contribute to the profitability of each and maximize our return."

在过去的两年里，分布在Park Hill区的Thespian剧院、Pizzazz比萨和Niblick高尔夫俱乐部业务都有所增长。因此Capital Idea应该投资分布在Irongate区的三家新企业：Poxy剧场、Slic-o比萨和Divot高尔夫俱乐部。先决条件是，我们应该要求它们参加一个特殊的活动：任何顾客在其中两家消费后将在第三家得到大幅折扣。通过刺激顾客在这三家店中消费，我们将增进每一家店的利润，使我们的收益最大化。

（A）First of all, the success of the Thespian Theater, Pizzazz Pizza, and the Niblick Golf Club in the Park Hill district does not guarantee the success of the Roxy Playhouse, the Slice-o'-Pizza, and the Divot Golf Club in the Irongate district.

（B）Secondly, the fact that the three businesses in the Park Hill district have all had business increases within the past two years does not warrant they will continue to be profitable in the coming years.

（C）Finally, the author unfairly assumes that customers will take equal interest in the three different new businesses. The fact is that consumers may patronize only one or two of the new businesses in the Irongate district.

---

126 The following appeared as part of an article in a newsletter for farmers.
以下内容摘自某份面向农民的时事通讯上的一篇文章。

"Users of Solacium, a medicinal herb now grown mainly in Asia, report that it relieves tension and promotes deep sleep. A recent study indicates that a large number of college students who took pills containing one of the ingredients in Solacium suffered less anxiety. To satisfy the anticipated demands for this very promising therapeutic herb and to reap the financial benefits, farmers in this country should begin growing it."

Solacium这种草药主要生长在亚洲。据使用者说它可以缓解紧张，促进深度睡眠。最近的研究显示，很多大学生在服用过含有Solacium中一种成分的药品后，焦虑程度都有所减轻。为了满足人们对这种非常有效的治疗草药的预期需求，并获得经济收益，这个国家的农民应该开始种植它了。

（A）The major problem with the argument is that the author fails to provide any evidence to support the assumption that growing this medicinal herb is profitable.

（B）Another problem with the argument is that there is no evidence to support the implicit assumption that there will be a great demand for this therapeutic herb.

（C）Thirdly, the argument relies on a dubious study. As Solacium is only one of the ingredients of the pills that college students have taken, it is presumptuous to say that Solacium can alleviate students' anxiety.

---

127 The following appeared in a memorandum from the president of Aurora, a company that sells organic milk（milk produced without the use of chemical additives）.
以下内容摘自出售绿色牛奶(不使用化学添加剂生产的牛奶)的Aurora公司总裁的一份备忘录。

"Sales of organic food products in this country have tripled over the past five years. If Aurora is to profit from this continuing trend, we must diversify and start selling products such as organic orange juice and organic eggs in addition to our regular product line. With the recent increase of articles in health magazines questioning the safety of milk and other food products, customers are even more likely to buy our line of organic products. And to help ensure our successful expansion, we should hire the founder of a chain of health-food stores to serve as our vice-president of marketing."

本国绿色食品的销售额在过去5年里增长了3倍。如果Aurora想从这种持续的趋势中获利，就必须做到多元化，并开始在我们原有生产线的基础上生产绿色橙汁，绿色鸡蛋。随着最近健康杂志上质疑牛奶和其他食品安全性的文章的增加，顾客们会更愿意购买我们的绿色系列食品。为了确保我们的扩展成功，我们应该雇用健康食品连锁店的创建者作我们的市场营销部副总裁。

（A）In the first place, the success in the sales of organic food products in the past five years can not guarantee the continuing success in the future.

（B）In the next place, it is true that consumers are affected by magazines. However, it is groundless to say that they are even more likely to buy Aurora's line of organic products.

（C）Thirdly, the author fails to make a case for the assumption that the founder of a chain of health-food stores is competent to serve as Aurora's vice-president of marketing.

128 **The following appeared in a memorandum from the human resources department of Diversified Manufacturing.**

以下内容摘自Diversified制造公司人力资源部的一份备忘录。

"Managers at our central office report that their emp-loyees tend to be most productive in the days immediately preceding a vacation. To help counteract our declining market share, we could increase the productivity of our professional staff members, who currently receive four weeks paid vacation a year, by limiting them to a maximum of one week's continuous vacation time. They will thus take more vacation breaks during a year and give us more days of maximum productivity."

我们中心办公室的经理报告说，他们的雇员在假期前几天工作效率最高。为了帮助扭转我们市场份额下滑的局面，通过限制我们的专业技术员工每次最长休假时间为一周，可以增加他们的生产力。他们目前一年有4周的带薪休假。由此，一年中他们休假的次数将增多，也给我们带来更多极富生产力的日子。

（A） For one thing, the author overemphasizes the importance of the stimulation caused by a vacation.

（B） For another, the argument rests upon an unwarranted assumption that employees will happily accept the idea of taking no more than one week of vacation at a time.

（C） Finally, the author ignores other factors contributing to the declining market share of Diversified Manufacturing.

129 **The following appeared in a memorandum from a regional supervisor of post office operations.**

以下内容摘自邮局运营部一位地区总监的一份备忘录。

"During a two-week study of postal operations, the Presto City post office handled about twice as many items as the Lento City post office, even though the cities are about the same size. Moreover, customer satisfaction appears to be higher in Presto City, since the study found fewer complaints regarding the Presto City post office. Therefore, the postmasters at these two offices should exchange assignments: the Presto City postmaster will solve the problems of inefficiency and customer dissatisfaction at the Lento City office while the Lento City postmaster learns firsthand the superior methods of Presto City."

为期两周的邮政运营研究发现，虽然Presto和Lento这两个城市的规模差不多，但前者处理的邮政业务是后者的两倍。而且，Presto市的顾客满意度看起来更高，因为研究结果表明，人们对Presto市邮局的投诉比较少。因此，两个邮局的局长应该交换位置。Presto市的局长将解决Lento市邮局的低效和顾客不满意的问题，而Lento市的局长可以从Presto市学习第一手的先进管理方法。

（A） First, the argument is based on a dubious study. Two weeks is not long enough to draw a convincing conclusion that the Presto City post office is always more efficient and provides better service than the Lento City post office.

（B） Secondly, the proposed exchanging of assignments between the two postmasters may cause unexpected results to both post offices, since neither of the postmasters is familiar with the other city's situation.

The following appeared in a memorandum written by the managing director of the Exeunt Theater Company.

以下内容摘自Exeunt戏剧公司管理者写的备忘录。

"Now that we have moved to a larger theater, we can expect to increase our revenues from ticket sales. To further increase profits, we should start producing the plays that have been most successful when they were performed in our nation's largest cities. In addition, we should hire the Adlib Theater Company's director of fund-raising, since corporate donations to Adlib have increased significantly over the three years that she has worked for Adlib."

既然我们已搬迁到一个更大的剧院，我们的票房收入就有望增加。为了进一步提高利润，我们应该开始排练在我国最大的城市演出时最成功的剧目。另外，我们应该聘用在Adlib戏剧公司主管筹资的经理，因为在她为Adlib工作的三年中，其他公司对Adlib的捐助显著增加。

（A）To begin with, a larger theater can not guarantee the increase of revenues from ticket sales.

（B）Secondly, the argument rests upon an unwarranted assumption that plays that have been most successful when they were performed in the largest cities will also be popular with audiences when the Exeunt Theater Company stages them in a larger theater.

（C）Thirdly, the author unfairly attributes Adlib's corporate donation increase to the director's perfor-mance.

（D）Finally, granted that it is the Adlib Theater Company's director that played a crucial role in bringing in the increased corporate donations, hiring her may contribute to but cannot ensure the success of the Exeunt Theater Company.

The following appeared in a memorandum from the human resources department of HomeStyle, a house remodeling business.

以下内容摘自一家房屋改建公司——HomeStyle人力资源部的一份备忘录。

"This year, despite HomeStyle's move to new office space, we have seen a decline in both company morale and productivity, and a corresponding increase in administrative costs. To rectify these problems, we should begin using a newly developed software package for performance appraisal and feedback. Managers will save time by simply choosing comments from a preexisting list; then the software will automatically generate feedback for the employee. The Human Resources department at CounterBalance, the manufacturer of the countertops we install, reports satisfaction with the package."

今年，尽管HomeStyle搬迁到了新的工作地点，但是公司员工的士气和生产率都有所下降，管理成本也随之增加。为了纠正这些问题，我们应该开始使用一个新开发的用于绩效评估和意见反馈的软件包。该软件可以节约经理们的时间——他们仅需从现有的表格中选取意见，这个软件就会自动生成他们对员工的反馈意见。CounterBalance（我们安装的工作台面的生产商）的人力资源部对这个软件包很满意。

（A）In the first place, the decline in both company morale and productivity and a corresponding increase in administrative costs at HomeStyle can simply be the result of the company's move, thus making the proposal to use the newly developed software package useless.

（B）In the next place, the fact that the software package seems unable to solve new problems out of the preexisting list makes it less reliable.

（C）Finally, the author commits a fallacy of false analogy. It is highly doubtful that the newly developed software package that works well at CounterBalance is applicable to HomeStyle. Differences between the two companies clearly outweigh the similarities, thus making the analogy less than valid.

132 The following appeared as part of an article in a weekly newsmagazine.
以下内容摘自某份新闻周刊上的一篇文章。

"The country of Oleum can best solve the problem of its balance of trade deficit by further increasing the tax on its major import, crude oil. After Oleum increased the tax on imported crude oil four months ago, consumption of gasoline declined by 20 percent. Therefore, by imposing a second and significantly higher tax increase next year, Oleum will dramatically decrease its balance of trade deficit."

Oleum国可以通过增加它的主要进口物原油的税收来解决贸易逆差问题。从四个月前Oleum增加了进口原油税以后，汽油的消费减少了20%。因此，下一年，通过征收第二种更高税率的税种，Oleum将大幅降低它的贸易逆差金额。

（A）First of all, the argument turns on an unwarranted assumption that consumption of gasoline will decline steadily if the tax on it increases over time.

（B）Secondly, if Oleum imposes a second and significantly higher tax increase on crude oil, other countries may retaliate against it by increasing their tax on products from Oleum. In this case, it is unlikely that Oleum will dramatically decrease its trade deficit.

（C）Finally, a further increase of the tax on imported crude oil may harm the development of the country's overall economy.

133 The following appeared as part of a business plan by the Capital Idea investment firm.
以下内容摘自Capital Idea投资公司的一份商业计划书。

"In recent years the worldwide demand for fish has grown, and improvements in fishing technology have made larger catches and thus increased supply possible: for example, last year's tuna catch was 9 percent greater than the previous year's. To capitalize on these trends, we should therefore invest in the new tartfish processing plant on Tartfish Island, where increasing revenues from tourism indicate a strong local economy."

最近几年，全球范围内对鱼的需求增加，而且捕鱼技术的提高使捕捞量增大，从而使鱼的供应量也有所增加：例如，去年的金枪鱼捕捞量比前年增加了9%。为了利用这个趋势赚钱，我们应该给Tartfish岛上新建的tartfish处理厂投资，那里旅游业收入的不断增长表明当地的经济很发达。

（A）For one thing, the argument rests upon a problematic assumption that the growing worldwide demand for fish indicates a growing demand for fish in general.

（B）For another, the fact that demand and supply are all increasing in recent years can not guarantee that fishing industry is and will be profitable. If supply exceeds demand, the price of fish will decline.

（C）Finally, the mere fact that Tartfish Island's revenues from tourism is increasing is not evidence that Tartfish Island's economy is strong.

134 **The following appeared in a speech by a stockholder of Consolidated Industries at the company's annual stockholders' meeting.**

以下内容摘自Consolidated工业公司的一个股东在本公司年度股东大会上的讲话。

"In the computer hardware division last year, profits fell significantly below projections, the product line decreased from twenty to only five items, and expenditures for employee benefits increased by 15 percent. Nevertheless, Consolidated's board of directors has approved an annual salary of over one million dollars for our company's chief executive officer. The present board members should be replaced because they are unconcerned about the increasing costs of employee benefits and salaries, in spite of the company's problems generating income."

去年计算机硬件部分的利润大大低于计划目标，生产线从20条减到5条，而发给员工的福利却增加了15％。尽管如此，Consolidated的董事会已经同意给我们公司首席执行官100万美元以上的年薪。现在的董事会成员应该被替换，因为尽管公司出现收入下降问题，他们仍然无视员工福利和工资的增长所带来的成本增加。

（A） First of all, the argument depends upon an unfounded assumption that the profitability of the computer hardware division represents that of the company as a whole.

（B） Secondly, the shareholder unfairly assumes that their company's chief executive officer is responsible for the decline of profits in the computer hardware division.

（C） Finally, the fact that Consolidated's board of directors has approved an annual salary of over one million dollars for the company's chief executive officer is insufficient to support the assumption that the present board members are unconcerned about the increasing costs of employee benefits and salaries. Therefore, it is imprudent to replace the present board members.

135 **The following appeared in a memorandum from the business planning department of Avia Airlines.**

以下内容摘自Avia航空公司商业规划部的一份备忘录。

"Of all the cities in their region, Beaumont and Fletcher are showing the fastest growth in the number of new businesses. Therefore, Avia should establish a commuter route between them as a means of countering recent losses on its main passenger routes. And to make the commuter route more profitable from the outset, Avia should offer a 1/3 discount on tickets purchased within two days of the flight. Unlike tickets bought earlier, discount tickets will be nonrefundable, and so gain from their sale will be greater."

在它们所在地区的所有城市中，Beaumont和Fletcher的新业务数量增长最快。因此，作为一种应对主要旅客航线最近蒙受损失的办法，Avia应该在这两个城市之间建立一条通勤航线。为了让通勤航线一开始就能多多获利，Avia应该给航班起飞前两天内购票的人提供1/3的机票折扣。不像在较早的时间购买的票，打折票是不可退的，这样，从机票销售中获得的利润会更大。

（A） In the first place, the author fails to establish a causal relationship between the fast business growth in Beaumont and Fletcher and the number of the commuters between the two cities.

（B） In the next place, the author provides no evidence to support the assumption that people who commute between Beaumont and Fletcher will use Avia Airlines.

（C） Finally, the author unfairly assumes that the practice of offering a 1/3 discount on tickets purchased within two days of the flight will make the commuter route more profitable from the outset. On the one hand, the discount policy is unlikely to motivate more people to travel by Avia Airlines. It is likely that the commuters will not increase the frequency of their commute between the two cities simply because the ticket price has been reduced. On the other hand, as commuters generally have regular routine, it is unlikely that most of the commuters between Beaumont and Fletcher would be pleased to purchase tickets at a 1/3 discount.

---

136 **The following appeared in a memorandum from the vice-president of Gigantis, a development company that builds and leases retail store facilities.**
以下内容摘自Gigantis(一家建造和出租零售店铺面的发展公司)副总裁的一份备忘录。

"Nationwide over the past five years, sales have increased significantly at outlet stores that deal exclusively in reduced-price merchandise. Therefore, we should publicize the new mall that we are building at Pleasantville as a central location for outlet shopping and rent store space only to outlet companies. By taking advantage of the success of outlet stores, this plan should help ensure full occupancy of the mall and enable us to recover quickly the costs of building the mall."

过去5年中，在全国范围内，专门经营打折商品的专卖店销售量增长显著。因此，我们应该把我们正在建造的Pleasantville宣传为专卖店中心，并且铺面只租给直销公司。利用专卖店的成功，购物中心的所有铺面都将被租用，从而我们可以很快收回建造购物中心的成本。

(A) To begin with, the argument relies on a gratuitous assumption that sales at outlet stores will continue to thrive simply because they increased significantly in the past five years.

(B) Secondly, even if the trend continues in the future, only renting store space to outlet companies is an extreme measure.

(C) Finally, the vice-president fails to establish a causal relationship between the nationwide success of outlet stores and the full occupancy of the new mall at Pleasantville.

---

137 **The following appeared in a memorandum written by the chair of the music department to the president of Omega University.**
以下内容摘自Omega大学音乐系主任的一份备忘录。

"Mental health experts have observed that symptoms of mental illness are less pronounced in many patients after group music-therapy sessions, and job openings in the music-therapy field have increased during the past year. Consequently, graduates from our degree program for music therapists should have no trouble finding good positions. To help improve the financial status of Omega University, we should therefore expand our music-therapy degree program by increasing its enrollment targets."

精神健康专家发现许多精神病人的症状在集体音乐治疗会后变得不太明显，而音乐治疗方面的工作机会在过去一年中也有所增加。相应的，我们音乐治疗学位课程的毕业生应该很容易找到一份好工作。因此，为了帮助改善Omega大学的经济状况，我们应该增加音乐治疗学位课程的入学人数来扩展该项目。

(A) First of all, the fact that job openings in the music therapy field have increased during the past year does not necessarily mean that graduates from Omega University's degree program for music therapists can easily find good positions in the job market.

(B) Secondly, the author fails to establish a causal relationship between the financial status of Omega University and the music-therapy degree program. Other relevant factors may also contribute to the improvement of the financial status of Omega University.

The following appeared in a memorandum to the work-group supervisors of the GBS Company.
以下内容摘自写给GBS公司的工人管理员的一份备忘录。

"The CoffeeCart beverage and food service located in the lobby of our main office building is not earning enough in sales to cover its costs, and so the cart may discontinue operating at GBS. Given the low staff morale, as evidenced by the increase in the number of employees leaving the company, the loss of this service could present a problem, especially since the staff morale questionnaire showed widespread dissatisfaction with the snack machines. Therefore, supervisors should remind the employees in their group to patronize the cart—after all, it was leased for their convenience so that they would not have to walk over to the cafeteria on breaks."

CoffeeCart流动车位于我们办公主楼的休息大厅内，它为员工们提供饮料和食物，因为入不敷出，所以这个流动车可能会终止在GBS的服务。由于员工士气很低——这点可以从离开公司的员工人数的增加中看出，这种服务的终止可能会带来问题，特别是员工士气调查表显示员工们普遍对快餐车不满。因此，管理员们应该提醒他们手下的员工惠顾这个流动车，毕竟租借流动车是为了员工们，以便他们不用在工休时去自助餐厅用餐。

（A）In the first place, the author fails to provide sufficient evidence to support the claim that the staff morale is low.

（B）In the second place, the argument rests upon a questionable assumption that encouraging GBS Company's employees to patronize the CoffeeCart would resolve the problem of staff morale.

The following appeared as part of an article in a consumer magazine.
以下内容摘自某份消费杂志上的一篇文章。

"During a recent trial period in which government inspections at selected meat-processing plants were more frequent, the amount of bacteria in samples of processed chicken decreased by 50 percent on average from the previous year's level. These results indicate that the trial schedule should be made permanent: by continuing with more frequent inspections, the government could thus cut in half the incidence of stomach and intestinal infections throughout the country. In the meantime, consumers of Excel Meats should be safe from infection because Excel's main processing plant has shown more improvement in eliminating bacterial contamination than any other plant cited in the government report."

在最近的受审期内，政府对选定的肉类加工厂的检查频率增加了，加工过的鸡肉样本内细菌含量比前一年下降了50%。这些结果表明，受审期应该被无限延长：通过频繁不断的检查，可以使全国肠胃感染的发病人数减少一半。同时，Excel Meats 的消费者应该不会被感染，因为政府报告显示，Excel的主要加工设备在灭菌方面的改善要优于其他任何工厂。

（A）To begin with, the argument rests upon a dubious trial. The author fails to indicate that the selected meat-processing plants were representative of meat-processing plants in general and that a sufficient number were included in the trial to warrant the claim that increased government inspections contribute to the decrease of the amount of bacteria in samples of processed chicken.

（B）Secondly, the author unfairly assumes that the government has enough inspectors and resources to carry out the proposed permanent inspections at all meat-processing plants.

（C）Finally, the fact that Excel's main processing plant has shown more improvement in eliminating bacterial contamination than any other plant does not prove that meat processed by Excel's other processing plants is free from contamination.

"Last year, the city contracted with Flower Power to plant a variety of flowers in big decorative pots on Main Street and to water them each week. By midsummer many of the plants were wilted. This year the city should either contract for two waterings a week or save money by planting artificial flowers in the pots. According to Flower Power, the initial cost for artificial flowers would be twice as much as for real plants, but after two years, we would save money. Public reaction certainly supports this position: in a recent survey, over 1, 200 Gazette readers said that the city wastes money and should find ways to reduce spending."

去年，本市和Flower Power签订合同，让其在主大道上的大装饰花瓶内种植多种花卉并每周浇水一次。没到仲夏，许多植物都枯萎了。今年，本市应当与他们签订合同，要么每周浇水两次，要么在花瓶内插上假花以节省费用。据Flower Power称，假花的初始费用为真花的两倍，但两年后，我们将开始省钱。公众显然支持这种解决方式：在最近的调查中，超过1200的本报读者认为本市浪费资金，应该设法减少开支。

（A）First, the author unfairly assumes that two waterings a week will prevent flowers in big decorative pots on Main Street from wilting.

（B）Second, the author is presenting a false dilemma by imposing an either-or choice between two waterings a week and planting artificial flowers.

（C）Thirdly, the results of the survey are questionable as the argument does not indicate that the readers who participated in the survey were representative of the general public and that a sufficient number were included in the survey to warrant the claim that the city wastes money and should find ways to reduce spending.

（D）Finally, granted that the results of the survey are reliable, it is imprudent to say that the general public would support the idea of using artificial flowers as substitutes for real ones.

"The Riverfront Festival drew 10, 000 visitors—not bad for your first year. You would double that number, however, by bringing in the Jolly Pirate Ship. In St. Clyde, the Harbor Week Festival averaged 30, 000 visitors per year over the last decade, but the attendance reached a high point of 45, 000 a couple of years ago, when the Jolly Pirate was at the Harbor Week Festival. One of the organizers reported that the ship was especially popular with school groups. Have the Jolly Pirate Ship sail into the Riverfront Festival next summer, and your festival will be much more successful."

Riverfront Festival吸引了1万名游客——这对你们的第一年来说并不算差。然而，如果引进了Jolly海盗船，就能使游客的人数翻倍。St. Clyde，Harbor Week Festival在过去的10年中平均每年有3万名游客，但是几年前当Jolly海盗船被引进Harbor Week Festival时，它的游客人数最高曾达到4.5万人。其中一位组织者指出，该船很受学校团体的欢迎。明年夏天让Jolly海盗船驶进Riverfront Festival吧，你们的会演将更加成功。

（A）In the first place, the argument suffers from the fallacy of "post hoc, ergo propter hoc". The consultant fails to establish a causal relationship between the number of the visitors to Harbor Week Festival and the fact that Jolly Pirate was at the Harbor Week Festival.

（B）In the next place, the consultant commits the fallacy of "all things are equal". The consultant unfairly assumes that facts drawn from the Harbor Week Festival will be applicable to the Riverfront Festival.

（C）Finally, granted that the Jolly Pirate Ship has contributed to the increase of visitors to the Harbor Week Festival a couple of years ago, it does not necessarily mean that this method will be effective in the coming years.

---

142 **The following appeared in a memorandum from the development director of the Largo Piano Company.**
以下内容摘自Largo钢琴公司开发经理的一份备忘录。

"The Largo Piano Company has long been known for producing carefully handcrafted, expensive pianos used by leading concert pianists. During the past few years, however, our revenues have declined; meanwhile, the Allegro Musical Instrument Company introduced a line of inexpensive digital pianos and then saw its revenues increase. In order to increase Largo's sales and in fact outsell Allegro, we should introduce a line of digital pianos in a variety of price ranges. Our digital pianos would be likely to find instant acceptance with customers, since they would be associated with the prestigious Largo name."

Largo钢琴公司在为最杰出的音乐会钢琴家精心手工制作昂贵钢琴这一领域久负盛名。然而，在过去的几年中，我们的收入下降了。同时，Allegro乐器公司推出了便宜的数码钢琴，接着它的收入就增加了。为了增加Largo的销售额，实际上是为了卖得比Allegro多，我们应该推出不同价位的数码钢琴。我们的数码钢琴很有可能会立刻被顾客接受，因为人们会把它们与声望很高的Largo这一名字联系在一起。

（A）To begin with, the author fails to establish a causal relationship between the line of inexpensive digital pianos and the revenue increase at Allegro Musical Instrument Company.

（B）Secondly, the argument relies upon an unwarranted assumption that strategy used in the Allegro Musical Instrument Company will be applicable to the Largo Piano Company.

（C）Thirdly, the author unfairly assumes that the demand for digital pianos will increase or at least level off.

（D）Finally, the Largo Piano Company's reputation among pianists can not guarantee that its digital pianos would be likely to find instant acceptance with customers. While the Largo Piano Company has long been known for producing handcrafted pianos, the Allegro Musical Instrument Company may be famous for its digital pianos.

---

143 **The following appeared in a memorandum from the CEO of Volare Airlines.**
以下内容摘自Volare航空公司执行总裁的一份备忘录。

"Even though our record last year of on-time takeoffs and arrivals was not as good as that of several other major airline companies, our total revenues were among the highest of any airline. Clearly, an on-time record is not the passengers' first concern, and so we should not risk reducing our revenues by trying to improve our record. Instead, we should try to attract new passengers by announcing a program of incentives and discounts. Consider that Flugel Airlines saw ridership increase last year after it lowered fares on its most popular routes, whereas Aero Airlines lost

尽管去年我们记录的航班准时起飞和到达的情况不如其他几个主要航空公司，我们的总收入却是所有航空公司中最高的。很明显，准时记录不是乘客首要关心的问题，因此我们不应为了提高准时记录而使我们的收入遭受损失。相反，我们应该通过发布奖励和打折信息来吸引更多的乘客。想一想，Flugel航空公司去年它降低了最受欢迎航线的机票价格后，乘客的数量就增加了。相反，即使Aero航空公司的董事长因为航班

customers even after its president appeared on television to apologize publicly for flight delays."

晚点而在电视上向公众公开道歉，它的乘客数量仍在减少。

（A）First, the fact that the total revenues of Volare Airlines were among the highest of any airline does not provide evidence to support the claim that an on-time record is not of concern to passengers.

（B）Secondly, the author is presenting a false dilemma by imposing an either-or choice between two courses of action that are not mutually exclusive. It is possible that Volare Airlines can increase revenues and improve their on-time record at the same time.

（C）Thirdly, the author fails to provide sufficient evidence to support the claim that a program of incentives and discounts can attract new passengers, as facts drawn from other companies are not necessarily applicable to Volare Airlines.

---

144 The following appeared in a memorandum from the marketing department to the general manager of the Swiftville Gazette.
以下内容摘自Swiftville报市场营销部给总经理的一份备忘录。

"In an effort to expand its readership, the Swiftville Gazette made plans to replace the current editor-in-chief and to launch a costly subscription drive. Neither of these measures is now necessary, however, newspaper readership is on the rise once again, as newly released results of a national study show that the top five daily newspapers in the country are enjoying increased circulation for the first time in years. Therefore, the Gazette can expect to become a profitable enterprise for the first time since the editor-in-chief was hired. Moreover, since people are once again interested in the news, we can streamline our operations by dropping some of our 'extras', such as the gardening column, the real estate section, and the local sports news."

为了增加读者人数，Swiftville 报计划撤换当前的总编，并开展一项耗资甚多的订阅运动。然而，目前这两种措施都是不必要的：报纸的读者人数又一次上升，因为最近发布的一项研究结果表明，位居全国前五名的日报发行量数年来第一次出现增长。因此，新主编上任以后，本报第一次有望成为一家盈利性企业。此外，因为人们再次开始对新闻感兴趣，所以我们可以简化工作，去掉一些"特别栏目"，比如园艺、房地产以及当地体育新闻。

（A）First of all, the fact that the top five daily newspapers in the country are enjoying increased circulation does not indicate that the readership of all the other newspapers in the country is also on the rise.

（B）Secondly, the rising readership trend does not guarantee that the trend will continue.

（C）Thirdly, even if it were the case that the Swiftville Gazette's readership is on the rise, this fact alone is not sufficient to support the claim that plans made by the Swiftville Gazette are unnecessary.

（D）Finally, the fact that people are once again interested in the news does not mean that they become less interested in the "extras" columns. These two things need not be mutually exclusive.

---

145 The following appeared as part of a business plan created by the general manager of the Multon Electronic Company.
以下内容摘自Multon电子公司总经理起草的一份商业计划书。

"In response to complaints from customers about the difficulty of installing and operating Multon's products, Multon Electronic Company tried an experiment. The Customer Service Department has long suspected that customers are not reading

针对顾客抱怨 Multon产品难于安装和操作这一问题，Multon电子公司做了一个实验。长期以来，客户服务部都怀疑顾客没有阅读每一款新购产品内所附的

the instructions that are included with every new purchase, and so it inserted a gift certificate at the end of every instruction manual. Because only 75 people returned the certificates in a three-month period last year, Multon Electronics has proved its point that customers are not bothering to read the instructions. The Customer Service Department can solve this problem by providing every new customer with an instructional video."

说明书，所以在每一本操作手册后面插了一个礼品认领书。在去年三个月的时间内仅有75名顾客寄回了认领书，从而Multon电子证明了它的顾客都不愿去读说明书这一观点。客户服务部可以通过给每一个新顾客提供操作录像的方法来解决这个问题。

（A） First of all, the manager provides no evidence to support the assumption that customers who have read the instructions will have no difficulty in installing and operating Multon's products.

（B） Secondly, the argument rests upon a dubious study. No evidence is provided to support the assumption that people who returned certificates have read the instructions while people who did not return the certificates did not read the instructions.

（C） Finally, the manager unfairly assumes that customers prefer watching instructional videos to reading instruction manuals.

---

146 **The following is a memorandum to the president of the EZ-Manufacturing Company from the manager of cafeteria services.**
以下内容摘自自助餐厅经理递交给EZ制造公司总裁的一份备忘录。

"Offering pizza in our cafeteria has proved extremely profitable. To further increase our profits from pizza sales, we should switch to PDQ Pizzeria to supply our pizza. PDQ pizza was twice voted the 'best pizza' in the neighboring town of Hamiltonia in on-line surveys of Hamiltonia Gazette readers. The PDQ branch in our town currently sells pizza for only slightly more than our cafeteria does and has begun offering free daily delivery. Switching to PDQ pizza will clearly improve satisfaction with our cafeteria and hence increase the cafeteria's profits."

在自助餐厅提供比萨已被证明是非常盈利的。为了进一步增加比萨销售利润，我们应该换用PDQ比萨为我们供应的比萨。在临镇Hamiltonia的Hamiltonia报纸在线调查活动中，PDQ比萨两次被读者评选为最佳比萨。PDQ在我们镇的分店所卖的比萨只比我们自助餐厅现在卖的贵一点点，而且它已经开始提供日间免费配送服务。换用PDQ比萨肯定会增加顾客对我们自助餐厅的满意度，从而增加自助餐厅的利润。

（A） In the first place, the argument depends on a problematic survey. There is no evidence to support the assumption that the tastes of Hamiltonia Gazette readers are representative of consumers' general tastes.

（B） In the second place, the argument suffers from the fallacy of "all things are equal". The success of PDQ in the neighboring town does not necessarily indicate that PDQ will also be popular in this town.

（C） Thirdly, the manager unfairly assumes that customers will accept PDQ pizza with great satisfaction. The fact is that customers to the cafeteria may be concerned with the price of the pizza rather than free daily delivery service.

（D） Finally, the manager fails to provide sufficient evidence to support the assumption that selling PDQ pizza will be more profitable than selling the current pizza.

The following appeared in a memorandum from the marketing department of Reel magazine.

以下内容摘自*Reel*杂志市场部的一份备忘录。

"In order to determine the cause of the recent decline in sales of our magazine, we sent a survey to customers who have canceled their subscription during the last nine months. Results indicate that 80 percent of the 450 respondents feel that Reel contains too many ads. In order to retain current customers and win back customers who have canceled their subscriptions, we should reduce the number of ads. This solution will not only improve customer satisfaction but also increase our revenue by boosting magazine sales."

为了确定我们杂志最近销售下降的原因，我们给过去9个月中取消订阅的顾客送去了一份调查表。结果显示，450个回答者中有80%的人觉得Reel上广告过多。为了留住现在的顾客并争取让那些取消订单的顾客重新订阅我们的杂志，我们应该减少广告量。这个方法不但能提高顾客对杂志的满意度，而且会提高杂志的销量，从而增加我们的收入。

（A）To begin with, the argument rests upon a problematic survey. The author provides no evidence to support the assumption that the respondents' views are representative of the views of all the customers who have canceled their subscriptions.

（B）Secondly, the author unfairly assumes that the readers who have not canceled their subscriptions also think that Reel contains too many ads.

（C）Finally, the author fails to make a case for the assumption that revenues from the increased sales will outweigh the loss caused by the reduction of ads.

---

148 **The following appeared in an article in a health and fitness magazine.**

以下内容摘自一份健康与保健杂志上的一篇文章。

"A recent study of balding men revealed that 80% had higher than normal levels of the chemical compound DHT in their bodies. A second study discovered that rats fed a diet high in animal fats produced elevated levels of the same chemical. In this second study, however, one group of rats did not produce DHT when they also ate portions of wheat germ—a food rich in vitamin E—along with the other foods high in animal fat. Viewed together, these studies show that the best way to maintain healthy hair and scalp is to reduce fat consumption sharply and to take daily vitamin E supplements."

最近一项对秃头男士的研究显示，80%的秃头者体内DHT这种化学物质的含量高于正常水平。还有一项研究发现，如果老鼠吃动物脂肪含量高的食物，那么它们体内这种化学物质的含量就会升高。然而，在后一项研究中，一群老鼠在吃动物脂肪含量高的食物的同时，也吃部分小麦胚——一种富含维生素E的食物，体内就没有产生DHT这种物质。总的来看，这些研究表明保持头发和头皮健康的最佳方法是大幅减少脂肪的摄入量，同时每天补充维生素E。

（A）First of all, the results of the first study are not sufficient to support the assumption that it is DHT that is responsible for balding. To strengthen the assumption, other factors that may contribute to balding should be considered and ruled out.

（B）The argument suffers from the fallacy of "false analogy". It is highly doubtful that the facts drawn from rats are applicable to bald people.

（C）Finally, the author unfairly assumes that it is vitamin E that contributes to the decline of DHT in rat bodies.

149 The following appeared in a memo from the vice president in charge of fund-raising at Waymarsh University.

以下内容摘自Waymarsh大学负责筹资的副校长的一份备忘录。

"Three years ago, as part of a very successful campaign to increase the amount of money donated for scholarships, Midas College used student volunteers to telephone selected alumni and request contributions. That year the total amount of money donated to Midas exceeded its annual goal by 150 percent. To reduce overhead costs for fund-raising and increase contributions, Waymarsh University should begin using student volunteers to make telephone requests in all our fund-raising efforts. Furthermore, since the enrollment at Waymarsh University is more than twice that at Midas College, we should be able to raise at least as much money each year as Midas did by using this same method."

三年前，Midas大学开展了一项活动，非常成功地增加了人们为奖学金捐款的金额。作为活动的一部分，Midas大学让学生志愿者给选定的毕业校友打电话，请求他们捐款。那一年，Midas收到的捐款总额超过了年度目标150%。为了减少为筹资而花费的高额费用，并增加捐款，Waymarsh也应该在所有筹资过程中让学生志愿者打电话请求捐款。此外，Waymarsh大学的入学人数是Midas大学的两倍，使用同样的方法，我们每年筹集到的资金至少应该和Midas一样多。

（A） In the first place, the vice president fails to establish a causal relationship between telephone requests for contributions and the amount of money donated to Midas College.

（B） In the second place, the argument suffers from the fallacy of "all things are equal". On the one hand, the fact that the campaign worked well at Midas College does not indicate that it will also be successful at Waymarsh University. On the other hand, methods which were effective three years ago may be ineffective in coming years.

（C） Finally, the author unfairly presumes that enrollment plays a crucial role in determining the amount of money donated. There is no causal relationship between the enrollment and the amount of money donated.

150 The following appeared in a letter to the editor of a newspaper.

以下内容摘自写给某报编辑的一封信。

"Last year when Washington County received a special appropriation for improving high-way safety, it spent all those funds to straighten sections of certain roads. Unfortunately, the number of traffic accidents in the county was actually higher than in the previous year. Although Adams County received a smaller appropriation for improving highway safety, it hired more police officers and enforced traffic laws more strictly. Last year Adams County reported 15 percent fewer traffic accidents than during the previous year. Since money for improving highway safety throughout the state is limited, the state can achieve greater success with less expenditure by using all such funds for stricter enforcement of speed limits."

去年，当Washington县收到一笔为提高公路安全性而设的专款后，把所有资金都用在了改直部分路段上。不幸的是，实际上该县的交通事故数量高于前一年。尽管Adams县收到的提高公路安全性的金额要少一些，但是它雇用了更多的警察来严格执行交通法规，所以该县所报道的交通事故比前一年减少了15%。因为全州用于提高公路安全性的资金是有限的，所以把所有这类资金都用于严格执行速度限制法规，本州就可以花较少的钱而取得较大的成功。

（A） First, the argument rests upon a problematic assumption that straightening certain roads fails to reduce traffic accidents.

（B）Secondly, the author unfairly assumes that stricter enforcement of traffic laws is the only factor that contributes to the decline of traffic accidents in Adams County. The mere fact that the strict traffic law enforcement precedes a decline in accidents is not sufficient to establish a causal relationship between the two events.

（C）Finally, the author commits the fallacy of "all things are equal". Granted that the strict enforcement of traffic laws led to a decline of accidents in Adamn County, it is imprudent to presume that the strategy will have similar results in Washington County, because these two counties are not necessarily similar.

---

151 The following appeared in a memo from a vice president of Mama Mia's, a chain of Italian restaurants.

以下内容摘自Mama Mia's —— 一家意大利餐馆连锁店副总的一份备忘录。

"Officials of the movie industry report that over 70 percent of the movies released last year targeted a teenage audience. Furthermore, national sales data indicate that the favorite food of teenagers is pizza. Since a branch store of Good Times Movie Rental opened on Center Street six months ago, sales of takeout pizza at our restaurant next door have been higher than at any other restaurant in our chain. Because the rental of movies seems to stimulate pizza sales, the best way to increase our profits is to open new Mama Mia's restaurants next to or very near all of the Good Times Movie Rental stores."

电影业的官员报道说，去年上演的电影中有70%以上将目标观众定位于青少年。此外，全国范围内的销售数据显示，青少年特别喜欢吃的食物是比萨。自从Good Times电影出租公司的一家分店六个月前在中心街开业以来，我们与之相邻的餐馆外售比萨饼的销量比我们连锁店中任何一家都高。因为电影出租似乎能刺激比萨的销售，所以提高我们利润的最佳方法是在与Good Times电影出租公司的店铺相邻或相近的地方开设新的Mama Mia's餐馆。

（A）In the first place, the vice president unfairly assumes that the Good Times Movies Rental on Center Street is responsible for the increased sales of takeout pizza. The evidence provided is insufficient to establish a causal relationship between the two events.

（B）In the second place, the information offered in the argument is too vague to guarantee that teenagers will go to Good Times Movie Rental because most of the movies are produced for them.

（C）Thirdly, granted that teenagers go to Good Times Movie Rental for movies, there is no evidence to support the assumption that this trend will continue in the coming years.

（D）Finally, the argument commits the fallacy of "all things are equal". The success of a certain store can not guarantee other stores using the same method will enjoy the same results.

---

152 The following appeared in a memo from the vice president of the Fizzle Soda Company.

以下内容摘自Fizzle Soda公司副总的一份备忘录。

"There is apparently a market for new beverages, as can be seen from the fact that other companies have recently introduced new juice drinks and sports drinks. Given this market and customer surveys indicating that many drinkers of regular Fizzle soda add chocolate syrup to their soda, we can increase our company's sales by creating a new chocolate-flavored soda, 'Choco-Fizz.' Choco-Fizz will help us attract

从其他公司最近推出了新的果汁饮料和运动饮料这一事实中可以看出，新型饮料显然很有市场。基于这个市场，再加上顾客调查显示许多普通Fizzle汽水的消费者会在他们的汽水中加入巧克力汁，我们可以通过制造新型的巧克力口味汽水"Choco-Fizz"来增加我们公司的销售额。Choco-Fizz有助于

new customers and keep our customers who might otherwise switch to our competitors' chocolate beverages. Also, Choco-Fizz will be more successful than Fizzle Plus, our most recently introduced flavor, because it will be easier to distinguish from regular Fizzle soda."

为我们公司吸引新顾客，同时可以防止我们公司的顾客转而选择我们竞争对手的巧克力饮料。并且，Choco-Fizz会比我们最近推出的风味饮料Fizzle Plus更成功，因为人们很容易把它与普通Fizzle汽水区分开来。

（A）To begin with, the author fails to establish a causal connection between the introduction of new drinks and the apparent market for new beverages.

（B）Secondly, the survey cited by the vice president is described in the vaguest possible terms. The argument does not indicate who conducted the survey, who responded, or how the survey was conducted.

（C）Thirdly, the mere fact that many drinkers of regular Fizzle soda add chocolate syrup to their soda is insufficient to conclude that the new chocolate-flavored soda will be popular.

（D）Finally, the author fails to make a case for the claim that Choco-Fizz will be more successful than Fizzle Plus.

---

153 **The following appeared in a memo from the president of the Meltaway Company, a producer of ice cream.**
以下内容摘自一家冰淇淋生产公司——Meltaway总裁的一份备忘录。

"Health concerns and convenience appear to be the key factors affecting sales of ice cream. Last year's publication of research suggesting that some types of fat can be beneficial to health must have made people more willing to eat regular ice cream, which contains fat. Over the past year, national sales of regular ice cream increased about 8 percent, while sales of fat-free or low-fat ice cream increased by only 1 percent. During the same time period, sales of ice cream were similarly affected by consumers' demand for convenience, as grocery stores increased their sales volume for ice cream by 9 percent, compared to a 3 percent increase for ice-cream parlors and other stores specializing in ice cream. Therefore, we can expect that most of our profits over the next few years will come from providing regular ice cream to grocery stores."

健康问题和便利性似乎是影响冰淇淋销售的主要因素。去年公布的研究结果显示，有些类型的脂肪对健康是有利的，该结果一定能使人们更乐意吃含有脂肪的普通冰淇淋。去年一年，全国普通冰淇淋的销售量增长了8%，而无脂或低脂冰淇淋的销售量仅增长了1%。与此同时，冰淇淋的销量还受顾客对便利性需求的影响，因为与冷饮店以及其他冰淇淋专卖店的销售额仅增长3%相比，杂货店的冰淇淋销售额增长了9%。因此，在未来的几年内，可以预期我们的大部分利润将来自向杂货店供应普通冰淇淋。

（A）In the first place, the president unfairly attributes sales increase of regular ice cream to the fact that last year's publication of research suggested that some types of fat can contribute to a healthy lifestyle.

（B）In the second place, the conclusion of the argument rests upon an unwarranted assumption that the net profit margin of grocery stores is higher than that of ice-cream parlors and other stores specializing in ice cream.

---

154 **The following appeared in a memo from a public health official.**
以下内容摘自某个公共健康官员的一份备忘录。

"A recent international study shows that 7, 000 children who brushed their teeth with a toothpaste containing altide had 40

最近一项国际研究表明：7000名使用含有altide的牙膏刷牙的儿童出现蛀牙

percent fewer cavities than 7, 000 other children who did not use a toothpaste with this ingredient. Furthermore, altide occurs naturally in the water from springs on the island of Mandiba, and residents of that island typically have very few dental fillings or artificially replaced teeth. Therefore, the cheapest and most effective way to improve the dental health of residents of nearby islands is to provide them bottled water from the springs on Mandiba."

的概率比另7000名使用不含该成分的牙膏的儿童低40%。此外，Mandiba岛上的泉水中天然就含有altide这种物质，且该岛居民通常很少需要补牙或换假牙。因此，增进附近岛屿居民牙齿健康最省钱最有效的方法是向他们提供来自Mandiba泉水的瓶装水。

（A）First, the survey cited by the public health official is too vague to draw a general conclusion that altide is conducive to dental health.

（B）Secondly, the author fails to establish a causal relation between spring water containing altide and the good dental health conditions of the residents on the island of Mandiba.

（C）Finally, granted that altide benefits dental health, the argument provides no evidence to support the claim that drinking bottled water from the springs on Mandiba is the cheapest and most effective way to improve the dental health of residents on nearby islands.

---

155 The following appeared in an article from a health magazine.
以下内容摘自某份健康杂志上的一篇文章。

"In a yearlong clinical trial of Mi-Quell, a new medicine for treating migraine headaches, researchers observed no significant side effects during the first five months. After six months, however, 20 percent of the subjects in the clinical trial began to report dizziness. Furthermore, during the final six months of the clinical trial, 43 of the subjects fell at least once and 18 were involved in automobile accidents. Such data indicate that Mi-Quell should be used to treat migraine headaches for up to six months, but after that time period doctors should prescribe another medicine."

经过对Mi-Quell——一种新的治疗偏头痛的药物一年的临床实验，研究者发现在前五个月没有什么明显的副作用，然而，六个月以后，接受临床实验的患者中有20%的人开始报告头昏眼花。而且，在临床实验的最后六个月期间，43位接受实验者都至少摔倒了一次，还有18位实验者卷入了汽车事故。这些数据表明，用Mi-Quell来治疗偏头痛最多只能用六个月的时间，六个月之后，医生应该给病人开其他药。

（A）To begin with, the argument relies on a problematic clinical trial. The author fails to prove that the subjects are representative of all patients suffering from migraine headaches.

（B）Secondly, the fact that researchers observed no significant side effects during the first five months is insufficient to guarantee the safety of this medicine during that period. There might be unseen side effects that could bring about health problems later in life.

（C）Thirdly, no evidence is provided to prove that the fact that 43 of the subjects fell at least once and 18 were involved in automobile accidents is due to the side effects of this medicine.

（D）Finally, it is imprudent to recommend doctors prescribe another medicine after using Mi-Quell for six months. Other medicines may be less effective than Mi-Quell in treating migraine headaches.

---

156 The following appeared in a memo from the budget planner of the city of Clearview.
以下内容摘自Clearview市预算计划者的一份备忘录。

"After a campaign to promote recycling of metal, paper, plastics, and glass, the city collected twice as much of these

经过促进回收金属、纸张、塑料以及玻璃的运动以后，本市去年从当地住宅区收集

recyclable materials from local homes last year as during the previous year. When the city sold these materials, the major buyer paid 30 percent more per pound for recycled aluminum and certain grades of paper. Within a few months the city also plans to annex and collect recyclable materials from a new housing area containing over 4,000 households. Thus, by collecting larger amounts of recyclable materials and selling them at higher prices, the city's recycling program should soon become profitable."

的可回收材料数量是前一年的两倍。当本市卖出这些材料时，主要的购买商以每磅高30%的价格购买了回收铝和某些级别的纸。在几个月内，本市计划开始在一个拥有4000住户的新住宅小区里收集可回收材料。这样，通过大量收集可回收材料，然后高价卖出，本市的回收项目很快就能盈利。

（A） For one thing, although the city collected twice as much of these recyclable materials from local homes last year as during the previous year, there is no evidence to support the implicit assumption that this trend will continue in the future.

（B） For another, the fact that the major buyer paid 30 percent more per pound for recycled aluminum and certain grades of paper—the high price does not indicate that the price of these materials will continue to rise or stay the same. The price of materials depends on the relation between supply and demand in the market.

（C） Furthermore, the new housing area containing over 4, 000 households may have less recyclable materials than the planner expects. New housing areas typically contain little recyclable materials.

（D） Finally, the mere fact that the amount of collecting and the obtaining from selling materials are both increasing is not sufficient to support the claim that the city's recycling program will soon become profitable. The expense of promoting and implementing the program must be considered.

157 The following appeared in a proposal from the sheriff of Adams County.
以下内容摘自Adams县县长提出的一条建议。

"Last year a course in driver's education became a requirement for graduation for all students at the Adams County High School, and the board of education purchased 10 new cars to provide students in the classes with on-the-road driving experience. Nevertheless, the number of teenage drivers involved in traffic accidents here in Adams County has increased by 200 percent this year, and officers from the sheriff's department have cited a record high number of teenagers for violations of traffic laws. Since the high school driver's education classes have been so ineffective in improving traffic safety, we should no longer require them and should spend our limited funds on other programs."

去年，驾驶员培训成为Adams县所有高中生毕业前必修的一门课，学校董事会购进了10辆新汽车以增加班上学生的路上实际驾驶经验。尽管如此，Adams县青少年涉及交通事故的数量在今年仍增加了200%，并且来自县委的官员宣称青少年违反交通法的人数达到了前所未有的高度。既然高中的驾驶员教育课程在提高交通安全方面是如此无效，那么我们不应该再要求他们必修此课，而把我们有限的资金用到其他项目上去。

（A） In the first place, there is no causal connection between the driver's education course at the Adams County High School and the number of teenagers who have violated the traffic laws in Adams County. On the one hand, not all students at the Adams County High School have passed the course in driver's education. On the other hand, not all teenagers in Adams County are from the Adams County High School.

（B） In the next place, even if it was the case that driver's education at the Adams County High School was ineffective in improving traffic safety last year, it does not indicate that driver's education will continue to be ineffective in the future.

158 **The following appeared in a memo from the president of Pampered Pooch Spas, a chain of luxury dog-grooming businesses.**

以下内容摘自一家高档狗美容连锁企业——Pampered Pooch Spas总裁的一份备忘录。

"Over 70 percent of the current households in the town of Philazoa have pets, many new families are moving into Philazoa, and kennels in the area continue to report brisk sales of puppies. Furthermore, the average family income in Philazoa is 50 percent higher than the national average, and a local store reports record-high sales of the most expensive brands of dog foods. With so many devoted pet owners and such liberal spending to take good care of those pets, Philazoa will be a profitable location for a new Pampered Pooch Spa—a dog-grooming business that offers premium care at higher than average prices."

Philazoa的现有家庭中超过70%都养有宠物，许多新的家庭正在迁入Philazoa，且该区狗市上小狗的交易活动仍然很活跃。此外，Philazoa的家庭平均收入比全国的平均收入高出50%，一家当地的商店报告说，最高档品牌的狗食销量达到了前所未有的高度。有这么多投入的宠物主人以及他们为照顾好这些宠物而不惜重金的行为，Philazoa将会成为Pampered Pooch Spa——一家以高于普通的价格提供一流护理的宠物狗美容企业的一个新的盈利地点。

（A） First, the author fails to establish a causal relation between family income and money spent on pets. On the one hand, there is no evidence to indicate that the families having higher income have pets. On the other hand, sales of the most expensive brands of dog foods in one local store can not be representative of the sales in all the stores in the town of Philazoa.

（B） Secondly, the evidence cited by the author is not sufficient to support the assumption that Philazoa will be a profitable location for a new Pampered Pooch Spa. For one thing, even if it were the case that pet owners are generally willing to buy the most expensive brands of dog foods for their dogs, it would not follow that they will also spend a lot of money on dog-grooming. They may tend to take care of the pets by themselves rather than sending it to a dog-grooming company. For another, the dog-grooming industry may be highly competitive. Whether the new Pampered Pooch Spa has a competitive advantage over other dog-grooming companies is open to doubt. Moreover, the new residents may not be potential consumers of the new Pampered Pooch Spa.

159 **The following appeared in a budget proposal for the country of Salutopia.**

以下内容摘自Salutopia的一份预算建议书。

"Over the past 20 years the birth rate in Salutopia has declined. During that same period, however, the number of physicians practicing in Salutopia has steadily increased, and the average number of patients treated by each physician has decreased by 30 percent. Meanwhile, average life expectancy in Salutopia has risen to 71 years, and the mortality rate fell significantly last year. Since such data indicate dramatic improvements in public health and a more than adequate supply of physicians in Salutopia, the national medical college need not expand and can perhaps even reduce its size."

在过去20年里，Salutopia的出生率下降了。然而，在同一时期内，Salutopia的开业医生人数却在稳步增加，平均每个医生治疗的病人人数下降了30%。同时，Salutopia人的平均寿命已上升到了71岁，去年的死亡率也显著下降。这些数据表明，Salutopia的公众健康水平得到了大幅的提升，医生也人满为患，所以本国的医学院不需要扩大规模，甚至可以缩小现有规模。

（A） To begin with, the trend over the past 20 years does not indicate this trend will continue in the following years.

（B）Secondly, the author assumes that the relative number of physicians practicing in Salutopia has steadily increased over the past 20 years, resulting in a more than adequate supply of physicians. While this is a reasonable assumption, it is by no means a certainty. The reason for the longer life expectancy may be the improvement of medical care, and the increased average life expectancy requires more medical care related to elders than ever.

（C）Supply is relative to demand. Therefore, it is reckless to claim that the national medical college need not expand and can perhaps even reduce its size.

160 The following appeared in a memo from the president of Elegant Seafoods, a chain of restaurants.

以下内容摘自一家连锁餐馆——Elegant Seafoods总经理的一份备忘录。

"We should proceed with our plan to open a new restaurant in the busy College Plaza shopping center near Waymarsh College. Although two restaurants in that location have closed in the past two years (one a pizza parlor, the other a deli), their failure does not mean College Plaza is an unsuitable location for our restaurant. After all, the Plaza Café has been in business at that location for twenty years. Furthermore, national reports from the restaurant industry show that college students are eating out more frequently than ever. It is likely, then, that we will be very successful at that location."

我们应该开始执行在Waymarsh大学附近繁华的College Plaza购物中心开一家新餐馆这一计划。尽管在过去的两年中那个地方有两家餐馆(一家比萨饼店,一家熟食店)关闭了,他们的失败并不意味着College Plaza不适宜我们开餐馆。毕竟,Plaza餐馆已经在那个地方经营20年了。此外,来自餐饮业的全国报道表明,大学生们去餐馆吃饭的频率要高于以往任何时候。因而,我们很有可能在那个地方取得成功。

（A）For one thing, other restaurants' failure does not mean that Elegant Seafoods is doomed to failure. Likewise, the Plaza Café's success does not indicate that Elegant Seafoods is bound to succeed.

（B）For another, the fact that college students are eating out more frequently than ever does not necessarily mean that they will choose Elegant Seafoods.

161 The following appeared in a newsletter distributed at a town meeting in River City.

以下内容摘自在River市某一个镇的会议上所分发一篇业务通讯。

"Recently Greenspace, Inc. purchased several hundred acres of undeveloped land on the outskirts of River City. Although Greenspace has announced that it is considering plans to turn this land into a park for the city, Greenspace is owned by Megacompany, Inc., which also owns other companies that make such diverse products as cosmetics and new houses and that have typically done little to preserve the environment. Thus, to protect the animal and plant species of River City from increased pollution, consumers should refuse to purchase any products that are made by Megacompany until Greenspace abandons its plan to develop housing on the land."

Greenspace有限公司最近在River市郊购买了几百英亩未开发的土地。尽管Greenspace宣布它计划将这片土地建成一个公园,但是Greenspace隶属于Mega-company有限公司,该公司还拥有生产其他不同产品的公司,如生产化妆品的公司,建造新住宅的公司等,这些公司通常在保护环境方面做的很少。因此为了保护River市的动植物不受污染不断增加带来的侵害,消费者应该拒绝购买Mega-company公司生产的任何产品,直到Greenspace放弃它在那片土地上开发房地产的计划为止。

（A）To begin with, the fact that the other companies owned by Megacompany have typically done little to preserve the environment does not indicate that Greenspace is not concerned about the environment.

（B）Secondly, the author unfairly assumes that Greenspace plans to develop housing on the land on the outskirts of River City.

（C）Thirdly, the author provides no solid evidence to support the implicit assumption that Greenspace's plan is going to pollute the environment.

（D）Finally, there is no evidence to prove the suggestion that consumers refusing to purchase Megacompany's products to force Greenspace to abandon the project is the best way to solve current environment problems.

162 The following appeared in a memo from a vice president of Omni Industries.
以下内容摘自Omni工业公司一位副总的一份备忘录。

"Last month's reports from Omni's top executives indicate that they spent more than 20 percent of their company travel time waiting in airports. Meanwhile, during the past year Hermes Airlines had twice as many on-time flights as any other airline. To avoid the irritation of excessive waiting, Omni should use Hermes Airlines for its company travel. Such a change should increase company profits by using employee time more productively and improving morale."

上个月来自Omni高级管理人员的报告显示，他们的商务旅行中有超过20%的时间是在机场等待。同时，Hermes航空公司去年准时的航班数目是其他所有航空公司的两倍。为了避免过多等待的烦恼，Omni应该选用Hermes航空公司来进行它的商务旅行。这样的改变应该可以提高公司的利润，因为这不但能更有效地利用员工的时间，而且还可以鼓舞他们的士气。

（A）In the first place, the statistics cited in the reports may not be applicable to the future.

（B）In the second place, the fact that Hermes Airlines had twice as many on-time flights as any other airline last year does not guarantee that its on-time rates are the highest among all the airlines.

（C）Finally, the author fails to establish a causal connection between using Hermes Airlines for Omni Industries' company travel and the company's profit increase.

163 The following is taken from Townsville Residential Carpet Cleaning's business plan.
以下内容摘自Townsville住宅地毯清洁公司的商业计划书。

"Homes built in this country last year were an average of 20 percent larger than those built just 10 years ago. At the same time, carpet manufacturers had greater overall profits than in any previous year. To meet the demand for home carpet-cleaning services and improve our own profitability, we should take out a loan to buy an additional truck for our fleet."

我们国家去年建造的住房平均比十年前大了20%。同时，地毯制造商的总利润也高于以往任何年份。为了满足人们对住宅地毯清洁服务的需求，提高我们公司的利润，我们应该贷款为我们的车队再购置一辆卡车。

（A）First of all, the fact that homes built in this country last year were an average of 20 percent larger than those built just 10 years ago does not mean that the demand for carpet is increasing. People may choose wooden floors rather than carpet for their new homes.

（B）Secondly, the fact that carpet manufacturers had greater overall profits does not guarantee the greater profits in carpet-cleaning services. It is possible that the carpet manufacturers' increasing profits come from the reductions of their costs.

（C）Finally, the author fails to provide any evidence to support the implicit assumption that trucks currently owned by the fleet can not meet the demand for increasing service.

---

164 **The following appeared in a memo from the manager of Smart Step, a retail shoe store.**
以下内容摘自一家零售鞋店——Smart Step的经理的一份备忘录。

"The advertising strategy of Legacy Car Dealers has always been to target first-time buyers who may then become loyal repeat customers. Using this strategy, Legacy has sold more cars than any other local dealer during the past 50 years, and its owners are quite wealthy. Thus, to insure steadily increasing sales in future years, Smart Step should direct its current advertising to a youthful audience. Furthermore, a good choice to carry out this advertising campaign is the Hang-10 agency, which has a young creative staff and has become famous for its memorable tunes in advertisements on radio."

Legacy Car经销商的广告策略通常是以第一次购买者为目标客户，他们有可能会变成忠实的回头客。运用这种策略，Legacy在过去50年里卖出的汽车数量比本地区任何其他的经销商都要多，并且它的老板非常富有。因此，为了确保销售能在将来的年份里稳步增长，Smart Step应该把它的广告转向年轻的听众。此外，Hang-10广告代理公司是完成这个广告项目的最佳选择，它拥有年轻且富有创造力的职员，还因在收音机广告中出现令人难忘的曲调而闻名。

（A）In the first place, the argument rests upon a false analogy. The advertising strategy that works well for Legacy Car Dealers is not necessarily applicable to Smart Step.

（B）In the second place, the author fails to establish a causal connection between the choice of Hang-10 agency and the success of the advertising campaign. The mere fact that the advertising agency has a young creative staff and has become famous for its memorable tunes in advertisements on radio is insufficient to support the claim that an advertising campaign targeting a youthful audience will be a success.

---

165 **The following is from a proposal made by a government official in the country of Cortin.**
以下内容摘自Cortin国一名政府官员起草的一份建议书。

"More than half of Cortin's inhabitants live near the seacoast, as is also the case in the country of Blandis. To solve the problem of ocean pollution along the Blandis seacoast, the government of Blandis recently purchased the X-2000, a new machine that identifies specific pollut-ants in seawater. In the year since the X-2000 was purchased, a substantial decrease in ocean pollution has been measured at various locations along the coast of Blandis. To ensure that Cortin's seacoast is a healthful and attractive place to live and to visit, our government should follow the example of Blandis and purchase an X-2000."

Cortin有超过一半的居民住在海岸附近，Blandis国的情况也是如此。为了解决沿Blandis海岸的海水污染问题，Blandis政府最近购买了X-2000 —— 一种可以鉴别海水中特定污染物质的新机器。自从购买X-2000那年起，Blandis海岸线不同地方的测试结果均表明海水的污染程度已大幅下降。为了确保Cortin海岸成为一个有益健康且适宜居住和旅游的地方，我们的政府应该仿照Blandis的做法，购买一台X-2000。

（A）The major problem with the argument is that the government official unfairly attributes the substantial decrease in ocean pollution in Blandis to the introduction of the X-2000.

（B）Another problem with the argument is that it depends upon a false analogy. The fact that the solution works well in Blandis does not indicate that it will also be effective in Cortin. There is no evidence to support the assumption that the Cortin and Blandis are analogous in all aspects.

166 **The following appeared as part of an editorial in the *Doddsville News.***

以下内容摘自*Doddsville News*的一篇社论。

"Last year's accidental introduction of a species of algae-eating fish into nearby Grand Lake has dramatically cleared the lake's once-murky waters. Since then, the number of swimmers at Grand Lake's beaches has increased by 23 percent. Given this success at Grand Lake, Doddsville should introduce algae-eating fish into Emerald Lake. Emerald Lake is already a popular place for fishing, but improving the water there will attract additional tourists interested in swimming and boating. The result will be an increase in business and profits for Doddsville hotels and merchants."

去年偶然把食藻鱼引进了附近的Grand湖中，该湖一度黑暗的湖面变得非常清澈了。从那以后，在Grand湖边游泳的人数增加了23%。鉴于Grand的这种成功，Doddsville也应该在Emerald湖中引进食藻鱼。Emerald湖已经是一个很受欢迎的钓鱼场所，但是湖水改善以后，它将吸引更多喜欢游泳和划船的游客。这样，Doddsville旅馆以及商人的业务和利润都将增加。

（A）In the first place, the argument rests on a false analogy. The approach that is practical in the nearby Grand Lake may not work for Emerald Lake.

（B）In the second place, even if it were the case that the introduction of algae-eating fish into Emerald Lake is successful in improving water quality, it does not follow that business and profits for Doddsville hotels and merchants will also increase.

167 **The following appeared in a consultant's report to the Regional Cuisine, Inc.**

以下内容摘自某位顾问递交给Regional Cuisine有限公司的一份报告。

"The number of tourists coming to Central Valley has increased 30 percent in the past three years, but no new restaurants have been opened during that time. To capitalize on the rapidly expanding tourist market, Regional Cuisine should immediately open a new restaurant in Central Valley, featuring traditional dishes of the Central Valley region. Regional Cuisine restaurants have been profitable in other tourist areas and thus we should expect to succeed in Central Valley as well."

在过去的3年中，到Central Valley参观的游客数量增加了30%，但是这段时间里却没有新餐馆在这个地方开业。为了利用这个快速发展的旅游市场赚钱，Regional Cuisine应该立即在Central Valley开设一个新餐馆，以Central Valley地区的传统菜肴为特色。Regional Cuisine餐馆在其他旅游景点均盈利，因此我们预期在Central Valley也可以取得成功。

（A）First, the argument suffers from the fallacy of "all things are equal". What happened in the past three years does not guarantee the same trend will continue in the future. Similarly, the success of Regional Cuisine restaurants can not ensure that the new restaurant in Central Valley will also be profitable.

（B）Secondly, the evidence cited by the argument is insufficient to support the claim that Central Valley will be a good location for a new restaurant. The fact that no new restaurants have been opened while the number of tourists has increased may indicate that the restaurant industry is saturated.

（C）Finally, the author unfairly assumes that traditional dishes will be popular with tourists in Central Valley.

The following editorial appeared in the sports section of the Winetta Daily News.

下面这篇社论摘自Winetta新闻日报的体育版。

"Because the Winetta Women's Biking Team lost most of its races this year, the team coaches need to improve team members' fitness by following the example of the Spandia Women's Biking Team. After five straight years of losing more races than it won, the Spandia team signed up for the 'Train to Win' workout program and, only six months later, started winning more of its races. To make sure that Winetta Women's Biking Team wins more races next year, the coaches should incorporate 'Train to Win' into the team's fitness program."

由于Winetta女子自行车队今年输掉了它的大部分比赛，该队的教练需要仿照Spandia女子自行车队的方法来提高队员的体能。在连续5年输多胜少的情况下，Spandia签约使用"为赢而练"的训练方案，仅仅六个月之后，它就开始赢得所参加的大多数比赛了。为了确保Winetta女子自行车队能在下一年赢得更多的比赛，该队的教练应该把"为赢而练"方案融汇到队员的体能训练计划中。

（A）To begin with, the argument relies on an unwarranted assumption that the failure of the Winetta Women's Biking Team is largely due to the fitness of its members. The fact is that fitness is not as important as technique.

（B）Secondly, the author unfairly attributes Spandia Women's Biking Team's success to the "Train to Win" workout program.

（C）Finally, the argument commits the fallacy of "all things are equal". The solution for the Spandia Women's Biking Team is not necessarily applicable to the Winetta Women's Biking team.

The following appeared in a memorandum from the president of Didactica, a company that publishes textbooks.

以下内容摘自一家教材出版公司——Didactica老总的一份备忘录。

"We have just taken an important step toward promoting our textbooks more effectively. Didactica has signed a contract with MousePrints, Inc., a company that supplies advertising-sponsored mousepads to schools free of charge. Each mousepad is printed with four age-appropriate, education-related ads that include Web site addresses, and since the mousepads are placed next to computers in classrooms and computer labs, the users of the computers are likely to visit Didactica's Website. This method of familiarizing students and teachers with our company will help us increase our sales revenues and our share of the textbook market."

我们刚刚在更加有效推广我们的教科书方面迈出了重要的一步。Didactica与MousePrints有限公司签订了合同，该公司向学校免费提供由广告资助的鼠标垫。每一个鼠标垫上都印上了四个与年龄相宜与教育相关的广告，其中包括网站网址。因为鼠标垫都放在教室和实验室的计算机旁，所以计算机用户很可能会访问Didactica的网站。这种使学生和教师认识我们公司的方法将会帮助我们增加销售收入以及我们的教科书的市场份额。

（A）In the first place, the mere fact that teachers and students have immediate access to Didactica's website address is not sufficient to support the assumption that teachers and students are likely to visit its websites.

（B）In the second place, even if teachers and students are likely to visit Didactica's website, there is no guarantee that they will buy more textbooks published by Didactica.

（C）Finally, the claim that Didactica has taken an important step toward promoting its textbooks more effectively is open to doubt. It is likely that Didactica's competitors will use the same type of promotion. Therefore, Didactica will have no advantage over its competitors in promoting textbooks.

The following appeared in a plan written by the business manager of a daily newspaper called *The Smallville Bulletin*.

以下内容摘自一份*The Smallville Bulletin*的日报的业务经理起草的一份计划书。

"Last year nationwide revenues from classified ads posted on the Internet rose 50 percent, but our revenues from daily and weekend classified ads for autos, jobs, and homes rose only 5 percent—the smallest rise in the past five years. The message is clear: we at *The Smallville Bulletin* can expect that within the next five years, revenues from our classified ads section will decline steeply. Since most of our revenues will therefore come from ads placed in the other sections of our newspaper, we can best ensure the survival of *The Smallville Bulletin* by printing only one classified ads section per week and by creating new sections on a different set of consumer-related topics such as fashion, home décor, and technology."

去年在全国范围内，互联网上分类广告的收入增加了50%，但是我们从汽车、工作以及住房每日和周末的分类广告中获得的收入却只增长了5%——这是过去5年中增长最少的一年。该信息表明：我们可以预期*The Smallville Bulletin*从分类广告版面所获得的收入在接下来的5年中会急剧下降。因而我们的大部分收入要来自我们报纸其他版面的广告。因此我们可以通过每周只印制一期分类广告，同时开创一系列不同的与消费者相关的新主题版面，比如时尚、家庭装修以及科技等，来确保*The Smallville Bulletin*的生存和发展。

（A）First, what happened last year does not guarantee the same trend will continue in the next five years.

（B）Secondly, the author unfairly presumes that it is the classified ads posted on the Internet that led to the falling revenues from classified ads posted on *The Smallville Bulletin*. Other factors other than the emerging rivalry, such as the efficiency of the daily newspaper, can also contribute to the decline of revenue.

（C）Finally, there is no guarantee that the other consumer-related topics will necessarily be a success for *The Smallville Bulletin*.

The following appeared in a business plan written by the manager of the Parker Hotel.

以下内容摘自Parker Hotel经理起草的一份商业计划书。

"Currently the Parker Hotel's restaurant has a certificate of merit awarded by *Bacchus*, a well-known magazine for wine enthusiasts, but such certificates mean little because hundreds of other restaurants around the world also have them. To enhance our restaurant's reputation and profitability, we should invest a million dollars in our wine inventory so that we will have a good chance of winning Bacchus' highest award—the Vin Noble Prize—and subsequently being featured in the magazine. We would not have to keep spending large sums to maintain a comparable wine inventory, because the magazine's inspectors do not regularly revisit Vin Noble Prize winners."

当前，Parker Hotel餐馆拥有一张*Bacchus*———一份在葡萄酒爱好者中非常出名的杂志———颁发的荣誉证书。但是这样的证书是毫无意义的，因为全世界有几百家其他餐馆也拥有这样的证书。为了增加我们餐馆的声誉和利润，我们应该斥资100万美元于我们的葡萄酒库存，以增加我们赢得*Bacchus*的最高奖项——Vin Noble奖的几率，然后我们餐馆就会被该杂志特别报导。我们没有必要不停地花大把钱来维持一个可观的葡萄酒库存，因为该杂志的检查员并不会定期重访Vin Noble奖的获得者。

（A）First of all, the fact that hundreds of other restaurants around the world also have certificates of merit awarded by *Bacchus* is not sufficient to support the claim that these certificates are meaningless.

(B) Also, the author fails to establish a causal connection between the profitability and reputation of certain restaurants and the highest award.

(C) Furthermore, it is risky to recommend that the restaurant should invest a million dollars in its wine inventory as the enlargement of wine inventory does not necessarily guarantee that the restaurant will win Bacchus' highest award.

(D) Finally, it is thoughtless to say that the restaurant does not have to maintain a comparable wine inventory just because the magazine's inspectors do not regularly revisit Vin Noble Prize winners. Additionally, this practice violates business ethics.

---

172 **The following appeared in a memorandum from the president of Sinecor, a computer-software company.**
以下内容摘自一家计算机软件公司 —— Sinecor总经理的一份备忘录。

"The amount of money Sinecor spent last year on paid vacations and medical benefits increased by 30 percent. To offset these expenses, we should increase to 30 percent the portion of our employees who are temporary or contract workers. Since we will not have to give these workers vacation time or medical benefits, we will save money by employing them. In addition, our regular employees will be motivated to work harder to preserve their jobs as well as their vacation and health benefits. These changes will improve Sinecor's overall profitability and ability to compete with other companies."

去年，Sinecor花在带薪假期和医疗福利上的钱增加了30%。为了弥补这一部分支出，我们应该将我们员工中临时工或合同工的比例增至30%。因为我们不必为这些员工提供假期以及医疗福利，所以雇用他们可以省钱。另外，我们的正式员工会由此受到激励而努力工作，以便保住他们的工作以及假期和健康福利。这些改变不但会提高Sinecor的整体盈利能力，而且能增加Sinecor与其他公司的竞争能力。

(A) First, the argument rests upon an unwarranted assumption that money saved by increasing the proportion of temporary or contract workers to regular employees can offset the expenses incurred by paid vacations and medical benefits.

(B) Secondly, whether the temporary or contract workers are immediately available and whether they can substitute for the regular workers is still open to doubt. More temporary or contract workers will exert a negative effect on the stability of work force in the company and will be harmful to the long-term development of the company.

(C) Thirdly, the practice of substituting temporary or contract workers for the regular ones is more likely to undermine rather than boost the regular employees' morale.

---

173 **The following appeared in a proposal from the sheriff of Adams County.**
以下内容摘自Adams县县长的一份倡议书。

"This year the number of teenage drivers involved in traffic accidents here in Adams County has increased by 200 percent, and officers from the county sheriff's department have cited a record high number of teenagers for violations of traffic laws. To deal with this increasingly serious problem, the now-optional driver's education course at Adams County High School should become a required course for all students before their graduation. Furthermore, the board of education should

今年在Adams县，十几岁的孩子驾车出现交通事故的数量比去年高出了200%，县长办公室的官员指出，青少年违反交通法规的人数也达到了前所未有的高度。为了解决这个日益严重的问题，Adams县高中应把目前选修性质的驾驶员训练课改为所有学生毕业前的必修课。此外，教育管理委员会应该购买10辆

purchase 10 new cars to provide all students in the classes with extensive on-the-road driving experience."

新车以便增加班里所有学生的道路驾驶经验。

（A）In the first place, statistics drawn from this year does not necessarily indicate that the number of teenagers violating the traffic laws is going to increase in the future.

（B）In the second place, the argument relies on an unfounded assumption that requiring all the students at Adams County High School to take the driver's education course will increase teenagers' safety on the road and prevent them from violating traffic laws.

（C）Finally, the sheriff unfairly assumes that 10 new cars are sufficient to provide all students in the classes with extensive on-the-road driving experience.

---

174 **The following appeared in a memorandum from the head of a human resources department at a major automobile manufacturing company to the company's managers.**
以下内容摘自一家大型汽车制造公司人力资源部主管递交给经理的一份备忘录。

"Studies have found that employees of not-for-profit organizations and charities are often more highly motivated than employees of for-profit corporations to perform well at work when their performance is not being monitored or evaluated. Interviews with employees of not-for-profit organizations suggest that the reason for their greater motivation is the belief that their work helps to improve society. Because they believe in the importance of their work, they have personal reasons to perform well, even when no financial reward is present. Thus, if our corporation began donating a significant portion of its profits to humanitarian causes, our employees' motivation and productivity would increase substantially and our overall profits would increase as well."

研究表明，当没有监视或评价时，非盈利组织和慈善机构员工的工作积极性要比盈利机构的员工高得多。对非盈利组织员工的访谈表明，他们之所以具有较强的工作动力是因为他们认为自己的工作有助于改善社会状况。因为他们认为自己的工作很重要，所以，即使没有金钱方面的奖励，他们也会出于个人原因而努力把工作做好。因此，如果我们公司从赢利中拿出相当大的一部分钱来捐助人道主义事业，我们公司员工的工作动力和生产力将大幅度提升，总利润也将随之增加。

（A）In the first place, the credibility of the studies cited above is open to doubt since the source of the studies is unclear.

（B）In the second place, the argument depends on the assumption that the employees of nonprofit organizations will perform well at work simply because they are highly motivated. However, there is no guarantee that this is always the case.

（C）Furthermore, the head of the human resources department fails to establish a causal relationship between the donation of money and an increase in motivation and productivity.

（D）Finally, increased motivation and productivity do not necessarily lead to increased profits.

---

175 **The following appeared in an editorial from a magazine produced by an organization dedicated to environmental protection.**
以下内容摘自一份致力于环保的杂志上的一篇社论。

"In order to effectively reduce the amount of environmental damage that industrial manufacturing plants cause, those who manage the plants must be aware of the

为了有效降低由工业制造工厂引起的环境破坏，这些工厂的管理人员应该知道他们生产中每一个流程所造成的环境破坏的

specific amount and types of damage caused by each of their various manufacturing processes. However, few corporations have enough financial incentive to monitor this information. In order to guarantee that corporations reduce the damage caused by their plants, the federal government should require every corporation to produce detailed annual reports on the environmental impact of their manufacturing process, and the government should impose stiff financial penalties for failure to produce these reports."

具体情况及类型。然而，几乎没有企业有足够的经济动机去监控这一信息。为了保证企业能减少工厂引起的环境破坏，联邦政府应当要求每个企业都做有关他们生产过程对环境所造成的影响的详尽年度报告，并且对那些没有提供这类报告的企业施以严厉的经济处罚。

Outline 1

(A) The argument is based on an unwarranted assumption that corporations will take actions only if they have financial incentives. Common sense and experience informs me that this might not always be the case, especially when those damages harm the companies in question. And it is also possible that some of the leaders of those corporations might feel that they have the responsibility to serve the communities by maintaining a livable environment.

(B) The author unfairly assumes that those corporations will take an objective stance when reporting the environment impact of their manufacturing process.

(C) The argument depends on the further assumption that after submitting their annual reports corporations will realize the significance of environment damages and will take corresponding actions to reduce these damages.

Outline 2

(A) Producing detailed annual reports on the environmental impact of their manufacturing process doesn't necessarily guarantee that corporations will actually take action to reduce the damage. It is highly possible that the cost of reducing the amount of environmental damage according to the report is so expensive that the company can not bear it, or that the costs far outweigh the financial penalties imposed by the government, even if those penalties are high. In these cases, companies generally will not reduce the damages outlined in the annual reports.

(B) There is no criterion for plant managers to determine how much damage the plants should reduce. Without such a criterion, it is possible that some plants will identify certain types of product as environmentally damaging whereas others will not. Different plants respond in various ways, thereby they may not necessarily achieve the federal government's goal.

(C) The author unfairly assumes that annual reports are sufficient for the plants to assess the environmental impact of their manufacturing process. For one thing, in their annual reports, managers may conceal some potential damage that their manufacturing process causes for the purpose of maximizing profits. For another, some environmental damage may be severe, and require taking immediate measures. Additionally, some other pollution may not cause harm to the environment in a short term, but the damage to the environment will be impossible to repair in the long run.

176 The following appeared in a memorandum from the information technology department of a major advertising firm.

以下内容摘自一家大型广告公司信息技术部的一份备忘录。

"The more efficient a firm's employees are, the more profitable that firm will be. Improvements in a firm's information technology hardware and software are a proven way to increase

公司员工的效率越高，公司的盈利能力将越强。有证据表明，改善公司在信息技术方面的硬件和软件能够有效地提

the efficiency of employees who do the majority of their work on computers. Therefore, if our firm invests in the most powerful and advanced information technology available, employee productivity will be maximized. This strategy ensures that every dollar spent on enhanced information technology will help to increase our firm's profit margins."

高那些主要用计算机进行工作的员工的效率。因此，如果我们公司能在目前最过硬、最先进的信息技术上投资，员工的生产效率将达到最大值。这种战略会保证在信息技术上花费的每一美元都有助于提高我们公司的利润率。

（A） The author provides no evidence to support the assumption that an increase in employees' efficiency will cause an increase in the firm's profitability.

（B） The argument depends on an unwarranted assumption that the most powerful and advanced information technology will certainly result in maximized employee productivity. Common sense informs me that the more advanced the information technology is, the more time the employees will need for training and getting used to it. If it takes employees 3 months or even longer to learn a new information technology, will the production efficiency also be improved by introducing this kind of new information technology?

（C） The author fails to establish a causal relationship between enhanced productivity and the increase in the firm's profit margins. The cost of introducing the most powerful and advanced information technology may well outweigh the profits produced by increased productivity.

177 The following appeared as part of an article in a health club trade publication.
以下内容摘自一篇来自关于健身俱乐部经营的刊物上的文章。

"After experiencing a decline in usage by its members, Healthy Heart fitness center built an indoor pool. Since usage did not increase significantly, it appears that health club managers should adopt another approach—lowering membership fees rather than installing expensive new features."

在经历其会员使用率的下降后，Healthy Heart健身中心修建了一个室内游泳池。使用率没有明显的上升，看来健身中心的经理们应该采用另外一种方法——降低会员费，而不是增加昂贵的新设施。

（A） The argument depends on a hasty generalization. Unless it can be shown that Healthy Heart is typical of all fitness centers, the fact that it experienced no increase in member usage is not grounds for concluding that all fitness centers will experience similar results.

（B） The fact that building an indoor pool is ineffective in increasing usage does not necessarily indicate that installing other new features is also futile.

（C） The argument commits a fallacy of false dilemma. The author ignores other factors relative to this issue that may be useful in helping fitness centers increase usage by their members.

178 The following appeared in a memorandum from the CEO of a consumer electronics manufacturing firm to the head of the company's human resources department, who is responsible for hiring new employees.
以下内容摘自一家消费电子产品制造公司的CEO给公司负责新员工招聘的人力资源主管的一份备忘录。

"Eight years ago, our firm's profits were increasing with each new employee we added. We discovered that each employee had the skills and motivation to generate more revenue

八年前，我们公司的利润随着新员工人数的增加而提高。我们发现每个员工都有技能和积极性去为公司创造高于

for the firm than his or her salary cost us. However, for the past two years, our profit margin has been falling, even though we have continued to add employees. Thus, our newer employees are not generating enough revenue to justify their salaries. We must not be hiring new employees with the same level of skills and motivation as those we used to attract. Clearly, then, failures in the human resources department account for our falling profits."

他们薪水的收益。然而，在过去的两年里，即使我们不断地增加员工，利润率还是下降了。因此，我们的新员工没有为公司带来与他们薪水相称的收益。我们雇用的新员工所具有的技能和积极性一定不如我们以前雇用的员工。显而易见，我们公司利润的降低应当归咎于人力资源部门的失败。

（A）The author fails to establish a causal link between the firm's profits and the increase in the new employees.

（B）The author unfairly attributes the firm's profit margin falling to the new employees. It is highly possible that the decrease in profits is caused by old employees, who can not keep up with the development of the firm. It is also possible that ever-increasing competition lead to the decrease in profits.

（C）Even assuming that the decrease in profits is indeed caused by new employees, we still can not safely draw the conclusion that the human resources department should be responsible for the firm's falling profits. No convincing evidence is provided to prove that the new employees lack the essential skills and motivations to work well for the firm. Perhaps, it is poor management that has led to the decrease in profits.

179 The following appeared in a memorandum from a company's marketing department.
以下内容摘自某个公司市场部的一份备忘录。

"Since our company started manufacturing and marketing a deluxe air filter six months ago, sales of our economy filter—and company profits—have decreased significantly. The deluxe air filter sells for 50 percent more than the economy filter, but the economy filter lasts for only one month while the deluxe filter can be used for two months before it must be replaced. To increase repeat sales of our economy filter and maximize profits, we should discontinue the deluxe air filter and concentrate all our advertising efforts on the economy filter."

自从我公司6个月前开始生产和销售豪华型空气过滤器以来，我们经济型过滤器的销售量和公司利润都显著下降了。豪华型过滤器比经济型贵50%，但是经济型过滤器仅使用一个月就得更换，而豪华型却可以用到2个月。为了提高经济型过滤器的再次销售并使公司的利润最大化，我们应该停止对豪华型空气过滤器的生产和销售，把所有的广告都集中到经济型过滤器上。

（A）The positive statistical correlation between the decrease of profit and the marketing of a deluxe air filter might just be a coincidence. Other reasons such as the severe competition should be considered and ruled out.

（B）The author's conclusion is based on a groundless assumption that consumers will resume buying the economy filter if the company stops manufacturing the deluxe air filter.

（C）Alternative strategies other than discontinuing the deluxe filter have not been considered by the author, thus making the conclusion unpersuasive. It is highly possible that other alternatives may enhance the profits of the company.

180 The following appeared in the editorial section of a local newspaper.
以下内容摘自某份当地报纸上的社论部分。

"The tragic crash of a medical helicopter last week points up a situation that needs to be addressed. The medical helicopter industry supposedly has more stringent

上周一架医用直升机的悲惨坠毁提醒我们一个需要注意的情况。医用直升机在飞行员训练以及设备维护方面应该有比其他

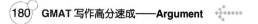

guidelines for training pilots and maintaining equipment than do most other airline industries, but these guidelines do not appear to be working: statistics reveal that the rate of medical-helicopter accidents is much higher than the rate of accidents for nonmedical helicopters or commercial airliners."

大多数类型的飞机更严格的指导方针。然而，这些指导方针看起来并没有起作用：统计数据显示，医用直升机的事故率要比非医用直升机或商业飞机高得多。

(A) In the first place, no concrete evidence is provided to support the assumption that inadequate pilot training or poor equipment maintenance is responsible for the higher rate of medical helicopter accidents. The author fails to rule out other factors that may have caused the medical helicopter accidents.

(B) In the second place, the argument depends on an incomplete comparison of medical helicopters and non-medical helicopters or commercial airliners. Therefore, the conclusion drawn from the comparison is open to doubt.

(C) Finally, the statistical evidence upon which the argument relies is too vague to be informative.

---

181 The following appeared in a letter from a part-owner of a small retail clothing chain to her business partner.
以下内容摘自一封由一家小型售衣连锁店的共有人给其商业伙伴的信。

"Commercial real estate prices have been rising steadily in the Sandida Heights neighborhood for several years, while the prices in the adjacent neighborhood of Palm Grove have remained the same. It seems obvious, then, that a retail space in Sandida Heights must now be much more expensive than a similar space in Palm Grove, which was not the case several years ago. So, it appears that retail spaces in Sandida Heights are now overpriced relative to those in Palm Grove. Therefore, it would be in our financial interest to purchase a retail space in Palm Grove rather than in Sandida Heights."

几年来，Sandida Heights附近的房地产价格稳步上升，而邻近的Palm Grove街区却保持价格稳定。显然，现在Sandida Heights的零售空地价格一定比Palm Grove相似的空地更加昂贵，这在几年前是不可能的。因此，与Palm Grove相比，Sandida Heights的零售空地看起来要价过高。因此，在Palm Grove购买零售空地将比在Sandida Heights买更有利。

(A) The argument commits the fallacy of hasty generalization. The fact that the commercial real estate prices in Sandida Heights have been rising while the prices in Palm Grove have remained unchanged is not sufficient to reach the conclusion that a retail space in Sandida Heights is now much more expensive than a similar space in Palm Grove.

(B) Even if a retail space in Sandida Heights is much more expensive than a similar space in Palm Grove, it is still unreasonable to assert that retail spaces in Sandida Heights are now overpriced. It is highly possible that retail spaces in Palm Grove are underpriced, while retail spaces in Sandida Heights are now normal relative to those in Palm Grove.

(C) Finally, even assuming that retail spaces in Sandida Heights are overpriced, it is still problematic to assert that purchasing a retail space in Palm Grove will be a wise financial decision.

---

182 The following appeared as part of an article in a daily newspaper.
以下内容摘自某份日报上的一篇文章。

"The computerized onboard warning system that will be installed in commercial airliners will virtually solve the

即将安装在民航客机上的计算机化机载警报系统将从根本上解决空中飞机相撞问

problem of midair plane collisions. One plane's warning system can receive signals from another's transponder—a radio set that signals a plane's course—in order to determine the likelihood of a collision and recommend evasive action."

题。为确定相撞的可能性和推荐回避措施，一架飞机上的警告系统可以收到另一架飞机上的异频雷达收发机——发信号表示飞机航线的无线电装置——传来的信号。

(A) The argument is based on the assumption that all the planes will be equipped with such a warning system. However, the author provides no evidence to support this assumption. It is highly possible that non-commercial airlines do not have this onboard warning system.

(B) Even if nearly all the planes are equipped with the warning system, there still exists the possibility that the midair collisions will take place. The author ignores the interface between pilots or flight specialists and the warning system. The pilots may be unfamiliar with the warning system, and may make mistakes when trying to deal with the problem of midair plane collisions.

(C) Furthermore, the author fails to consider the likelihood that the warning system itself may fail to function.

---

183 The following appeared in a presentation by the chief production manager of a machine parts manufacturing company at a management meeting.
以下内容摘自一家机器零件制造公司生产总经理在一次管理会议上的发言。

"Our factory in Cookville is our most advanced and efficient. It is capable of producing ten drill bits for each dollar of production costs, whereas none of our other factories can produce more than seven drill bits per dollar of production costs. Therefore, we can reduce our overall drill bit production costs by devoting the Cookville factory entirely to drill bit production. Since reducing the production costs of individual machine parts is the only way to achieve our larger goal of reducing our overall production costs, dedicating the Cookville factory entirely to drill bit production and shifting all other machine part production to our other factories will help us to attain that larger goal."

我们在Cookville的工厂是我们最先进和效率最高的厂。它能用1美元的生产成本造出10个钻头。然而，在我们其他的工厂中，没有一家工厂可以用1美元的生产成本制造出7个以上的钻头。因此我们能够通过将Cookville的工厂全部投入到钻头生产来降低总的钻头生产成本。因为减少单个机器零件的生产成本是我们实现降低总成本这一宏伟目标的唯一方法，因此让Cookville工厂全部投入到钻头生产中，而将其他机器零件转移到我们其他的工厂生产，将有助于实现我们的宏伟目标。

(A) First of all, the argument is based on an incomplete comparison between Cookville factory and factories in other places. Perhaps, in the Cookville factory, there are only one or several skilled workers who are capable of producing ten drill bits for each dollar of production costs, and they have already reached their full potential. Or maybe, the quality of drill bits produced by the Cookville factory is poor compared to those produced by other factories. Without ruling out all these and other possibilities, the author's recommendation that dedicating the Cookville factory entirely to drill bit production will reduce the company's overall production costs is untenable.

(B) Even if all the workers are proficient in producing quality drill bits at high speed, we still can not draw the conclusion that dedicating the Cookville factory entirely to drill bit production will reduce the company's overall production costs. It is highly possible that workers in the Cookville factory are more skilled at producing other machine parts. In order to achieve the higher goal of reducing the company's overall production costs, it may be better off with assigning the task of producing drill bits to other factories.

(C) Furthermore, the manager claims that reducing the production costs of individual machine parts is the only way to achieve the company's greater goal of reducing overall production costs. However, experience and common sense informs me that this is not necessarily the case.

The following appeared in a memorandum to a team developing accounting software for SmartPro Software, Inc..
以下内容摘自SmartPro Software软件公司会计软件开发小组的一份备忘录。

"Currently, more professional accountants use Smart-Pro accounting software than any other brand. However, in the market for personal accounting software for non-professionals to use in preparing their income tax returns, many of our competitors are outselling us. In surveys, our professional customers repeatedly say that they have chosen SmartPro Software because our most sophisticated software products include more advanced special features than competing brands. Therefore, the most effective way for us to increase sales of our personal accounting software for home users would clearly be to add the advanced special features that our professional software products currently offer."

当前，较多专业会计师选择使用SmartPro的会计软件。然而，在非专业人士用以准备所得税申报表（income tax return）的个人会计软件市场上，我们很多竞争者的销量都超过了我们。在调查中，我们的专业客户反复表示，他们选择SmartPro Software是因为我们最完善的软件产品所具有的高级特殊功能比其他竞争品牌多。因此，把我们目前只在专业软件产品中提供的高级特殊功能添加到个人家庭会计软件产品中去，无疑是提高个人家庭会计软件产品销售额的最有效方法。

（A）In the first place, the reliability of the surveys is open to doubt. The surveys cited by the author are described in the vaguest possible terms. The author does not indicate who conducted the surveys, who responded, or how the surveys were conducted. Until these questions are answered, the survey results are worthless as evidence for professional customers' opinion about SmartPro Software.

（B）In the next place, even if the results of the surveys are reliable, the argument depends on the further assumption that professional customers' opinion represents that of non-professional customers. However, the author provides no evidence to support this assumption.

（C）Finally, even assuming that non-professional customers are interested in advanced special features that professional software products currently offer, there is no guarantee that adding the advanced special features to personal accounting software for home users is the most effective way to increase sales. Other factors—such as friendly interface, manageability, customer service—may play a decisive role for some people in their choice of accounting software.

The following appeared in a letter to the editor of a local newspaper.
以下内容摘自一封给一家当地报纸编辑的信。

"Our city council's neglect of the impoverished Railroad Flats neighborhood has left businesses with little incentive to locate there. Building a new professional football stadium in the neighborhood would solve this problem. Thousands of football fans would travel to the area to see games, and they would buy from local merchants, encouraging new busin-esses to open. So our city council should move quickly to fund the construction of a professional football stadium in Railroad Flats in order to help the neighborhood develop a thriving economy."

我们的城市委员会对Railroad Flats附近穷困地区的漠视使得商家不愿在那里开业。在附近建一个新的专业足球场将解决这一问题。数千名球迷将跑到那里去看球，他们会购买当地的商品，从而鼓励新的商家在那开业。因此，为了促进Railroad Flats附近地区的经济繁荣，我们的城市委员会应当尽快筹资在Railroad Flats建一个专业足球场。

（A） The argument rests on the assumption that the construction of a professional football stadium is sufficient to help the neighborhood develop a thriving economy. However, other factors, such as frequency of the football games, and football's popularity in the city also determine the ultimate success of the plan. Moreover, even assuming that football is popular in the city, whether the new professional football stadium will attract a large number of fans to travel to the area to watch football games is open to doubt. Finally, in the light of the particularity of football games, if there are not perfect facilities and better management, conflicts between football fans may worsen the stability of the local society. Therefore, in order to make the recommendation more persuasive, the author must take many other factors relevant to this issue into consideration.

（B） The argument commits the fallacy of hasty generalization. The author fails to consider other ideas which can help attract businesses to the town. It is highly possible that alternative methods may be more effective in promoting the economic development of the Railroad Flats neighborhood. The author has to compare those potential plans, and more analysis should be carried out before the final decision is made.

---

186 The following appeared in a memorandum from the marketing department of a children's clothing manufacturer.
以下内容摘自一家儿童制衣厂市场部的一份备忘录。

"Our HuggyBunny brand is the bestselling brand of children's clothing. Parents everywhere recognize the HuggyBunny logo as a mark of quality, and most of our customers show great brand loyalty. Sales reports have shown that parents are more likely to buy children's clothes with the familiar HuggyBunny brand and logo than otherwise identical clothes without it. Therefore, if we use the HuggyBunny brand name and logo for the new line of clothing for teenagers that our company will soon be introducing, that clothing will sell better than it would if we labeled it with a new brand name and logo."

我们的HuggyBunny品牌是儿童服装中卖得最好的品牌。各地的家长都将HuggyBunny的标识看作是质量的标志，而且我们绝大多数客户都表现出了极强的品牌忠诚度。销售报告表明，与其他没有HuggyBunny商标和标识的相同衣服相比，家长们现在更倾向于购买具有HuggyBunny商标和标识的儿童服饰。因此，如果我们在即将引进的十几岁青少年衣服生产线所生产的衣服上打上HuggyBunny商标和标识，那么这些衣服的销售情况要比我们使用一个新的品牌和标识好。

（A） First of all, the credibility of the sales reports is open to doubt since the author did not indicate who published the reports. The fact that parents regard the HuggyBunny logo as a mark of quality is not sufficient to support the assumption that parents are more likely to buy children's clothes with the familiar HuggyBunny brand and logo than otherwise identical clothes without it. It is highly possible that children's clothing manufactured by HuggyBunny is too expensive and most of the parents can not afford to buy it even the clothing is of high quality.

（B） Secondly, even assuming that parents are more likely to buy their children's clothes with the familiar HuggyBunny brand and logo, it does not follow that parents will continue to buy their teenage children clothing of the same brand. While young children like to wear HuggyBunny clothing, teenagers may have outgrown wearing clothing labeled with the HuggyBunny brand and logo. Therefore, using the HuggyBunny brand name and logo for the new line of clothing for teenagers can not guarantee that the clothing will sell better than it would if it is labeled with a new brand name and logo.

187 **The following appeared in a research paper written for an introductory economics course.**

以下内容摘自某篇为一门经济学导论课程所写的研究论文。

"For the past century, an increase in the number of residential building permits issued per month in a particular region has been a reliable indicator of coming improvements to that region's economy. If the monthly number of residential building permits issued rises consistently for a few months, the local unemployment rate almost always falls and economic production increases. This well-established connection reveals an effective method by which a regional government can end a local economic downturn: relax regulations governing all construction so that many more building permits can be issued."

在过去一个世纪，某一特定地区每月发放的住宅建筑许可证的增长数量已经成为那个地区经济即将增长的一个可靠标志。如果每月发放的住宅建筑许可证数量在几个月中持续增加，则当地的失业率几乎总会下降，经济产量提高。这种确凿的关系揭示了一个地区政府可用以结束当地经济低迷的有效方法：放松对所有建设进行管制的法规，这样就会发放更多的住宅建筑许可证。

（A）The major problem with the argument is that the author assumes that there is a causal relationship between the number of residential building permits issued per month and improvements to the local economy. However, the author provides no concrete evidence to support this assumption.

（B）Moreover, even assuming that the increased building permits do cause reduced unemployment and economic production increases, further relaxing of regulations governing building permits will not necessarily lead to an overall economic revival, since other industries will suffer.

（C）Finally, even if increased building permits have caused reduced unemployment and economic production increases during the last 100 years, the argument depends on the further assumption that this trend will continue in the foreseeable future. However, no evidence is supplied to prove that this is the case.

附录　GMAT 写作必备 300 句

下面是笔者精心收集的300句经典句子。建议考生背熟这些句子，达到可以随口背诵的地步。为了便于背诵，笔者把中英文对照排列。考生可以按照下面推荐的方法进行背诵，促进写作和口语的共同提高。

- **分单元背**：把300个句子根据你自己的进度制订计划——每天背多少个新句子，复习多少个已经背过的句子；
- **英汉互译练习**：刚开始时，可以试着把英文译成中文，读过几遍后再试着把中文译成英文；
- **口头背诵**：出口成章并熟练应用是我们背诵这些句子的终极目标。

1. A large number of people tend to live under the illusion that they completed their education when they finished their schooling. Obviously, they seem to fail to take into account the basic fact that a person's education is a most important aspect of his life.

许多人存在这样的误解，认为离开学校就意味着完成了他们的教育。显然，他们忽视了教育是人生重要组成部分这一基本事实。

2. In recent years, there is a growing tendency for parents to ask their children to accept extra educational programs.

近些年，父母要求孩子接受额外教育的趋势呈增长之势。

3. A proper part-time job does not occupy too much of a student's time. In fact, it is unhealthy for them to spend all of time on studying. As the old saying goes: All work and no play makes Jack a dull boy.

一份适当的业余工作并不会占用学生太多的时间。事实上，把全部时间都用到学习上并不健康，正如那句老话：只工作，不玩耍，聪明的孩子会变傻。

4. Statistics show that 30 percent of the population does not have strong standpoint.

统计数据表明，30%的人口并没有坚定的立场。

5. According to a recent survey, four million people die each year from diseases linked to smoking.

最近的一项调查表明，每年有四百万人死于与吸烟有关的疾病。

6. Additional social stresses may also occur because of the population explosion or problems arising from mass migrat-ion movements though modern means of transportation have greatly alleviated that particular problem.

由于人口猛增或大量人口流动(现代交通工具使这种流动相对容易)引发的种种问题也会对社会造成新的压力。

7. Although many experts from universities and institutes consistently maintain that it is an inevitable part of an independent life, parents in growing numbers are starting to realize that people, including teachers and experts in education, should pay considerable attention to this problem.

尽管来自高校和研究院的许多专家坚持认为这是独立生活不可避免的一部分，然而，越来越多的家长开始意识到，包括教师和教育专家在内的人，都该认真对待这一问题。

8. It must be noted that improvements in agriculture seem to not be able to catch up with the population increases in rural areas and that there are millions of peasants who still live a miserable life and have to face the dangers of exposure and starvation.

必须指出，农业的发展似乎赶不上农村人口的增加，仍有上百万农民过着缺衣少食的贫寒生活。

9. Parents should be encouraged to send their children to nursery

应该鼓励父母将孩子送到幼儿园，这

schools, which will bring about profound impacts on children and families, and even society as a whole.	将对孩子、家庭，甚至整个社会产生深远的影响。
10. Many sociologists point out that rural emigrants are putting pressure on population control and social order; that they are threatening to take already scarce city jobs; and that they have worsened traffic and public health problems.	许多社会学家指出，民工正给人口控制和社会治安带来压力。他们威胁着本已萧条的工作市场，恶化了交通和公共卫生状况。
11. Although this view is widely held, this is little evidence that education can be obtained at any age and at any place.	尽管这一观点被广泛接受，很少有证据表明教育能够在任何地点、任何年龄进行。
12. An increasing number of experts believe that migrants will have a positive effect on the city construction. However, this opinion is now being questioned by more and more city residents, who complain that the migrants have brought many serious problems like crime and prostitution.	越来越多的专家相信移民将对城市的建设起到积极作用。然而，越来越多的城市居民却怀疑这种说法，他们抱怨民工给城市带来了许多严重的问题，如犯罪和卖淫。
13. There is a general discussion these days about education in many colleges and institutes. One of the questions under debate is whether education is a lifetime study.	当前，高校和研究机构对教育存在着大量争论，其中一个争论点就是教育是否是一个终身学习的过程。
14. An investigation shows that female workers tend to have a favorable attitude toward retirement.	一项调查显示，女性劳动者对退休持积极态度。
15. There is a lot of discussion about science and technology. One of the questions under debate is whether traditional technological methods are bound to die out when a country begins to develop modern science and technology.	关于科学技术存在许多争论，其中一个问题是，当国家发展现代科学技术时，传统的技术方法是否可能会消亡。
16. An investigation shows that many older people express a strong desire to continue studying at a university or a college.	一项调查显示，许多老人都有到大学或学院继续学习的愿望。
17. Anthropologists have discovered that fear, happiness, sadness, and surprise are universally reflected in facial expressions.	人类学家已经发现，恐惧、快乐、悲伤和惊奇都会行之于色，这对于全人类是共通的。
18. According to a recent survey, a growing number of people express a strong desire to take another job or spend more time on the job in order to get more money to support their family.	根据最近的一项调查显示，越来越多的人表达了想从事另外的工作或加班以赚取更多的钱来补贴家用的强烈愿望。
19. Parents should emphasize that their children maintain a balance between play and study. As an old saying goes: All work and no play makes Jack a dull boy.	任何家长都应重视保持孩子学习与玩耍的平衡，正如那句老话：只工作，不玩耍，聪明的孩子会变傻。
20. As a member of society, everybody should shoulder the responsibility for one's own behavior. Responsibility is society's ethical foundation. Without responsibility, or morals, society will be paralyzed, and not run well. Fortunately since the human civilization began, everyone's responsibility in	作为社会的一分子，每个人都应该为自己的行为负责。责任是社会道德的基础。没有责任就没有道德，那么这个社会就会陷入瘫痪，无法正常运转。好在自从人类文明开始，在法律制度之下，

societies with a legal basis is to accept the consequences of one's behavior.

社会中每个人都有对自己的行为后果负责的义务。

21. There are several reasons for this problem. One of the main reasons is that the number of vehicles is increasing much more rapidly than roads are being built. Another primary reason is that there seems to be too many private cars and not enough public buses.

关于这个问题，有很多原因。其中一个主要原因是车辆增加的数量远快于道路的建设。另一个主要原因是私家车过多而公交车不够。

22. As a popular saying goes, "There are two sides of everything." Now the public is benefiting more and more from scientific and technological inventions. On the other hand, science and technology can cause a lot of problems. People in many countries are suffering from public hazards because of these problems.

常言道：凡事都有两面性。如今，人们从科技发明中得到了越来越多的好处。另一方面，科技进步也给我们带来了许多麻烦。许多国家的人民正在遭受科技问题带来的公害之苦。

23. There is a general discussion about fashion in recent years. One of the questions under debate is whether a person should choose comfortable clothes, which he or she likes, regardless of fashion.

近些年，关于时尚问题存在着广泛的争论。其中一个问题就是一个人是否应选择他/她喜欢的舒适衣服，而不管是否时尚。

24. As for me, I'm firmly convinced that the number of foreign tourists should be limited, for the following reasons.

就我而言，我坚定地认为应当限制国外旅游者的数量，理由如下。

25. From what has been discussed above, we may safely draw the conclusion that a part-time job can have a far-reaching impact on students and they should be encouraged to take part-time job, which will benefit students and their families, even society as a whole.

通过上面的讨论，我们不难得出以下结论：兼职会对学生们会产生深远的影响，我们应鼓励学生从事兼职工作，这将有利于学生和他们的家庭，甚至整个社会。

26. There is a general debate on campus today over the phenomenon of college or high school students having part-time jobs.

对于大学生或高中生打工这一现象，校园里一直进行着广泛的争论。

27. An increasing number of people are beginning to realize that education does not end with graduation.

越来越多的人开始意识到，教育不能随着毕业而结束。

28. Although modern science and technology have proved that such methods are absurd, there are still millions of people in many remote places that use these methods.

尽管现代科学技术已经证明了这些方法是愚昧的，在许多偏僻的地方，仍有数百万的人在使用这些方法。

29. As is so often pointed out, knowledge is a two-edged sword which can be used equally for good or evil. It is now being used indifferently for both.

正像人们常常指出的，知识是一把双刃剑，它可以用来造福，也可以用来为害。人们现在正漠然地把知识用于这两个方面。

30. As the time and cost of making a chip drops to a few days and a few hundred dollars, engineers may soon be free to let their imaginations soar without being impeded by expensive failures.

随着芯片的制造时间和费用降低到了几天和几百美元，工程师们可能很快就可以任他们的想象驰骋而不会被昂贵的失败所束缚。

31. People seem to fail to take into account the fact that education does not end with graduation.

人们似乎忽视了教育不应该随着毕业而结束这一事实。

32. At the time when technology means ever more harmful carbon in the air we breathe, we need these forests more than ever.

当技术的发展意味着我们会吸入更多有害的碳元素时，我们比任何时候都更需要森林。

33. Because of the space crunch, the Art Museum has become increasingly cautious in considering acquisitions and donations of art, in some cases passing up opportunities to strengthen its collections.

由于空间不足，艺术博物馆在考虑购买和接受捐赠的艺术品时越来越慎重，有些情况下会放弃进一步改善收藏的机会。

34. Before giving my opinion, I think it is important to look at the arguments on both sides.

在给出我的观点之前，我想有必要看看双方的观点。

35. At the same time, along with the benefits of such machines, employees must study these machines so that they are able to control them.

同时，随着这些机器带给我们的好处，员工们也必须学习与之相关的知识来使用它们。

36. Besides, the living standard of the average Chinese person is still not high enough to be able to afford the many different sorts of expenses incurred during long distance travels.

此外，中国人民的生活水平还没有高到足以使普通中国人有钱支付长途旅行的各种开支的地步。

37. Bicycles can't be compared to other means of transportation like cars and trains for speed and comfort.

在速度和舒适度方面，自行车是无法和汽车、火车这样的交通工具相比的。

38. But is it really the case? The information I've collected over last few years leads me to believe that artistic and cultural projects may be less useful than many governments think. In fact, basic infrastructure projects play an extremely important role and should be given priority.

但这是真的吗？这些年我收集的信息让我相信文化、艺术项目并没有许多政府想象的那么有用。事实上，基础设施建设非常重要，应该放在首位。

39. When asked what kind of school they are willing to send their children to, many parents say they would choose a boarding school rather than day schools for their children.

当被问到愿意将孩子送到哪种学校时，许多父母认为他们会选择寄宿学校而不是日制学校。

40. But what these people fail to see is that international tourism may bring about a disastrous impact on our environment and local history.

但是这些人忽视了国际旅游可能会给当地环境和历史造成的灾难性影响。

41. By taking a major-related part-time job, students can not only improve their academic studies, but get experience, experience they will never be able to get from the textbooks.

通过做一份和专业相关的兼职，学生不仅能够提高他们的专业能力，而且能获得从课本上得不到的经验。

42. Children are undergoing rapid physical development; and lack of physical exercise may produce disastrous results later in life.

孩子们正处于身体快速发育的时期，缺乏体育锻炼可能会对他们未来的生活造成严重影响。

43. Although many people tend to live under the illusion that traditional technology and methods are still playing an extremely important role in their lives, increasing evidence shows that it is less useful than many people think.

尽管许多人保持着传统观念，认为传统技术方法仍在人们生活中发挥着重要作用，但是越来越多的证据显示，它并没有人们想象的那么有用。

44. There is a growing tendency these days for many people who live in rural areas to come into and work in city. This problem has caused wide public concern in most cities all over the world.

农民进城打工正成为一个不断增长的趋势，这一问题在世界上大部分城市已引起普遍关注。

45. Children with parents whose guidance is firm, consistent, and rational are inclined to possess high levels of self-confidence.

父母的教导如果坚定、始终如一和理性，孩子就有可能充满自信。

46. Civilized men like this kind of life. While they enjoy the comfort and banal luxury of their dwelling, they do not realize that they are deprived of the necessities of life.

文明人喜欢这样一种生活方式。在享受舒适和庸俗的豪华时，却没有意识到自己被剥夺了生活所必需的东西。

47. Consequently, the extra money obtained from a part-time job will strongly encourage students to continue to study.

因此，兼职挣来的钱将强有力地激励学生们继续他们的求学生活。

48. Due to high tuition fees, most ordinary families cannot afford to send their children to boarding schools.

由于较高的学费，大部分普通家庭支付不起孩子上寄宿学校的费用。

49. Editors of newspapers and magazines often go to extremes to provide their readers with unimportant facts and statistics.

报刊杂志的编辑常常为了向读者提供一些无关紧要的事实和统计数字而走向极端。

50. Environmental experts point out that increasing pollution not only causes serious problems such as global warming but also could threaten to end human life on our planet.

环境学家指出：持续增加的污染不仅会导致全球变暖这样严重的问题，而且还将威胁到人类在这个星球上的生存。

51. Only in a peaceful environment can people lay emphasis on sports events. The Olympic Games is a convincing example because it has been compelled to be cancelled several times in its history due to wars.

只有在和平环境里，人们才有精力去重视体育赛事。奥运会就是一个很有说服力的例子，在历史上它数次由于战争而被迫取消。

52. Even the best graduates need to continue learning before they become educated persons.

即使是最优秀的毕业生，在成为博学的人之前也要不断地学习。

53. This issue is becoming a matter of concern for more and more people, especially for parents and experts in education.

这一问题已被越来越多的人关注，尤其是父母和教育专家。

54. For lack of a distinct culture, some places can not attract tourists any more. Consequently, a quick rise in the number of foreign tourists may eventually lead to a decline in local tourism.

由于缺乏独特的文化，一些地方不再吸引旅游者。因此，国外旅游者数量的快速增加可能最终会导致当地旅游业的衰败。

55. There is no denying the fact that air pollution is an extremely serious problem and city authorities should take strong measures to deal with it.

无可否认，空气污染是一个极其严重的问题。城市当局应该采取有力措施来解决它。

56. For the majority of people, reading or learning a new skill has become the focus of their lives and the source of their happiness and contentment after their retirement.

对大多数人来讲，退休以后，阅读或学习一项新技术已成为他们生活的中心、快乐的来源。

57. From what has been discussed above, I am fully convinced that the leisure lifestyle is undergoing a decline with the progress of

通过以上讨论，我完全相信，随着现代社会的进步，悠闲的生活方式正在

modern society, and that this decline is not necessary a bad thing. | 消失，这并不是件坏事。

58. As for me, it is essential to know, at first, what kind of problems young students might encounter on campus. | 我认为，首先应看看学生们在校园可能会遇到哪些问题。

59. For people who want to adopt a healthy and meaningful lifestyle, it is important to find time to acquire new knowledge. As the old saying goes: It is never too old to learn. | 对于那些想过上健康而有意义的生活的人们来说，找时间学习一些新知识是很重要的。正如那句老话：活到老，学到老。

60. As for me, I'm in favor of the opinion that education is not over at graduation, for the following reasons. | 就我而言，我同意教育不应该随着毕业而结束的观点，理由如下。

61. From psychological aspect, the majority of children tend to have an unfavorable attitude toward additional educational activities. | 从心理上讲，大部分孩子似乎对额外的学习没有什么好感。

62. From what has been discussed above, we may safely draw the conclusion that both day schools and boarding schools are important to train young students for our society. | 通过以上讨论，我们可以得出结论：寄宿学校和日制学校对我们社会培养年轻学生都是重要的。

63. As for me, the declining of traditional technology and methods is not a bad thing; it is the natural result of society's progress. | 我认为，传统技术方法的消亡不一定是坏事——这是社会进步的必然结果。

64. There is a growing tendency for parents to stay at home to look after their children instead of returning to work earlier. | 现在，父母留在家里照顾孩子而不愿过早返回工作岗位正成为一种流行趋势。

65. Furthermore, people who are addicted to fashion have to spend more time going shopping and paying more attention to the impression they make on others. As a result, it is impossible to devote enough time and energy in their studies and jobs. | 而且，沉湎于时尚的人们不得不花费更多时间逛商店，更加注意自己给别人的印象。因此，他们不可能有足够的时间用于学习或工作。

66. In democratic countries any efforts to restrict the freedom of the press are rightly condemned. However, this freedom can easily be abused. | 在民主国家里，任何限制新闻自由的企图都理所当然地受到谴责。然而，这种自由很容易被滥用。

67. A government's protection of ancient culture does not merely safeguard one's own culture, it also promotes modern civilization. | 政府对古代文化的保护不仅保留了自己文化的独特性，而且能促进现代文明的发展。

68. However, there is an even more insidious kind of pollution that particularly affects urban areas and invades our daily lives, and that is noise. | 但是，还有一种更加隐蔽且有害的污染，它专门影响城镇地区，侵袭我们的日常生活，那就是噪音。

69. However, this idea is now being questioned by more and more experts, who point out that it is unhealthy for children who always stay at home with their parents. | 然而，这一想法正遭受越来越多的专家的质疑，他们指出，孩子总是和父母一起待在家里是不健康的。

70. I am always amazed when I hear people saying that sport creates goodwill between the nations, and that if only the common peoples of the world could meet one another at | 每当听到体育运动能够在国家间建立起友好感情、世界各地的普通人只要能在足球场或板球场上相遇就会没有

football or cricket, they would have no inclination to meet on the battlefield.

兴趣在战场上相遇这样的话，我都倍感诧异。

71. From what I have mentioned above, we can see clearly that violence on TV has a major influence on youngsters' behaviors.

从上面所提到的，我们可以清楚地看到，电视暴力对青少年行为的影响是极其深远的。

72. I find young people exciting. They have an air of freedom, and they have not a dreary commitment to mean ambitions or love of comfort. They are not anxious social climbers, and they have no devotion to material things.

我觉得年轻人令人振奋。他们带有自由的气息，不会为狭隘的野心和贪恋享受而孜孜以求。他们不会焦虑地向上爬，不会对物质性的东西难舍难分。

73. If we glimpse the unutterable, it is unwise to try to utter it, nor should we seek to invest with significance that which we cannot grasp. Beauty in terms of our human meanings is meaningless.

如果我们瞥见了只可意会不可言传的事物，企图把它说出来，那是不明智的；对于我们不理解的事物，我们不应该去赋予它某种意义。用只对我们人类有意义的词句来解释美是没有意义的。

74. At the same time, there are still many people who live under the traditional ideas that day schools play an extremely important role in children's study.

同时，仍有许多人持传统观点，认为日制学校对孩子的学习有着极其重要的作用。

75. In addition to the obvious problem—loneliness—another major obstacle, in my opinion, is the alien environment of the campus.

除了孤独这一明显的问题之外，我认为另一个困难是对校园环境的不熟悉。

76. At the same time, young people should be encouraged to communicate with their peers and develop their interpersonal skills, which may help them greatly reduce dependence on their parents and is essential for maintaining a healthy mental condition.

同时，应该鼓励年轻人和他们的同龄人交往，发展他们的交际能力，这将帮助他们极大地减少对父母的依赖，保持健康的精神状态。

77. If you want to achieve something or intend to fulfill one of your ambitions, you must work hard and be prepared. Otherwise, you will not be able to take advantage of opportunities when they arrive.

假如你想要取得成就或实现你的雄心壮志，就必须努力工作、做好准备。否则，机遇来临时你将无法抓住。

78. In conclusion, we must rationally take this problem into account and place more emphasis on peasants' lives. Any government that is blind to this point will pay a heavy price.

总之，我们应理智地考虑这一问题，重视农民的生活。任何政府如果忽视这一点都将付出巨大的代价。

79. However, unfair competition will cause social Darwinism and the strong will prey on the weak, which is unfavorable to society's harmonious development.

然而，不正当的竞争将会引起社会达尔文主义，弱肉强食，不利于社会的和谐发展。

80. In fact, we have to admit that quality of life is as important as life itself.

事实上，我们必须承认，生命的质量和生命本身一样重要。

81. In my opinion, there are plenty of opportunities for everyone in our society, but only those who are adequately prepared and

我的观点是：在我们的社会里，人人都有许多机遇，但是只有那些做好充

highly qualified can make use of them. 分准备并且高度称职的人才能抓住这些机遇。

82. Extra studies bring about an unhealthy impact on the physical growth of children. Educational experts point out that it is equally important to have some sport activities instead of extra studies when children spend the whole day in a boring classroom. 额外的学习对孩子们的身体发育是不利的。教育专家指出，孩子们在枯燥的教室里待了一整天后，参加一些体育活动而不是额外的学习，同样是非常重要的。

83. If you can do without the few pastoral pleasures of the country, you will find the city can provide you with the best that life can offer. 如果你愿舍弃乡下生活那一点点乐趣的话，那么你会发现城市可以为你提供生活中最美好的东西。

84. In the last few decades, advances in medical technology have made it possible for people to live longer than in the past. 在过去的几十年，先进的医疗技术已经使人们比过去活得更长成为可能。

85. With the development of our national economy, all these problems will certainly be solved step by step. 随着我国经济的发展，这些问题必将逐步解决。

86. From what has been discussed above, I firmly believe that time will prove that traditional technology and methods will die out with the development of modern science and technology. The maintenance of the traditional technology and methods is futile. 通过以上讨论，我坚定地相信时间会证明传统技术方法将会随着现代科学技术的发展而消亡，坚持传统技术方法是徒劳的。

87. There seems to be too many people without job and not enough available job positions. 失业的人似乎太多，而又没有足够的工作岗位。

88. In view of such a serious situation, environmental-friendly transportation tools like bicycles are more important than ever before. 考虑到这些严重的状况，我们比以往任何时候都更需要自行车这样的环保型交通工具。

89. Insects would make it impossible for us to live in the world; they would devour all our crops and kill our flocks and herds, if it were not for the protection we get from insecteating animals. 昆虫将使我们无法在这个世界上居住；如果我们没有受到以昆虫为食的动物的保护，昆虫就会吞食掉我们所有的庄稼并杀死我们饲养的牲口。

90. It is commonly accepted that no college or university can educate its students by the time they graduate. 人们普遍认为高校是不可能在毕业的时候教会他们的学生所有知识的。

91. In view of the seriousness of this problem, effective measures should be taken before things get worse. 考虑到问题的严重性，就必须在事态进一步恶化之前采取有效的措施。

92. Whatever the source of noise, one thing is certain: silence, it seems, has become a golden memory. 不管噪声来自何方，有一点是肯定的：寂静似乎已变成一种珍贵的回忆。

93. It is desirable to build more hospitals, shopping centers, recreation centers, cinemas and other public facilities to meet the public's growing needs. 人们希望建立更多的医院、购物中心、娱乐中心、电影院和其他公用设施，来满足人们日益增长的需求。

94. In addition, in order to attract tourists, a lot of artificial facilities have been built, which have unfavorable effects on the environment. 另外，为了吸引旅游者而修建大量人工设施，这对环境是不利的。

95. It is fairly clear that sleeping period must have some function, and because there is so much of it the function would seem to be important.

很清楚，睡眠必然具有某种作用。睡眠占去那么多时间，所以其作用似乎还很重要。

96. In conclusion, we must lay emphasis on this problem and try our hardest to help them enjoy their first days on campus.

总之，我们应重视这个问题，并尽最大努力帮助他们平稳度过最初的校园生活。

97. It is generally believed that the chief reason for the increase in population in developed countries is not so much the rise in birth rates but the decline in death rates resulting from improvements in medical care.

人们普遍认为，在发达国家，人口增长的主要原因与其说是出生率的上升，还不如说是由于医疗保健的改善使死亡率下降了。

98. In the first place, school authorities should provide more services to help freshmen to get used to their new life as soon as possible.

首先，学校应提供更多服务，帮助新生尽快适应新的生活。

99. It is hard to imagine a student focusing his or her energy on a textbook while other children are playing.

当别的孩子在玩耍的时候，很难想象一个学生能集中精力在课本上。

100. Tourism, however, gives rise to a number of problems. For instance, it becomes a burden to inefficient transportation systems.

然而，旅游业也引起许多问题。例如，它增加了我国本来效率就不高的运输系统的负担。

101. It is impossible to say simply for the fun and exercise: as soon as the question of prestige arises, as soon as you feel that you and some larger unit will be disgraced if you lose, the most savage combative instincts are around.

没有可能仅仅为了娱乐或锻炼而运动：一旦出现了声望问题，一旦你觉得你的失败会使你和你所属团体有失体面，你最野蛮的好斗本能就会被激发出来。

102. It is suggested that governments ought to make efforts to reduce the increasing gap between cities and the countryside. They ought to set aside an appropriate amount of funds for improving the standard of peasants' lives. They ought to invite experts in agriculture to share their experience, information, and knowledge with peasants, which will contribute directly to the economic growth of rural areas.

政府被建议应该努力减小正在拉大的城乡差距：应该划拨适当的资金提高农民的生活水平；应该邀请农业专家向农民介绍他们的经验、知识和信息，这些将直接地帮助发展农村经济。

103. Many people claim that with rapid economic development the number of people who use bicycle is decreasing and bicycles are bound to die out. However, the information I've collected leads me to believe that the bicycle will continue to play an extremely important role in modern society.

尽管许多人认为随着经济的高速发展，骑自行车的人数会减少，自行车可能会消失。然而，我收集的一些信息让我相信，自行车仍然会继续在现代社会发挥极其重要的作用。

104. Moreover, many people, including drivers and cyclists, do not obey the traffic rules properly, especially at busy intersections. This undoubtedly worsens an already grave situation.

而且，许多人，包括司机和骑自行车的人，不能很好地遵守交通规则，特别是在繁忙的十字路口。这无疑使本已严重的状况雪上加霜。

105. It is true that during their explorations they often faced difficulties and dangers of the most perilous nature, equipped in a manner which would make a modern climber shudder at the thought, but they did not go out of their way to court such excitement.

确实，他们在探险中遇到了极具威胁性的困难和危险，而他们的装备会让一个现代登山者想一想都浑身颤栗。不过他们并不是刻意去追求刺激。

106. Many experts point out that physical exercise contributes directly to a person's physical fitness.

许多专家指出体育锻炼能直接地有助于身体健康。

107. No one can deny the basic fact that it is impossible for average workers to easily master high-technology skills.

没有人能否认这一基本事实：对于一般工人来讲，轻松掌握这些技术是不可能的。

108. An advantage of children's participating in some paid work is that this practice can cultivate their independence, self-determination and sense of responsibility.

孩子参加有偿劳动的一个优点是这种实践可以培养小孩的独立性、自主性和责任感。

109. Take cars, for example. They not only pollute the air in cities, but make them crowded. Furthermore, they are responsible for a lot of traffic accidents. Car noise disturbs residents living on both sides of streets all day and night.

就拿汽车为例。汽车不仅污染城市空气，而且使城市拥挤不堪。此外，汽车造成了许多交通事故。汽车所产生的噪音使居住在街道两旁的居民日夜不得安宁。

110. Long before children are able to speak or understand a language, they communicate through facial expressions and by making noises.

儿童早在能说或能听懂语言之前很长一段时间，就会通过面部表情和发出声音来与人交流了。

111. In the first place, some aspects of traditional technology and methods are harmful and hamper the development of modern technology and science.

首先，传统技术方法有些部分是有害的，并且会阻碍现代科技的发展。

112. It is indisputable that there are millions of people who still have miserable lives and have to face the dangers of starvation and exposure.

无可争辩，现在有数百万的人仍过着挨饿受冻的悲惨生活。

113. Many city residents complain that there are few buses in their city that they have to spend too much time waiting for a bus, which is usually crowded with a large number of passengers.

许多市民抱怨城市的公交车太少，以至于他们要花很长时间等一辆公交车，而车上可能已满载乘客了。

114. Although people's lives have been dramatically changed over the last decades, it must be admitted that, shortage of funds is still one of the biggest challenges students face because tuition fees and book prices are rising by the day.

近几十年，尽管人们的生活有了惊人的改变，但必须承认，由于学费和书费日益飞涨，资金短缺仍然是学生们面临的最大问题之一。

115. Many government leaders go into raptures at the mere mention of artistic and cultural projects. They are forever talking about the nice parks, the smart sculptures in the central city and the art galleries filled with valuable rarities. Nothing, they maintain, is more essential to economic growth than these projects.

只要一提起艺术和文化项目，一些政府领导就会兴奋不已。他们滔滔不绝地说着美丽的公园、城市中心漂亮的雕塑、还有满是稀世珍宝的艺术展览馆。他们认为在经济发展中，没有什么比这些艺术项目更重要了。

116. Many parents believe that additional educational activities provide obvious advantages. With extra studies, they maintain, their children are able to obtain many kinds of practical skills and useful knowledge, which will put them in a beneficial position in the job markets when they grow up.

许多家长相信额外的教育活动有许多优点。他们指出，通过课外学习，他们的孩子可以获得很多实践技能和有用的知识，当他们长大后，这对他们就业是大有好处的。

117. It is widely acknowledged that computers and other machines have become an indispensable part of our society, which make our life and work more comfortable and less laborious.

人们普遍认为计算机和其他机器已经成为我们社会必不可少的一部分。它们使我们的生活和工作更舒适、更轻松。

118. Many people believe that international tourism produces positive effects on economic growth and local government should be encouraged to promote international tourism.

许多人认为国际旅游对经济发展有积极作用，应鼓励地方政府发展国际旅游。

119. Although rural immigrants contribute greatly to the economic growth of the cities, they may also bring about many negative impacts.

尽管民工对城市的经济发展做出了巨大贡献，然而他们也带来了一些负面影响。

120. It is commonly thought that our society has been dramatically changed by modern science and technology, and human beings have made extraordinary progress in knowledge and technology during recent decades.

人们普遍认为现代科技使我们的社会发生了巨大的变化。近几十年人类在知识科技方面取得了惊人的进步。

121. Many surveys show that people in increasing numbers are beginning to recognize that boarding schools provide a better environment and facilities for children.

许多调查显示，越来越多的人开始意识到寄宿学校能给他们的孩子提供较好的学习环境和设施。

122. There are two reasons for the improvement in people's living conditions. In the first place, we have been carrying out reform and opening-up policy. Secondly, there has been a rapid expansion of our national economy. Further-more, the birth rate has been brought under control.

人民生活状况改善的原因有两点。首先，我们一直在贯彻执行改革开放政策。其次，国民经济正在迅速发展，而且出生率已经得到控制。

123. Many values associated with traditional technology are out of date and should be replaced by modern science.

许多传统的技术方法已经过时，应被现代科技所取代。

124. From what has been discussed above, we can safely draw the conclusion that, although parents' desire to look after children by themselves is understandable, its disadvantages far outweigh the advantages.

通过以上讨论，我们可以得出这一结论：尽管家长想亲自照看孩子的愿望是可以理解的，但是这样做的缺点远大于优点。

125. Many young people go into raptures at the merely mention of buying clothes. And they seem to be attracted by colorful material and various styles of fashion. There is nothing, they maintain, that can be compared with clothes. In fact, fashion has become an indispensable part of youngsters' lives.

许多年轻人一提到时尚服饰就兴高采烈。他们似乎被时尚服饰那多彩的面料、不同的款式所吸引。他们认为没有什么东西可以与时尚的服饰相比。实际上，时尚的服饰已成为年青人生活中不可或缺的一部分。

126. Meanwhile, the number of people who have access to their own cars has risen sharply in recent years.

同时，拥有私人轿车的人数这几年快速增长。

127. Millions of people have to spend more time and energy on studying new skills and technology so that they can keep up in today's job market.

上百万的人们不得不花费更多的时间和精力学习新的技术和知识，以使自身在就业市场保持优势。

128. Modern civilization advocates materials. Without the government's intervention and protection to the cultural tradition legacy, the destruction to it will be too ghastly to contemplate.

现代文明崇尚物质。如果没有政府对文化传统遗产的干预与保护，对它的破坏将是不堪设想的。

129. Moreover, children will have less time to play and communicate with their peers due to extra studies, consequently, it is difficult for them to develop and cultivate their character and interpersonal skills. They may become more solitary and even suffer from mental illness.

而且，由于要额外学习，孩子们没有多少时间和同龄的孩子交流玩耍，导致很难培养他们的个性和交际能力。他们可能变得孤僻，甚至产生某些心理疾病。

130. The thought, the mankind's intelligent quintessence, whether it is accepted by the contemporary people, it will be wonderful works in the history of progress of mankind.

思想，人类智慧的精华，不管它是否被当代人接受，都将是人类进步史上的奇葩。

131. Most important of all, apart from their hometown and parents, students don't see any familiar faces and suffer from homesickness, which might cause serious mental problems.

最重要的是，离开了家乡和父母，看不到任何熟悉的面孔，学生们不得不忍受思家之苦，这可能会导致严重的精神疾病。

132. My suggestions to deal with the problem are as follows. To begin with, it is urgent to create nature reserves. Secondly, certain rare wild animals that might become extinct should be collected, fed and reproduced artificially. Finally, those who hunt them should be punished severely.

我对解决这个问题的建议如下：首先，迫在眉睫的是建立自然保护区。其次，一些濒临灭绝的珍稀野生动物应该收捕、人工喂养并繁殖。最后，对于捕猎珍稀野生动物的人必须严惩。

133. Many people seem to overlook the basic fact that clothing's major function is to keep us warm and comfortable.

许多人似乎忽视了这个基本事实：衣服的基本功能是使我们保持温暖舒适。

134. From what has been discussed above, we may safely draw the conclusion that the advantages of bicycles far outweigh their disadvantages and they will still play an essential role in modern society.

通过以上讨论，我们可以得出结论：自行车的优点远大于缺点，并且在现代社会仍将发挥重要作用。

135. No one can doubt the essential fact that the traffic problem over the last few years has caused public concern all over the world. Experts in increasing numbers are beginning to believe that this situation will lead to unfavorable effects on economic growth in local areas.

没有人能否认这一重要事实：最近几年交通问题在全世界受到了普遍关注。越来越多的专家开始相信这种状况将对当地的经济发展产生不利影响。

136. The senior and junior students could share their own experiences with the new students about how to overcome the difficulties they encountered, and how to adjust to the new environment.

高年级学生可以与新生一起分享他们的经历：如何克服遇到的困难，如何适应新的环境。

137. The story of a poor family that acquired fame and fortune

(下面)这户穷人一夜之间发财出名的

overnight, dramatically illustrates the power of the press.

故事戏剧性地说明了媒体的威力。

138. Not only can walking fish live out of water, but they can also travel short distances over land.

行鱼不仅可以离开水存活,还可以在岸上短距离移动。

139. People in growing numbers are beginning to believe that learning new skills and acquiring knowledge contributes directly to enhancing their job or promotion opportunities.

现在,越来越多的人开始相信学习新的技术和知识能直接帮助他们获得工作或提升的机会。

140. Although parents would be able to devote much more time and energy to their children, it must be admitted that, parents have less experience and knowledge of educating and supervising children, when compared with profess-ional teachers working in kindergartens or nursery schools.

尽管父母能在他们孩子身上投入更多时间和精力,但是必须承认,与在幼儿园工作的专职教师相比,他们在如何教育管理孩子上缺乏经验和知识。

141. It is true that the *Fifth Amendment* states that the government may not take private property for public use without compensation, but it is the government that defines private property.

没错,《第五修正案》指出政府不得无偿把私有财产取作公用,但为私有财产下定义的是政府。

142. People differ in their attitudes towards failure. Faced with it, some of them can stand up to it, draw useful lessons from it, and try hard to fulfill what they are determined to do. Others, however, lose heart and give up.

人们对失败持有不同的态度。面对失败,有人能够经得起考验,从失败中吸取教训,并努力去完成他们下定决心要做的事情。然而,另一些人却丧失信心而退却了。

143. Nowadays, many students go into raptures at the mere mention of going to high school or college. Unfortunately, for most young people, their first day on campus is not a pleasant experience.

当前,一提到即将开始的高中或大学生活,许多学生都会兴高采烈。然而,对多数年轻人来说,学校生活刚开始的日子并不是什么愉快的经历。

144. On the one hand, it is indisputable that boarding schools are exerting a growing influence, especially in last few years.

一方面,寄宿学校正在发挥越来越重要的作用,尤其是最近几年,这是无可争辩的。

145. From what has been discussed above, we may safely draw the conclusion that although extra studies provide many obvious advantages, its disadvantages shouldn't be ignored and far outweigh its advantages. It is absurd to force children to take extra studies after school.

通过以上讨论,我们可以得出结论:尽管额外学习的确有很多优点,但它的缺点同样不可忽视,且远大于它的优点。放学后强迫孩子额外学习是不合理的。

146. No one can deny the fact that a person's education is the most important aspect of his or her life.

没有人能否认,教育是人生最重要的一方面。

147. One of the great early writers wrote: "Work is the grand cure of all the maladies and miseries that ever beset mankind. " If this is true, then the present situation should make us wonder whether the rule that the average worker is obliged to retire at the age of 50 is reasonable.

一位伟大的作家曾写道:工作是医治人间一切病痛和疾苦的万应良药。如果是这样的话,那么就现在的状况我们应该想一想,强迫普通工人50岁退休是否合理。

148. Parents are firmly convinced that sending their children to kindergartens or nursery schools will have an unfavorable influence on their growth.

父母们坚信把孩子送到幼儿园对他们的成长不利。

149. The problem of international tourism has caused wide-spread public concern in recent years.

近些年，国际旅游问题引起了广泛关注。

150. People believe that computer skills will enhance their job and promotion opportunities.

人们相信拥有计算机技术可以获得更多的工作和晋升的机会。

151. Proper measures must be taken to limit the number of foreign tourists and great efforts should be made to protect local environments and historical sites from the harmful effects of international tourism.

应该采取适当的措施限制外国旅游者的数量，努力保护当地环境和历史遗址不受国际旅游业的不利影响。

152. Real statesmen have the political faith and ambition, but do not use it like a vulgar tool.

真正的政治家有政治上的信仰和追求，而不是把政治当作庸俗的工具。

153. Rich as our country is, our quality of life is by no means satisfactory.

虽然我们的国家很富有，但是我们的生活质量却无法令人满意。

154. Scientists do not know why dinosaurs became extinct, but some theories postulate that changes in geography, climate, and sea levels were responsible.

科学家不知道恐龙为何灭绝，但是一些理论推断这是由地理、气候和海平面的变化造成的。

155. A sense of justice, consciousness of responsibility, and sympathy bring up the basic factors of a statesman.

正义感、责任感和同情感是造就政治家的最基本因素。

156. Since it is unnecessary to consider a student's routine life, day school can lay stress on teaching instead of other aspects, such as dormitory and cafeteria management.

由于无需考虑学生的日常生活，日制学校可以将重点放在教学上而不是宿舍和食堂管理这些方面。

157. Stone does not decay, and so the tools of long ago have remained when even the bones of the men who made them have disappeared without trace.

石头不会腐烂，所以以前的（石器）工具能保存下来，虽然它们的制造者已经消失得无影无踪。

158. Students attending a boarding school should cultivate their independence apart from their parents.

离开父母上寄宿学校的学生应培养他们的独立性。

159. The information I've collected over last few years leads me to believe that this knowledge may be less useful than most people think.

从这几年我搜集的信息来看，这些知识并没有人们想象的那么有用。

160. Television is more than just an electronic appliance; it is a means of expression, as well as a vehicle for communication, and as such becomes a powerful tool for reaching other human beings.

电视不仅仅是一件电器，它是表达的手段和交流的载体，并因此成为联系他人的有力工具。

161. Competition and cooperation are ways of mankind progresses. To lay more stress on one or the other oversi-mplifies the issue and is detrimental to society's forward progress.

竞争与合作是人类进步的重要方式。过多偏重任何一方都会将问题简单化，不利于社会向前发展。

162. Cooperation across boundaries will help to resolve various problems which have been puzzling the society for a long time.

国家间的合作有利于解决困扰整个社会已久的各种问题。

163. The critic appreciates and appraises artistic work via their unique criteria, thus providing a context to evaluate a work's social value.

批评家用自己独特的视角去鉴赏、评价艺术作品，从而给出评价一件作品社会价值的背景。

164. Since the examination is around the corner, I am compelled to give up sports.

考试迫在眉睫，我不得不放弃做运动。

165. The critic has set up a kind of creation norm and cultural rule, thus playing a driving role to the artist's creation to a certain extent.

批评家建立了一种创作规范与文化规则，这在一定程度上对艺术家的创作起着推动作用。

166. The difference between a man who succeeds and one who does not lies in the way each one treats opportunities. The successful person always makes adequate preparations to meet opportunities as they arrive. The unsuccessful person, on the other hand, works little and just watches as opport-unities pass by.

成功者与失败者的区别在于对待机遇的态度。成功者总是做好充分准备迎接机遇的适时来临；而失败者工作懒散，只能眼睁睁看着机遇擦身而过。

167. The Europe Investment Bank has provided loan of about eighty million Euros to Estonia for the renovation and expansion of the electric power transmission-line system.

欧洲投资银行向爱沙尼亚贷款8000万欧元，用于更新和扩建输电网。

168. When it comes to education, the majority of people believe that education is a lifetime pursuit.

说到教育，大部分人认为它是一个持续终生的追求。

169. The greater the population there is in a locality, the greater the need there is for water, transportation, and disposal of refuse.

一个地方的人口越多，对水、交通和垃圾处理的需求就会越大。

170. The latest surveys show that quite a few children have unpleasant associations with homework.

最近的调查显示，相当多的孩子对家庭作业没什么好感。

171. The majority of students believe that a part-time job will provide them with more opportunities to develop their interpersonal skills, which will put them in a favorable position in the job market.

大部分学生相信兼职工作会使他们有更多机会发展人际交往能力，而这对他们未来找工作是非常有好处的。

172. Television, the most pervasive and persuasive of modern technologies, and marked by rapid change and growth, is moving into a new era, an era of extraordinary sophistication and versatility that promises to reshape our lives and our world.

电视，这项以迅速变化和成长为标志的最普及和最有影响力的现代技术，正在步入一个新时代，一个极为成熟和多样化的、必将重塑我们生活和世界的时代。

173. The number of private cars in urban areas should be limited while the number of public buses should be increased.

城市私家车的数量应得以控制，而公交车的数量应该增加。

174. An investigation shows that many immigrants think that working in city provides them with not only a higher salary but also the opportunity to learn new skills.

一项调查显示，许多民工认为在城市打工不仅有较高的收入，而且能学到一些新技术。

175. "The people who get on in this world are the people who get up and look for the circumstances they want, and if they cannot find them, make them." This is a remark made by Bernard Shaw, a great writer, and his view is shared by more and more people as time goes by.

著名作家萧伯纳曾说过："在这个世界上取得成功的人，都努力去寻求他们想要的机会，如果找不到，他们就自己创造机会。"这一观点现在正为越来越多的人所接受。

176. There is only one difference between an old man and a young one: the young man has a glorious future before him and old one has a splendid future behind him, and maybe that is where the rub is.

老人和年轻人之间只有一个区别：年轻人前面有辉煌的未来，老年人灿烂的未来却已在他们身后。这也许就是困难之所在。

177. These days, people in growing numbers are beginning to complain that work is more stressful and less leisurely than in past. Many experts point out that with the development of modern society it is an inevitable result and there is no way to avoid it.

现在，越来越多的人开始抱怨工作比以前压力更大，业余时间比以前更少。许多专家指出这是现代社会发展的必然结果，无可避免。

178. From what has been discussed above, it would be reasonable to believe that basic projects play a far more important role than artistic and cultural projects in people's lives and economic growth.

通过以上讨论，我们有理由相信，在人们的生活和经济发展方面，基础建设能比艺术文化项目发挥更大的作用。

179. The reason why we have to grow trees is that they can supply fresh air for us.

我们必须种树的原因在于它们能给我们提供新鲜的空气。

180. Those urban planners who are blind to this point will pay a heavy price, one they cannot afford.

那些城市的规划者们如果忽视这一点，将会付出无法承受的代价。

181. To average people, they often tend to live under the illusion that proficiency in English often means a good opportunity for one's career, is this really the case?

对于一般人来说，他们常常以为掌握英语就意味着一份好的工作，然而这是真的吗？

182. Today an increasing number of people have realized that law education is of great importance. In order to keep law and order, every one of us is supposed to get a law education.

现在，越来越多的人认识到法制教育的重要性。为了维护法律和社会治安，我们每个人都应该接受法制教育。

183. Tourism brings China a lot of benefits. First, it enables Chinese people to know more about the outside world and promotes friendship and understanding. Secondly, it is financially beneficial to China, which needs more foreign currency for its modernization program.

旅游业给中国带来许多好处。首先，它使中国人了解外界，并有助于促进友谊和理解。其次，它在经济上也有利于我国，因为中国现代化建设需要大量的外汇。

184. This whole process by which machines can be used to work for us has been called automation.

机器用来为我们工作的整个过程叫自动化。

185. Unfortunately, there is very little evidence that big companies are willing to invest huge sums of money in a place without sufficient infrastructure, such as basic electricity and water supplies.

不幸的是，很少有证据表明大公司愿意把巨额的资金投到一个连水电这些基础设施都不完善的地方去。

186. Using a bicycle contributes greatly to people's physical fitness as well as easing traffic jams.

使用自行车有助于人们的身体健康，并极大地缓解交通阻塞。

187. Those who are in favor of artistic and cultural projects argue that the cultural environment will attract more tourists, which will bring huge profits to local residents. Some people even equate the building of such projects with economic improvements.

那些赞成建设文化艺术项目的人认为文化环境会吸引更多的游客，这将给当地居民带来巨大的利益。一些人甚至把建设文化艺术项目与发展经济建设等同起来。

188. Whether a large family is a good thing or not is a very popular topic, which is often talked about not only by city residents but by farmers as well.

家庭人口多好还是少好是一个非常通俗的话题，不仅是城里人，连农民也经常讨论这个问题。

189. It has always been a mystery to me why city dwellers, who appreciate all these things, obstinately pretend that they would prefer to live in the country.

城里人心里对这一切很明白，却偏要执拗地装出他们喜欢住在乡村的样子，这对我来说一直是个谜。

190. Furthermore, students living in their own homes would have access to a comfortable life and have more opport-unities to communicate with their parents, and that has a beneficial impact on the development of their personal character.

而且，学生住在自己家中，有舒适的生活，有更多机会和父母交流，这对他们个性的培养有利。

191. What's more, living at school can save them a great deal of time on the commute between home and school, so they would be able to concentrate more time and energy on their academic work.

而且，生活在学校里能节省每天往返于学校和家的大量时间，使他们有更多的时间和精力学习。

192. It has been estimated that the weight of all the insects destroyed by spiders in Britain in one year would be greater than the total weight of all the human beings in the country.

据估计，在英国，蜘蛛一年里所消灭的昆虫的重量超过这个国家所有人口的总重量。

193. With the opening and reform policy being carried out, thousands upon thousands of foreign visitors are crowding into our country. They are eager to see this old mysterious land with a splendid culture of more than 5,000 years.

随着改革开放政策的贯彻执行，数以万计的外国游人涌入中国。他们渴望参观这个有着5000多年灿烂文化的神秘古国。

194. Without something of this kind, searching for intelligence on other planets would be like trying to meet a friend in London without a pre-arranged rendezvous and absurdly wandering the streets in the hope of a chance encounter.

没有这种手段，要想寻觅其他星球上的智慧生命，就如同去伦敦见一位朋友，事先未约定地点，而荒唐地在街上游逛，期待碰巧遇上一样。

195. In the organization of industrial life, the influence of the factory upon the physiological and mental state of the workers has been completely neglected.

在工业生活的组织中，工厂对工人生理和精神状态的影响完全被忽视了。

196. This caused the construction of gigantic buildings where too many human beings are crowded together.

这导致许多摩天大厦拔地而起，大厦内众多的人挤在一起。

197. Modern industry is based on the idea of maximum production at the lowest cost, in order that an individual or a group of individuals may earn as much money as possible.

现代工业的基本概念是：以最低成本获取最多产品，为的是让某个个人或某一部分人尽可能地多赚钱。

198. Young men who have reason to fear that they will be killed in battle may justifiably feel bitter in the thought that they have cheated of the best things that life has to offer. But in an old man who has known human joys and sorrows, and has achieved whatever work it was in him to do, the fear of death is somewhat abject and ignoble.

有理由害怕自己会死在战场上的年轻人想到自己被剥夺了生活所能给予的最美好的东西时感到痛苦，这是可以理解的。可是老年人已经饱尝了人间的甘苦，一切能做的都已经做了，如果怕死，就有点儿可怜又可鄙了。

199. When anyone opens a current account at a bank, he is lending the bank money, repayment of which he may demand at any time, either in cash or by drawing a cheque in favour of another person.

任何人在银行开一个活期账户，就等于把钱借给了银行。这笔钱可以随时提取，提取的方式可以是现金，也可以是开一张以他人为收款人的支票。

200. Primarily, the banker-customer relationship is that of debtor and creditor—who is which depending on whether the customer's account is in credit or is overdrawn.

银行与储户的关系主要是债务人和债权人的关系。究竟谁是债务人谁是债权人，要看储户是有结余还是透支。

在前面反复说过，要想写作得高分，就得长短句相结合。下面的这100句话短小精悍，表达力强，是考生写好句子不可或缺的参考资料。

201. A much better and brighter future awaits us.

一个更加美好和光明的未来就在我们眼前。

202. There is no doubt that the increase in demand caused the rise in prices.

毫无疑问，需求的增长导致价格的上涨。

203. We should do our best to achieve our goals in life.

我们应竭尽全力来实现我们的人生目标。

204. We should get into the habit of keeping good hours.

我们应该养成早睡早起的习惯。

205. By exercising, we can always stay healthy.

通过体育锻炼，我们能始终保持健康。

206. This issue has caused widespread public concern.

这个问题已经引起了公众的广泛关注。

207. Listening to music enables us to feel relaxed.

听音乐能使我们放松。

208. We should convince people of the value of working hard.

我们应该让人们知道努力的价值。

209. The harder you work, the more progress you make.

越努力，进步就越大。

210. Summer is sultry. That's the reason why I don't like it.

夏天很闷热，这就是我不喜欢的原因。

211. Smoking has a great influence on our health.

抽烟对我们的健康影响很大。

212. So precious is time that we can't afford to waste it.

时间如此珍贵，我们不能浪费。

213. Pollution poses a great threat to our existence.

污染对我们的生存造成了巨大威胁。

214. People equate success in life with the ability to operate a computer.

人们把会使用计算机与人生成功相提并论。

215. Reading is beneficial to our mind.

读书对心灵有益。

216. Overwork harms our health.

过度工作对健康有害。

217. The progress of the society is based on harmony.

社会的进步是以和谐为基础的。

218. On no account can we ignore the value of knowledge. 我们绝对不能忽视知识的价值。

219. Nothing is more important than education. 没有什么比接受教育更重要。

220. It is universally acknowledged that trees are indispensable. 全世界都知道树木对我们是不可或缺的。

221. Adler is correct in this assertion that education does not end with graduation. Adler的这句话很正确，教育不能随着毕业而结束。

222. An advantage of using the solar energy is that it won't create any pollution. 太阳能的优点在于它不会产生任何污染。

223. There is no denying that our quality of life has gone from bad to worse. 无可否认，我们的生活品质已经越来越糟。

224. Any government, which is blind to this point, may pay a heavy price. 任何政府若忽视这一点，都将付出巨大的代价。

225. As is known to all, fake and inferior commodities harm the interests of consumers. 众所周知，假冒伪劣商品损害了消费者的利益。

226. We should spare no effort to beautify our environment. 我们应该不遗余力地美化我们的环境。

227. When an opportunity comes, it brings a promise but never realizes it on its own. 每当机遇降临，伴之而来的是成功的希望，但是机遇不能自行实现成功。

228. This phenomenon has caused widespread public concern in many parts of the world. 这一现象已经在全世界许多地方引起了广泛关注。

229. This view is now being questioned by more and more people. 这一观点正受到越来越多人的质疑。

230. Despite many obvious advantages of bicycles, they are not without problems. 尽管自行车有许多明显的优点，但是它也存在着问题。

231. For my part, I agree with the latter opinion for the following reasons. 我同意后者，理由如下。

232. There is no doubt that our educational system leaves something to be desired. 毫无疑问，我们的教育制度无法令人满意。

233. This is a matter of life and death—a matter no country can afford to ignore. 这是一个生死攸关的问题，任何国家都不能忽视。

234. It is time the authorities concerned took proper steps to solve the traffic problems. 该是有关当局采取适当的措施来解决交通问题的时候了。

235. It must be noted that learning must be done by a person on his or her own account. 必须指出的是，学习只能靠自己。

236. It is conceivable that knowledge plays an important role in our lives. 可想而知，知识在我们的一生中扮演着重要的角色。

237. No invention has received more praise and abuse than the Internet. 没有一项发明像互联网一样同时受到如此多的赞扬和批评。

238. On the other hand, the contribution of day schools can't be ignored.

另一方面，日制学校的贡献是不能忽视的。

239. We cannot overemphasize the importance of protecting our eyes.

我们再怎么强调保护眼睛的重要性也不为过。

240. Freshmen often get lost on campus and fail to find their way to the dormitory or the library.

新生常常在校园迷路，不知道去宿舍或图书馆该怎么走。

241. Pollution is the price we pay for an overpopulated, over-industrialized planet.

污染是我们为这个人口过密、过度工业化的星球所付出的代价。

242. That all great has this power of suggesting a world beyond is undeniable.

不可否认，一切伟大的艺术都具有使人遐想进入天外世界的魅力。

243. Working hard doesn't mean sacrificing your social life.

努力工作并不意味着牺牲你的社会生活。

244. Professional success and personal life are mutually related.

职业成功与个人生活是相互联系的。

245. The literal meaning of self-esteem is respecting oneself.

自尊的字面意思是尊重自己。

246. Some paintings are garbage and others are masterpieces.

有些绘画没有任何价值，有些绘画却是传世佳作。

247. These products are very expensive and time-consuming.

这些产品不但花费甚多，而且非常耗时。

248. Schools also provide an environment of reciprocal study.

学校也提供了一个相互学习的环境。

249. Students learn best in a highly structured environment.

学生们在具有高度组织性的环境中学得最好。

250. In the relationship between humans and machines, humans are the leaders.

在人类与机器的关系中，人类占主导地位。

251. The things that history records and reveals have historical limitations.

历史记录的和揭示的东西都具有历史局限性。

252. Businesses must become more involved in helping to prevent it.

企业必须更多地参与到防止其发生的行动中来。

253. Most societies would probably be much better off.

大多数社会可能会更富裕。

254. It is a concern to the whole society.

这是整个社会所关注的。

255. Private cars are an extension of family life.

私家车是家庭生活的延伸。

256. Nudes are considered a kind of art by many people.

很多人认为裸体画是一种艺术。

257. Working with high efficiency will speed up the procedure.

高效率的工作将会加速进程。

258. A crime is not punished accordingly.

罪行并没有得到相应的惩罚。

259. Creativity is not part of work that employees are asked to do.

创造力并不是员工要完成的工作的一部分。

260. Ironing shirts is a hateful job. 烫衬衣是一件烦人的工作。

261. The desire for peace transcends political differences. 对和平的渴望超越了政治分歧。

262. Borrowing too much also damages the quality of their retired lives. 借款过多会降低他们退休后的生活品质。

263. This knowledge might bring us respect and recognition. 这些知识会使我们受到尊重和认可。

264. With hard work she won herself a place at university. 通过努力学习，她在大学赢得了一席之地。

265. The overall social atmosphere will become better. 整个社会的风气会好转。

266. The process can bring us enjoyment and challenge. 这个过程会带给我们快乐和挑战。

267. I did not get much enjoyment out of that book. 我并没有从那本书中得到太多的乐趣。

268. What is the final objective of business? 商业的最终目标是什么？

269. Our objective is to achieve full employment. 我们的目标是实现全部就业。

270. We have succeeded in our main objectives. 我们已经成功完成了我们的主要目标。

271. They prefer idling around all day long. 他们喜欢整日游手好闲，无所事事。

272. The cat was creeping silently towards the mouse. 那只猫悄悄地向那只老鼠爬去。

273. They overlook important spiritual values. 他们忽视了精神方面的价值。

274. There will be chaos and no cooperation. 这里将只有混乱，而没有丝毫的合作。

275. The same salary grade will discourage people. 相同的工资等级会打消人们的积极性。

276. The work asks for a high amount of cooperation among employees. 这项工作要求员工通力合作。

277. There are no openings at present for secretaries at the bank. 目前，这家银行没有秘书职位空缺。

278. Personal interviews are much too subjective. 个人面试过于主观。

279. We fail to look beyond short-term goals. 我们不能看到近期目标以外的东西。

280. New employees might not work hard. 新员工可能不会积极地工作。

281. They tried to intimidate him into doing what they wanted. 他们试图通过威胁使他按他们的命令行事。

282. Being an employee in the company does not make the worker a lesser person. 作为这家公司的一员，公司并没有使这名员工低人一等。

283. The deficiencies in the system soon became obvious. 这个系统的缺陷很快就暴露了出来。

284. Any company is an organic whole. 任何一家公司都是一个有机的整体。

285. Any company has unified regulations or rules to follow. 任何公司都有需要统一遵守的规章或制度。

286. It fosters an atmosphere of trust and respect. 它有助于促成一种信任和尊重的气氛。

287. Teamwork is a key component of success.　　协力合作是成功的关键因素。

288. All of the people on earth are interconnected.　　全世界的人都是相互联系的。

289. His behavior brings shame to his family.　　他的行为使他的家人蒙羞。

290. It goes on without your being aware of it.　　它在你没有意识到的时候发生。

291. The company may suffer from those problems.　　该公司可能会受到这些问题的困扰。

292. Forcing them to work at a young age will stunt their growth.　　迫使他们在年少时工作将有碍他们的发育。

293. The negative messages may inevitably hurt some people.　　负面消息会不可避免地伤害到某些人。

294. Consumers can persuade sellers to accept their requests.　　消费者可以说服销售者接受他们的要求。

295. They visit adult entertainment sites and online gambling sites.　　他们访问成人娱乐网站并参与在线赌博。

296. There is no one but longs to go to college.　　人人都希望上大学。

297. The more books we read, the more learned we become.　　书读得越多，就越有学问。

298. Those who violate traffic regulations should be punished.　　违反交通规则的人应该受到处罚。

299. Our traffic conditions leave much to be desired.　　我们的交通状况令人不满。

300. Exercising is closely related to health.　　运动与健康息息相关。

《GMAT官方指南（综合）》（第13版）

GMAC（美国管理专业研究生入学考试委员会）编著

◎ GMAC（GMAT考试的命题机构）中国大陆唯一授权
◎ GMAT必备参考书，体现最新改革趋势
◎ 900道全真试题，涵盖GMAT考试所有题型，并配有全面的答案解析
◎ 提供辅助学习网站，内含50个综合推理问题
◎ 测试练习部分帮助考生评估从何着手复习重点
◎ 针对GMAT数学部分，进行综合性数学复习
◎ 全新的语法复习涵盖GMAT语文部分所有概念
◎ 真实作文题目、回答范例及评分信息

定价：**228元** 开本：**16开** 页码：**840页**

《GMAT官方指南（语文）》

GMAC（美国管理专业研究生入学考试委员会）编著

◎ GMAC（GMAT考试的命题机构）中国大陆唯一授权
◎ 300道全真试题，涵盖GMAT考试语文部分所有题型，并配有全面的答案解析
◎ 题目按难易程度排列，节省考生时间
◎ 全新的语法复习涵盖GMAT语文部分所有考点
◎ 原汁原味的作文题目、回答范例及评分信息

定价：**99元** 开本：**16开** 页码：**336页**

《GMAT官方指南（数学）》

GMAC（美国管理专业研究生入学考试委员会）编著

◎ GMAC（GMAT考试的命题机构）中国大陆唯一授权
◎ 300道全真试题，涵盖GMAT考试数学部分所有题型，并配有全面的答案解析
◎ 题目按难易程度排列，节省考生时间

定价：**99元** 开本：**16开** 页码：**216页**

《GMAT官方题库范文精讲》

Mark Alan Stewart 等 编著 **江奇 杨毅** 译注

◎ 国际权威GMAT研究机构授权出版
◎ 北美GMAT写作专家创作，新东方GMAT写作名师讲评
◎ 精选233篇GMAT作文真题写作范文
◎ 权威专家讲授GMAT考试高分作文要诀

定价：**42元** 开本：**16开** 页码：**300页**

《GMAT词汇精选》

俞敏洪 编著

◎ 中英文释义确保词义理解的准确性
◎ "词根+联想"加深记忆效果
◎ 精彩附录，分类梳理GMAT常考词汇

定价：**40元** 开本：**32开** 页码：**392页**

《词以类记：GMAT词汇》

张红岩　编著

◎ 全面收录GMAT最新核心词汇，提高备考效率

◎ 按学科和意群分类，细分至最小同义词区间，符合记忆规律

◎ 结合全球顶级商学院学习经历，提炼MBA核心应用词汇表

◎ 精心设计自测练习，提高记忆效果

定价：35元　开本：32开　页码：416页

《GMAT逻辑推理——分类思维训练及试题解析》

陈向东　编著

◎ 归纳总结GMAT逻辑推理解题分析思路

◎ 梳理GMAT逻辑推理出题原则及解题步骤

◎ 分类讲解GMAT逻辑推理重点难点试题

◎ 提供15套考前模拟冲刺试题及精准译文

定价：59元　开本：16开　页码：532页

《GMAT语法改错精解》

刘振民　编著

◎ 深入讲解GMAT句子改错题目特点，全面介绍解题方法

◎ 分类剖析典型题目，补充必需语法知识

◎ 科学设置仿真试题，模拟真实考场情境

定价：40元　开本：16开　页码：332页

《GMAT数学高分快速突破》

陈向东　编著

◎ GMAT数学考试必备辅导用书

◎ 详尽梳理归纳GMAT数学考点

◎ 分项强化GMAT数学题目思维训练

◎ 全面总结GMAT数学术语、解题技巧

◎ 科学设置与考试难度相当的仿真模考题

定价：40元　开本：16开　页码：300页

《GMAT阅读高分指导与精练》

翟少成　编著

◎ 详解GMAT阅读考试内容及文章特色

◎ 揭秘GMAT阅读解题技巧及备考策略

◎ 剖析GMAT阅读题型特点及解题方法

◎ 精讲《GMAT官方指南》阅读理解题目

定价：45元　开本：16开　页码：320页

读者反馈表

尊敬的读者:

您好! 非常感谢您对**新东方大愚图书**的信赖与支持,希望您抽出宝贵的时间填写这份反馈表,以便帮助我们改进工作,今后能为您提供更优秀的图书。谢谢!

为了答谢您对我们的支持,我们将对反馈的信息进行随机抽奖活动,当月将有 20 位幸运读者可获赠《**新东方英语**》期刊一份。我们将定期在新东方大愚图书网站 www.dogwood.com.cn 公布获奖者名单并及时寄出奖品,敬请关注。

来信请寄:　　北京市海淀区海淀东三街 2 号新东方南楼 19 层　北京新东方大愚文化传播有限公司
图书部收

邮编:100080　　　　　　　　　　　　　　　　　　　　E-mail:bj62605588@163.com

姓名:＿＿＿＿＿　年龄:＿＿＿＿＿　职业:＿＿＿＿＿　教育背景:＿＿＿＿＿　邮编:＿＿＿＿＿

通讯地址:＿＿＿＿＿＿＿＿＿＿＿＿＿＿＿＿＿＿＿＿＿＿＿＿　联系电话:＿＿＿＿＿＿＿

E-mail:＿＿＿＿＿＿＿＿＿＿＿　您所购买的书籍的名称是:＿＿＿＿＿＿＿＿＿＿＿

1. 您是通过何种渠道得知本书的(可多选):
   □书店　□新东方网站　□大愚网站　□朋友推荐　□老师推荐　□@新东方大愚图书(http://weibo.com/dogwood)
   □其他＿＿＿＿＿＿＿＿＿

2. 您是从何处购买到此书的?　□书店　□新东方大愚淘宝网　□其他网上书店　□其他＿＿＿＿＿＿＿＿

3. 您购买此书的原因(可多选):
   □封面设计　□书评广告　□正文内容　□图书价格　□新东方品牌　□新东方名师　□其他＿＿＿＿＿＿＿＿

4. 您对本书的封面设计满意程度:　□很满意　□比较满意　□一般　□不满意　□改进建议＿＿＿＿＿＿＿＿＿

5. 您认为本书的内文在哪些方面还需改进?　□结构编排　□难易程度　□内容丰富性　□内文版式　□其他＿＿＿＿

6. 本书最令您满意的地方:□内文　□封面　□价格　□纸张

7. 您对本书的推荐率:□没有　□1 人　□1-3 人　□3-5 人　□5 人以上

8. 您更希望我们为您提供哪些方面的英语类图书?
   □少儿英语类　□初高中英语类　□四六级类　□考研类　□IELTS 类　□TOEFL 类　□GRE、GMAT 类　□SAT、SSAT 类
   □留学申请类　□BEC、TOEIC 类　□实用英语类　□商务英语类　□休闲欣赏类　□英语读物类　□其他＿＿＿＿＿＿＿
   您目前最希望我们为您出版的图书是:＿＿＿＿＿＿＿＿＿＿＿

9. 您在学习英语过程中最需要哪些方面的帮助?(可多选)
   □词汇　□听力　□口语　□阅读　□写作　□翻译　□语法　□其他＿＿＿＿＿＿＿＿

10. 您最喜欢的英语图书品牌:＿＿＿＿＿＿＿＿＿＿＿
    理由是(可多选):□版式漂亮　□内容实用　□难度适宜　□价格适中　□对考试有帮助　□其他＿＿＿＿＿＿＿

11. 您对新东方图书品牌的评价:＿＿＿＿＿＿＿＿＿＿＿＿＿＿＿

12. 您对本书(或其他新东方图书)的意见和建议:＿＿＿＿＿＿＿＿＿＿＿＿＿＿＿
    ＿＿＿＿＿＿＿＿＿＿＿＿＿＿＿＿＿＿＿＿＿＿＿＿＿＿＿＿＿＿＿＿
    ＿＿＿＿＿＿＿＿＿＿＿＿＿＿＿＿＿＿＿＿＿＿＿＿＿＿＿＿＿＿＿＿

13. 填表时间:＿＿＿＿年＿＿＿＿月＿＿日